The Practice of the Body of Christ

Princeton Theological Monograph Series

K. C. Hanson, Charles M. Collier, D. Christopher Spinks,
Robin Parry, and Rodney Clapp, Series Editors

Recent volumes in the series:

Koo Dong Yun
*The Holy Spirit and Ch'i (Qi):
A Chiological Approach to Pneumatology*

Stanley S. MacLean
*Resurrection, Apocalypse, and the Kingdom of Christ:
The Eschatology of Thomas F. Torrance*

Brian Neil Peterson
*Ezekiel in Context: Ezekiel's Message Understood in Its Historical Setting
of Covenant Curses and Ancient Near Eastern Mythological Motifs*

Amy E. Richter
Enoch and the Gospel of Matthew

Maeve Louise Heaney
Music as Theology: What Music Says about the Word

Eric M. Vail
Creation and Chaos Talk: Charting a Way Forward

David L. Reinhart
*Prayer as Memory: Toward the Comparative Study of Prayer
as Apocalyptic Language and Thought*

Peter D. Neumann
Pentecostal Experience: An Ecumenical Encounter

Ashish J. Naidu
*Transformed in Christ: Christology and the Christian Life
in John Chrysostom*

The Practice of the Body of Christ
Human Agency in Pauline Theology after MacIntyre

Colin D. Miller

Foreword by
Stanley Hauerwas

☙PICKWICK *Publications* • Eugene, Oregon

THE PRACTICE OF THE BODY OF CHRIST
Human Agency in Pauline Theology after MacIntyre

Princeton Theological Monograph Series 200

Copyright © 2014 Colin Miller. All rights reserved. Except for brief quotations in critical publications or reviews, no part of this book may be reproduced in any manner without prior written permission from the publisher. Write: Permissions, Wipf and Stock Publishers, 199 W. 8th Ave., Suite 3, Eugene, OR 97401.

Pickwick Publications
An Imprint of Wipf and Stock Publishers
199 W. 8th Ave., Suite 3
Eugene, OR 97401

www.wipfandstock.com

ISBN 13: 978-1-61097-267-3

Cataloguing-in-Publication data:

Miller, Colin.

    The practice of the body of Christ : human agency in Pauline theology after MacIntyre / Colin Miller; foreword by Stanley Hauerwas

    x + 218 pp. ; 23 cm. Includes bibliographical references.

    Princeton Theological Monograph Series 200

    ISBN 13: 978-1-61097-267-3

    1. Agency (Philosophy). 2. Bible. Romans—Theology. 3. MacIntyre, Alasdair C. I. Title.

BS2665.52 M54 2014

Manufactured in the U.S.A.

Ἐπεφάνη γὰρ ἡ χάρις τοῦ θεοῦ σωτήριος πᾶσιν ἀνθρώποις παιδεύουσα ἡμᾶς, ἵνα ἀρνησάμενοι τὴν ἀσέβειαν καὶ τὰς κοσμικὰς ἐπιθυμίας σωφρόνως καὶ δικαίως καὶ εὐσεβῶς ζήσωμεν ἐν τῷ νῦν αἰῶνι.

—Titus 2:11–12

Contents

Foreword by Stanley Hauerwas   ix

Introduction   1

1. MacIntyrian Challenges to the Modern Study of Paul   7
2. A Gifted Obedience: Rereading Romans 5:12–21   61
3. Practicing Participation: The Virtues of Romans 6–8   99
4. Romans 12–15 as the Practice of the Body of Christ   136
5. Some Synthetic and Prospective Conclusions   197

Bibliography   209

Foreword

I WAS ONCE BADGERING HERBERT MCCABE, O.P. TO WRITE THE BOOK only he could write on Aquinas. Herbert was not about to be intimidated by me, observing that he had discovered that if you are patient the books that allegedly only you can write end up being written by your students. I should like to think this marvelous book by Colin Miller is a book I should have written but now I do not have to write it because he has done it for me.

The only trouble with that way of putting the matter is that I could not have written this book. Herbert could have written the book on Aquinas, but I could not have written this book on Paul. I could not have written this book because I do not have the scholarly skills necessary to write a book on Paul. In fact, I do not have the familiarity with the text of Romans to write a book like this. So I thank God that Colin has written a book I could not write.

I should like to think, however, that Colin was able to write this book partly because he has read some of the books that have been important for my work. Aristotle and MacIntyre are obviously crucial conversation partners for how Colin reads Paul. Of course Colin's ability to read Aristotle and MacIntyre is not surprising given he majored in philosophy as an undergraduate. Colin's ability to read Paul as a representative of the tradition of the virtues has, I suspect, everything to do with his background in philosophy. The constructive account of Paul Colin has given us in this book makes me think that the best preparation for those that would do graduate work in Scripture is to spend a year reading philosophy.

For it is surely the case that Colin's ability to help us see the inner connections between apocalyptic, Christology, and ecclesiology for Paul's understanding of the formation of Christians in the virtues is the result of how Aristotle and MacIntyre have taught him to think. I am not suggesting that Colin has made Paul out to be little more than a precursor to MacIntyre's account of the virtues. Rather I am suggesting that Colin is able to see what Paul is about because of what he has learned from MacIntyre. In fact there is a great gulf between Paul and MacIntyre just to the extent

Foreword

MacIntyre, at least insofar as he is a philosopher, cannot account for what is central for Paul, that is, Paul's apocalyptic Christology.

Accordingly, Colin's account of Paul helps us see how apocalyptic makes the everyday possible for Christians. Exactly because Christians, and Paul in particular, believed they had seen the end in Jesus' cross and resurrection, they were able to take the time, time demanded by our bodily character, to acquire the habits necessary to sustain a community of people who live between the times. To so live, according to Colin's account of Paul, requires the participation in a community shaped by the work of the Holy Spirit. The new time that apocalyptic names is the time of the Spirit.

I am often accused of having an inadequate account of the Holy Spirit. I have never been sympathetic with that criticism because I should like to think that everything I have to say depends on the work of the Spirit. But let me go on record that Colin's account of the work of the Spirit in Paul is an account in which I am in full agreement. Moreover I think he is right that there is no reason to assume that the gift of the virtues by the Spirit negates our agency. Rather, as Paul (and Aquinas) assumed, our agency and the agency of the Spirit are not in a competitive relation. The Spirit, particularly when the work of the Spirit is understood to animate the church, makes our agency possible.

There is no reason for me to try to summarize the argument Colin has developed so well concerning how Paul should be read. I can, however, strongly recommend this book not only for Colin's account of Paul but just as importantly for how his portrayal of Paul's understanding of the church as a school for the virtues has significant implications for us. For I am sure his account of the relation between Paul's Christology and ecclesiology has profound implications for the way we think and live as Christians today.

Although I would be wrong to take credit for the wonderful work contained in this volume, I should like to think that what I have tried to do in my own work, that is, remind us of the significance of the church for how we think about ethics, is confirmed by Colin's account of Paul. This is a book only someone like Colin, a philosophically sophisticated biblical scholar and priest, could have written. And for that we should be profoundly grateful.

Stanley Hauerwas

Introduction

THIS REVISED VERSION OF MY DISSERTATION SEEKS TO FORGE CONNECtions between two movements in today's theological disciplines. The first is the so-called "apocalyptic" interpretation of Paul and the second is often called "virtue ethics." "Apocalyptic" names the movement of scholarship that followed on the heels of the work of Ernst Käsemann in the middle of the last century and was given formation most notably by J. Christiaan Beker and J. Louis Martyn.[1] Recently Douglas Campbell in his way and Susan Eastman in hers have taken up and extended this interpretive school.[2] Close to the heart of such exegesis is the concern for the centrality of the revelation of Jesus Christ as the all-determining and world-making reality. In other words, sometimes directly and sometimes indirectly, in Paul these apocalypticists find Karl Barth's emphasis on the absolute primacy of Christology. As such, God's self-revelation in Jesus Christ cannot be secondary or subordinate to any prior systems of meaning, ideas, ethics, beliefs or principles. Christ *himself* is the reality, and everything must be seen in his dominating epistemic light. In the field of Pauline studies, this has often meant doing battle with the still-influential (even if disavowed) residue of Bultmannian Existentialism, often transposed into the various hermeneutical guises of a pesky and hard-to-nail-down liberal Protestantism. Equally, however, such a Christological primacy places these apocalypticists at odds with so-called "Lutheran"[3] interpretations of Paul that subordinate Christ to an *ordo salutis* wherein natural law always precedes revelation. Furthermore, the same sort of Christological relativization,

---

1. The major works are Martyn, *Galatians*; idem, *Theological Issues*; Beker, *Paul the Apostle*; idem, *Apocalyptic Gospel*; idem, *The Triumph of God*.

2. Campbell, *Deliverance*; Eastman, *Mother Tongue*.

3. I am no scholar of Luther, and I am aware that his thought is complex, voluminous and itself the subject of rigourous debate. Though I try to say as much along the way, mentions of Luther in this book should not be taken as claims about what Luther himself thought, but rather to the particular named aspects of *appropriatations* of Luther, which I take to be fairly consistent with the *presentation* of Luther in the secondary sources I cite. The same is true of the word "Lutheran," as in the present instance. My apologies to my Lutheran brothers and sisters for this necessary oversimplifcation.

apocalypticists claim, is discernable in certain sociological hermeneutics of the so-called New Perspective wherein Christ's "meaning" is determined by his place in salvation history.

Virtue ethics, while something of a misnomer (see below), is nevertheless a "field" that has grown up in the last thirty years or so largely following the publication of Alasdair MacIntyre's *After Virtue*. It usually finds its place within moral philosophy as one school among deontological and utilitarian alternatives. Broadly, MacIntyre and others seek to revive the ancient or classical ethical theory wherein character, community and narrative play central parts. Both in its Christian and non-Christian guises, the revival of virtue reaches back to the resources of Aristotle and St. Thomas Aquinas.

My claim is that a virtue ethic, or, as I will refer to it below, a classical account of human agency, has much to contribute to an apocalyptic reading of Paul's letters. Martyn and others have rightly recovered the centrality of Christ for Paul. But they have been less clear about the place of the church and more specifically about human agency in such an account (see chapter 1). At times we are left wondering what such an emphasis on the revelation of Christ *looks like* apart from simply emphasizing its reality. Furthermore, as I suggest in chapter 1, Martyn and other have sometimes struggled to articulate a coherent place for genuine human action in God's apocalypse of Christ. In spite of protests to the contrary, it sometimes looks as if the human being is simply an individual, passive bystander being acted upon but never truly acting.

Martyn himself, in a recent article, appears poised to address this. There he begins to develop the notion of the Spirit's "participation" in human action, a participation in which Christians truly do *act*.[4] He points to a "Christological dual agency" in which "God has elected to participate in the *corporate morality of a community as community* . . . the *Corpus Christi*."[5] In the community we find that God has made a "newly competent moral agent."[6] A central contention below is that in Alasdair MacIntyre's work we find needed resources for unpacking what such a competent Pauline moral agent might look like in much more detail. Specifically, on the whole, apocalyptic interpretations of Paul need a thicker ecclesiology in order to avoid coming up short in considering agency. An ethic of virtue moves us beyond such problematics by giving us a coherent account of

---

4. Martyn, "Gospel Invades Philosophy," 28.
5. Ibid., 30–31, italics original.
6. Ibid., 31.

Introduction

the formation of a genuine agent that takes her place within the context of corporate ecclesial practices.

Of course, a compelling synthesis of apocalyptic and virtue is in many ways already embodied in the theology of Stanley Hauerwas (though he does not work it out through exegesis of Paul). Douglas Harink's essay "Apocalypse: Galatians and Hauerwas" in his *Paul Among the Postliberals* points to the Christological emphasis Hauerwas shares with Martyn and other apocalypticists.[7] For both, apocalyptic names the "authentic Christian . . . mode of taking seriously Christ's Lordship over the public, the social, the political . . . Apocalyptic theology treats issues of concrete enslavement and power within a political-cosmic horizon and in terms of final judgment. It disavows all privatization of Christian faith . . . it rejects notions of the cosmos as a 'seamless web of causal relations.'"[8] This much is exactly right, and such similarity is due in part, as Harink notes, to the shared influence of Barth.[9]

Harink's account obscures, however, an important difference between what each party means by "apocalyptic." While for each this centrally denotes the place of Christ, for Hauerwas this Christological focus is nuanced by a strong ecclesiology and appreciation for the human actor. Thus, for Hauerwas "church becomes the necessary correlative of an apocalyptic narration of existence. It is the eucharistic community that is the epistemological prerequisite to understanding 'how things are.'"[10] Harink rightly remarks that for Hauerwas "the truth about 'the way things are' with the universe can finally be told only through concentrated attention on God's action in the life, death and resurrection of Jesus Christ, by those caught up of the life and practices of the new creation people called church."[11]

While this is certainly descriptive of Hauerwas, it is hard to find such an ecclesial emphasis in Martyn and his followers. For the latter the church, and an account of human agency therein, has not yet found its proper footing.[12] We are left wondering what *difference* it makes that for Paul Christ is the one-off, non-negotiable, invasive, world-determining power. What is the force, that is, of the emphasis that "Jesus Christ *is* the

---

7. Harink, *Paul*, 67–103.
8. Ibid., 74.
9. Ibid., 83.
10. Ibid., 75.
11. Ibid., 76.
12. Eastman, *Mother Tongue*, e.g., 165, 197, is perhaps poised to make the church central with her comments about the the "relational matrix" that exists "in Christ."

apocalypse for Paul?"[13] Vitally important as it is to get this (nonfoundationalist) claim straight, such Pauline exegesis has for the most part yet to see that Paul's answer over and over again is "church." The church is the site of the formation of Christians as they are habituated into holy practices.

This, I claim, among other things, is what MacIntyre's account of human action helps us to see. The church is a community of practice and to become skillful at such practice is to live what MacIntyre calls the life of virtue and what Paul in Romans calls the life of δικαιοσύνη, justice. My more specific claim in this book will be that we find in Romans a classical account of human action in many ways like the one MacIntyre develops in his work, but not finally reducible to it. In other words, I am trying to push something like a MacIntyrian virtue ethic through Paul via Romans.

The particulars of my thesis develop as follows. Chapter 1 sets up the problem by first providing an account of MacIntyre's work on human action and then offering a critique of human agency in modern Pauline scholarship in light of MacIntyre's work. The following three chapters offer a re-reading of central chapters of Romans that seeks to establish that it is possible to situate Paul within a classical model of human agency.

Chapter 2 is on Romans 5:12–21 and takes the first step of establishing that for Paul the church is recognizable by its qualitative difference from those in Adam in that it is *just* and so performs just deeds. The grace of God in Rom 5:12–21 does not effect an abstract forensic transaction, nor result in an "imputed status" before God. Rather, I suggest Paul argues that Christ makes possible for the church a *just practice*. This reading reconfigures the usual assumptions regarding the relationship of divine and human in this passage, since the just practice in which the church actively participates is an obedience that is always already gifted.

If chapter 2 tells us *that* Christ has made the church just, chapter 3 takes up Rom 6–8 and argues that here Paul tells us *how* it is that this has come about. I press here for what I call "participation [in Christ] by practice." I argue that by "sin" and "justice" in Rom 6 Paul does not name cosmic powers to which the church is or is not enslaved, but habits of the body inclining Christians to behave in certain just or sinful ways. Paul goes on in Romans 8 to say that these habits are the product of the church's cooperation with the Spirit, wherein it puts to death its passions, which have their seat in the body. By killing the body in this way the bodies that make up the church die with Christ, and at the same time are made alive by his Spirit. The church thus imitates Christ's death by the death of its

---

13. Harink, *Paul*, 78.

own sin-tending bodies in a way that literally and physically connects it to (participates it in) Christ.

Chapter 4 picks up here and argues that Rom 12–15 gives the specifics of what the just life looks like—its "content" in day-to-day ecclesial actualization. I argue that Rom 12–15 is not the "result," the "outworking," or the "implication," of salvation, but its very content. This section in some ways parallels parts of Plato's or Cicero's *Republic*, or Aristotle's *Politics*: it prescribes roles, chastises certain vices, and commends certain virtues. This section of the letter, therefore, provides the final complement of a classical theory of human action: a description of the virtues and vices, specific actions and rules that make up a "practice" in the MacIntyrian sense. At the heart of this section stands the practice of ἡ ἀγάπη, the "love feast" or Eucharistic meal, from which the rest of Paul's exhortation gains its sense.

Finally, in the conclusion, I bring these various exegetical threads together, offering preliminary theological syntheses and pointing to directions for further study. I suggest we can see that Paul has a classical account of human agency, centered in the church as the pneumatic body of Christ, but that the exact contours of this agency need further development along theological lines. As such, it is important to see this book is not so much *doing* Pauline virtue ethics as arguing that he has such an ethic in the first place. In this regard, I argue that to try to "fit" Paul's account of the church in Romans into a MacIntyrian practice is ultimately to domesticate it in a Pelagian direction.

As I develop an account of Pauline agency through Romans I am concerned to avoid, and push beyond, two common and in some ways opposite undesirable readings: (1) A view of the Pauline agent in terms of something like a *simul iustus et peccator* dynamic wherein the Christian agent makes very little or no progress in holiness; (2) a radical and rather instantaneous transformation wherein human agency and training gives way to a sort of magical theosis. Both of these, I argue, are hyper-Augustinian soteriologies foreign to Paul.[14]

---

14. This concern to sort out what holiness actually looks like and how it works (the basic questions of agency) is shared by Eastman, *Mother Tongue*, 3: "How does one sustain such change over time? This difficulty concerns the intersection of Paul's language of death and new life with the daily lives of individuals and communities—lives that of necessity unfold in at least a somewhat linear fashion. Without some such linearity and continuity, one cannot speak of genuine transformation, but only of a continual replacement of the 'old' by the 'new.' But without a radical break with the past, one may slip into a kind of determinism, or at the least an evolutionary model of history, that is quite foreign to Paul's apocalyptic convictions."

The Practice of the Body of Christ

Finally, my hope is that this project stands in the position of contributing to the theological project of giving the apocalyptic movement in Pauline theology some ecclesiological legs. This includes spelling out a coherent account of human agency in Pauline theology and in developing more fully what Paul expected the church's on-the-ground practice to look like (a project only half-begun here, since our focus is on agency). In other words, this is a first step at developing a Pauline and apocalyptic theological ethics after MacIntyre.

1

MacIntyrian Challenges to the Modern Study of Paul

Introduction

IN 1981 ALASDAIR MACINTYRE DROPPED A BOMB ON THE EMERGING post-modern world. The effects of *After Virtue* continue to be recognizable not just in philosophical ethics, but across the humanities through the sciences and out into the non-university world.[1] His claim was not just that the two main options in modern ethics, deontology and utilitarianism, were two sides of the same dead-end coin. His claim was no less than that the modern world had lost the ability to make sense of what it was doing or saying.

My claim is that, among these other effects, MacIntyre's work raises significant challenges for readings of Paul. In particular, MacIntyre shows how notions of human agency and the moral life have changed with the abandonment of a classical model that spoke of human action in terms of virtues and vices, desires and passions, reason and intention. Thus, for instance, one obvious challenge for readers of Paul seems to lie in the most basic concept of virtue as a disposition of the person to consistently act in particular ways. Modern Pauline studies for the most part has no way of making sense of a notion of habit and the sort of human agency implied therein, and this creates insurmountable difficulties to understanding

---

1. *After Virtue*, hereafter *AV*; 2nd edition 1983, 3rd edition 2007. In academic philosophy see Cunningham, ed., *MacIntyre*; Knight, *Aristotle to MacIntyre*; Smith, *Virtue Ethics*. In Christian ethics see Murphy et al.,*Virtues and Practices*; Lutz, *Tradition*; Hauerwas and Pinches, *Christians*. In education see MacIntyre and Dunn, "Alasdair MacIntyre," 1–19. As an inspiration of the "new monastic movement" see Wilson, *Living Faithfully*.

some central areas of Pauline theology. The purpose of this chapter is to demonstrate and illustrate this claim.

I proceed as follows. First, because MacIntyre does not think his challenge can be articulated except in the form of a story, we are involved in a selective retelling of MacIntyre's narrative of the development of the highly intertwined topics of an "ethic of virtue", grace and human agency, and the notion of the self or subject as they are pertinent to the study of Paul. I set out MacIntyre's account in these specific areas rather fully since many New Testament scholars will be unfamiliar with this work. At points it will be helpful to fill out his argument by drawing on the work of others who have told similar stories with differences that are important for us. Second, I examine major trends in academic Pauline theology in light of MacIntyre. As will become clear, a history of the sort MacIntyre provides significantly illuminates the modern construal of Paul's theology. A central purpose of my use of MacIntyre's account is to show just how contingent and, often, arbitrary, most current work on Pauline theology in these areas is. Thus I argue that, because New Testament scholars tend to ignore such issues, they often end up reconstructing Paul in their own "common sense" modern grammar of human agency and the moral life. It is precisely the obviousness of this grammar and hence its appropriateness for reading Paul that I want to call into question. Beyond this, however, the review of contemporary scholarship in the light of MacIntyre's work allows me to expose several errors in Pauline research regarding the relation between divine and human agency. The first is a reading of Paul usually ascribed to Luther in which Christians are saved in a state of sin and are more or less destined to remain sinners for the rest of their lives: on this view, justification happens only forensically, "before God." The second sees Christians as transformed from a previously sinful state—and very radically so—by an invasive infusion of the Spirit that almost magically realizes the creation of holy lives. Both of these are hyper-Augustinian soteriologies and both, I will suggest, are unPauline. A third type, however, will variously insist that holiness is a part of Paul's theology without insisting on magical moral change, but also without any explanation of how and why Paul should think such a change occurs. I argue that none of these three moves are able to make sense out of Paul because they lack any account of human action in classical terms. It is to the details of such an account that we now turn.

The Classical Tradition of the Virtues

MacIntyre uses "virtue" as a shorthand for a whole tradition. While sometimes scholars contrast a "virtue ethic" with an "ethic of obligation," we will see that this is both too simple and does not go to the heart of the matter.[2] Nor is it just the case that virtue names a moral philosophy in which account is made for the fact that people have certain dispositions to act in certain ways. Rather, for MacIntyre "virtue" names a particular way of talking about human action that is ultimately incommensurable with modern and post-modern accounts of the same. These differences come out below.

MacIntyre's account of the virtues has to arise from and take place within a historical narrative because for him there can be no such thing as moral theory as such.[3] Accounts of human action are always accounts of specific historical practice that arise within and as a part of concrete political, economic and social conditions (it is thus no surprise that he has learned much from Marxism). Action theory cannot fail to be part of such conditions, and it is because of this that it is helpful at times to read his account of virtue as a particular narrative account of the "self."[4] In other words, we are dealing here with moral psychology.

Aristotle

MacIntyre's story about the development of what we are calling a classical account of the virtues begins, more or less, with Homer and "heroic society," but it fits our purposes to begin with his important and substantial account of Aristotle. For Aristotle the central question is not just, as with Homer, about what it means to be good as father or craftsman or fisherman but what it means to be good as a *human being*. Answering such a question is the goal of the *Nichomachean Ethics*, which provides for MacIntyre's a sort of archetype and point of reference for every other account of the virtues. Other accounts will continually orient themselves to this work, sometimes heuristically and sometimes evaluatively.

---

2. MacIntyre labors at times to dispel the notion that a virtue ethic is to be contrasted with one based on rules, especially in his later work. See *Dependent Rational Animals*, 103–5. Hereafter *DRA*.

3. See MacIntyre's *Three Rival Versions*, esp. 170–215. Hereafter *TRV*.

4. MacIntyre himself does this from time to time. See *AV*, 129; *DRA*, 83–87.

Aristotle says that every activity aims at some good since human beings naturally aim at some goal. The good is defined in terms of the nature of the goal. This teleological or means-ends reasoning that is simply a given part of human nature makes up for Aristotle what MacIntyre calls a basic "metaphysical biology."[5] Human beings are simply hardwired (biology) to pursue certain goods (metaphysics). The highest good is happiness (εὐδαιμονία), since happiness is that for the sake of which we do everything else and which we do not pursue for the sake of any other end. Virtues are then those dispositions that tend to the attainment of the end, and vices the contrary. Virtues are, however, not merely instrumental to, but constitutive of, the good life, since for Aristotle one cannot attain the good short of its practice.[6] Thus virtues are part of the *definition* of the good life, and, as with Homer, actions are evaluable *factually* in terms of whether or not they do or do not contribute to the attainment of the end.[7]

The anatomy of Aristotelian virtue involves several essential elements. Virtues are dispositions of the soul (as the "form" of the body) to both *act* and *feel* in particular ways in particular circumstances. These habits of disposition determine what we find pleasant or desirable: our tastes are determined by our virtues.[8] The central reason for this is that for Aristotle the way we acquire virtue is not, as on some readings of Plato, by the simple apprehension of the good, but rather by means of training and discipline. This is what it takes to form our habits so that to be (say) a just person simply is to have habits to act justly, which is to act a certain way in particular situations.[9] The capacity for figuring out which situations require which sort of habited action belongs to the virtue of prudence. There are, in other words, no absolute rules for the application of particular kinds of actions, so prudence is necessary for the exercise of the virtues; without it there can be no application of the right acts to the right circumstances, which is of course to say that there can be no right

---

5. It is to be noted that in *AV* (148) MacIntyre had argued that such metaphysical biology could be discarded while retaining much of the rest of Aristotle's ethics. He retracts this, however, in *DRA* (x), saying that "I now judge that I was in error in supposing an ethics independent of biology was possible".

6. MacIntyre, *Short History*, 61–63. Hereafter *SHE*.

7. *AV*, 150.

8. Ibid., 149–50. So there is no necessary conflict between reason and desire as there was for Plato. On the soul see *SHE*, 64.

9. *SHE*, 64.

acts at all (for part of the definition of the latter is that they must be wisely applied).[10]

For each virtue there are two corresponding vices, since for Aristotle the virtues are the mean between two extremes. Hence, for instance, courage is the mean between cowardice and rashness. But this example illustrates well the point made above that such a disposition to courage requires the habituation of both what we would call "reason" and what we would call "emotion" (the passions). So reason is habituated to rule over emotions and the emotions themselves are thereby habituated to respond differently than they would if untrained. It is important to note that such training of the passions is not repudiation thereof. The passions are neither good nor bad *per se* but must be made to tend to the end of the good.[11]

MacIntyre points out that friendship is the most important virtue for Aristotle because it is the presupposition of the initial constitution of community.[12] It is, in fact, the presupposition for the exercise of the cardinal virtues of justice, temperance, prudence and courage. Justice, in other words, presupposes the conditions set by friendship and only the existence of friendship allows that virtue to be practiced. Such a relationship means that for Aristotle outside the *polis* there can ultimately be no justice in the strict sense.[13] The *polis* is the fundamental context in which the pursuit of the virtues makes sense, because they can only be attained in a community in search of the common good.[14]

---

10. Ibid., 66–68; *AV*, 155; see of course the extended treatment "Aristotle on Practical Rationality" in MacIntyre's *Whose Justice? Which Rationality?*, 124–45. Hereafter *WJWR*.

11. It is vitally important to understand the deep difference between what we now call "emotions" and what the ancients meant by its various approximations that are variously rendered as "passions," "desires," or "emotions." Modern emotions are often viewed as untreatable, largely uncontrollable, entirely passive feelings set off by external stimuli to which we might be able to learn to change our behavioral *reaction*, but which are themselves just a given part of our psychophysical, historically conditioned, existential temperament, to which teaching and argument are irrelevant. In the classical view, however, emotions were highly if difficultly treatable, and it was the task of the philosophical school to provide such a remedy. There is of course a massive literature on the topic, but foremost studies include Nussbaum, *Therapy*; Sorabji, *Emotions*; Engberg-Pedersen, *Hellenistic Philosophy*.

12. *AV*, 156; *DRA*, 147–55.

13. *WJWR*, 141–43.

14. Thus justice that attains between (say) Athens and Sparta is only justice named metaphorically and derivative of justice internal to Athens itself. On the other hand, however, the ideal of friendship to the pursuit of happiness allows Aristotle to solve the most pressing practical problem he faced in the *Ethics* and that is that the polis that he

This is the basic Aristotelian account that is so important for MacIntyre both positively and negatively. Moreover, something like this basic account of human action can be found across the ancient world as we approach the Middle Ages. Whether in a Platonic or Aristotelian configuration, what emerges is a common vocabulary of action-description in terms of passions and desires, virtue and vice, ultimate and proximate ends, training and habituation. We may call this the classical account of human action. We can so name this classical tradition because the language it uses to describe human action has much more in common, from Aristotle to Aquinas, than all its component authors do with the moral language of the modern world.

Augustine

MacIntyre writes that Augustine developed a critique of a Stoic description of action (most explicitly in the *City of God* where he sees it as the general form of pagan philosophy).[15] The direction and order of human desires is for Augustine the work of *voluntas*: desires are voluntary and so implicitly a part of the process of reasoning and action. Aristotle (and Plato) had been unable to explain convincingly how someone might know what is best and yet fail to do it. They had to refer either to an imperfection of knowledge or inadequate training. But Augustine held that the passions were *misdirected* by the will. And to position the will in the right direction is the job of God's grace, for only by being so directed can human action ever hope to be rightly ordered. Because the human practice of the good is the product of grace at such a fundamental level, the central vice is a vice of the will as well, pride, which is opposed to the most fundamental virtue, humility. So the "[practical] rationality of right action . . . is not the fundamental determinate but a secondary consequence of right willing."[16]

In leveling such a critique against the stoics, concomitant with his newly expanded notion of *voluntas*, Augustine also broke with his own Platonic heritage. What this means is that we genuinely seem to have "a new account of the genesis of action."[17] Specifically, contra Plato, Augustine saw in the *Confessions* and in the lives of others that the full apprehension

---

concludes is necessary for the good life does not exist. Only friendships can hold out the hope of such attainment.

15. *WJWR*, 154.
16. Ibid., 158.
17. Ibid., 154.

of the form of justice is itself not sufficient to generate right action. Rather, we have to direct our love, or rather have it directed, towards that form, and this by directing it towards a life that embodies that form in act, the life of Christ.[18]

MacIntyre leaves much of Augustine's account of the virtues implicit. But because Augustine will play such an important role later in the history of the concepts we are interested in, both in Aquinas and especially in MacIntyre's account of the Reformation, it is useful to set this out a bit more fully in regard to two key points. First, it is important to see that Augustine has a fully-fledged doctrine of the virtues. The second point, which is tightly bound up with the first, is to see the way that his doctrine of grace is integrated therein. This takes us beyond MacIntyre, but is of great import for contemporary Pauline scholarship.

Augustine has a doctrine of the virtues as dispositions of an agent to act in accordance with the good. What is important for us is the plain fact that for Augustine advancement toward God in the life of the virtues is necessary for salvation. The church is visibly different from the earthly city precisely in the fact that its practices are different: the church is holy, virtuous. This means, as Jennifer Herdt says, that "talk of habituation and human striving must go hand in hand with talk of conversion . . . Augustine's defense of Christian virtue as true virtue rests on the fact that we are responsive to grace rather than passive in the face of grace; our own agency, striving to imitate exemplars of virtue, remains central, and our final good, enjoyment of God, is possible only through our own active involvement."[19] Thus Augustine says in the *City of God* that "eternal life is the Supreme Good and eternal death the Supreme Evil, and . . . *to achieve the one and escape the other we must live rightly.*"[20] One is trained and habituated by the practices of the church.[21]

The virtues have their place for Augustine within the dynamic of the divine interaction of God with humanity. Many contemporary portrayals of Augustine's theology of grace are complicit in readings of the anti-Pelagian writings as a discourse in which a disembodied, abstract, divine agency called "grace" interacts with other similar hypostizations like "sin", "will" and "man". This schema is then interpreted as a one-sided rebuttal of Pelagius in favor of the irresistibility of grace to the exclusion of any

18. Ibid.
19. Herdt, *Virtue*, 47–48.
20. Augustine, *City of God* XIX.4; quoted in Herdt, *Virtue*, 50.
21. Herdt, *Virtue*, 67, 70–71.

genuine human agency.²² It is at such a view of Augustine that Michael Hanby takes aim in his book *Augustine and Modernity* by placing Augustine's response to the Pelagian controversy within the broader context of his Trinitarian theology and ecclesiology. He writes that

> [f]ew contemporary analyses of the doctrine of grace acknowledge the ontological stakes of the question, just as few analyses of Augustine's ontology consider the relevance of his doctrine of grace. As a consequence, the former almost inevitably turn on the attempt to dissect the willed movement into action and passion, delineate the human from the divine contribution and, quite predictably, protect the human contribution from violation by the causality of grace.... Presuming that the ontic and ontological status of humanity, nature and God are self-evident, [these sorts of studies] then implicitly reduce God to one object among others, dialectically juxtaposed to creation. Coextensive with this reduction is the reduction of grace to an immanently causal force, is an impoverished view of causality, whose precise connection to its effects is presumed to be accessible. This manner of framing the issue has the a priori effect of making God less than transcendent and immutable... Briefly put, this attempt to delineate and make discrete the respective contribution of the "two agents" is simply bad theological grammar. We are therefore warranted in viewing the Pelagian problem within the context of the larger question of causality.²³

In other words, the reason the Pelagian controversy is so important to Augustine is that it calls into question a traditional Christian understanding of creation and Trinity. The Pelagian controversy is, for Augustine according to Hanby, a debate about God.²⁴

---

22. See, for instance, Weaver, *Divine Grace*: "As the Augustinian scheme developed, the connection between human actions and their outcome in eternity diminished, for at every point grace exercised sovereignty over the self, its desiring, its meritorious activity, and its reward" (67).

23. Hanby, *Augustine*, 82.

24. We can see this more clearly by considering ways that Hanby takes up concerns in common with Kathryn Tanner's similar concerns in *God and Creation*: "For *creatio ex nihilo* entails the notion of divine immutability as a corollary. Creaturely existence or prime matter can have no prior claim to God's activity without locking God into a real relation to his creation... Hence the relation of divine cause to created effect cannot be dialectical.... Rather, God's causality of temporal effects cannot in any way be thought to effect a change in God's own agency, or a compromise of God's simplicity. Augustine's incessant rebuttal of the Pelagian position, that grace cannot originate with us, simply transposes this logic into the category of sanctification. Human merit

Hence, dealing with the problem of divine and human agency requires a reconfiguration of our speech about God. In the first place, it means that God cannot be properly spoken of as "cause" in any normal sense of the word, and certainly any modern sense of the word. "There is no proper analogy by which a 'causal mechanism' for creation from nothing can be brought into view. Creating, as opposed to merely causing, remains a mystery in the most profound sense."[25] What Hanby points out is that to speak of God as cause is to risk misunderstanding because the normal grammar of causal relations holds between *creatures*. But God is not a creature—not one "being" among others, however different—and so framing the issue this way is dangerous, for our language is bound to fool us. Equally though, to speak of God's agency merely contrastively, as not-finite, not-material, and so on, is, as Tanner has shown, to bring God down "to the level of the world and the beings within it in virtue of that very opposition: God becomes one being among others within a single order. Such talk suggests that God exists along side the non-divine, that God is limited by what is opposed to it [*sic*], that God is as finite as the non-divine beings with which it is being contrasted . . ."[26] A proper interpretation of Augustine, that is, cannot characterize God "by contrast with any sort of being, [so that God] may be the immediate source of being of every sort."[27]

Such is the case, argues Hanby, for Augustine. God's grace does not compete with human agency because God's transcendence means he is not limited to cause and effect as it operates in his creatures. Hence, to set up the Creator-creature relationship as cause-effect or action-passion is to misunderstand Augustine. Rather, we should really say that "God is not *an* agent. This God is not one actor alongside others, whose agency can be treated as an efficient quantifiable force in relation to the force of other agencies. Nor are creatures patients awaiting actualization prior to God's gift of being."[28] Put positively, because, and just as, God is the creator (since the logic of transcendence in relation to creation is the same in relation to grace), God "brings being out of nothing. This 'causal' activity is manifest in the creature as effect, *precisely in the creature's own actuality*

---

cannot be antecedent to the activity of grace without similarly rendering the divine act finite and reactive" (Hanby, *Augustine*, 83).

25. Hanby, *Augustine*, 84.
26. Tanner, *God and Creation*, 84.
27. Ibid., 45–46.
28. Hanby, *Augustine*, 85.

and activity."²⁹ God's agency, for Augustine, is the very condition of the possibility for creation's contingency in general and human freedom in particular. God, in his transcendence, is able to cause our very contingency. In other words, because there is no competition, no *zero sum* cooperation (this does not exclude other types of cooperation), it is right and proper for a creature to claim action and being as *his own*. In this way we can and should

> understand creatures to exhibit their status as creatures, as received effects, in their active response to the call to form from the divine *vox*. Paradoxically, this movement is utterly distinct and yet utterly indistinguishable from the movement of the *vox* in them. In consequence it is a response, a movement which *belongs to creatures precisely insofar as it belongs to God*. Hence Augustine says that 'whatever the soul possesses, and whatever it receives, is from God; and yet the act of receiving and having belongs, of course, to the receiver and the possessor.³⁰

Indeed, to deny this in most cases would be to deny God's transcendence and capability of bringing about free will in his very act. Ironically, then, so many pious disavowals of agency and competency (sc. virtues, holiness) turn out to be derived from, and ascribed to, a domesticated deity.³¹

This means that in a significant sense it is false to claim that for Augustine God's grace *causes* our good acts. There is no simple "mechanism" in play, no way we can speak merely of the respective contributions of the "two agents." Rather, God's "agency" (which is not a creaturely agency) is the condition of the possibility of any genuine human action at all. Moreover, Augustine's "self", in Hanby's terms, is always un-integrated prior to doxological formation. In less prolix terms, the only thing that can unify the self and make it truly "free" is participation in the practices of the

---

29. Creation itself exists for Augustine *within* the Trinity, in the Father and Son's reciprocal love and delight, which is the Holy Spirit. So to exist is to exist in such a relation and sanctification is the Spirit's drawing us into this plentitude of love, so that we literally are more than we were before. So selfhood, being at all, is doxological: "It is only through delight in Christ, a gift of the mutual delight between the Father and the Son, that 'I' can finally be myself" (Hanby, *Augustine*, 91).

30. Hanby, *Augustine*, 89.

31. Thus, Hanby argues that to divide action from passion is actually the precondition for the Pelagian opposition to Augustinian grace. "With no real reciprocal relation between the related terms, there is no causal connection, no immanent force, and thus no immanent exclusivity or competition, between cause and effect." The language of "domestication" is that of Placher, *Domestication*, who takes up much the same concern. See esp. his chapter on "Grace and Works in Modern Thought" (146–63).

church, which is to act in Christ to move toward a desire for God. This is, in the end, the only action that is both fully mine and fully rational. Augustine

> invokes christological mediation as the answer to his own dissipation. This move once again situates both the self and its knowledge within the ambit of trinitarian gift, and makes the means to the acquisition of that knowledge neither a self-objectification nor a sacrificial self-negation, but a sacrifice of praise and thanksgiving. To recover oneself in this sense, however, is only to further the soul's ecstatic reversal by opening it in charity to the Body's participation in the doxological sacrifice of its Head.... [S]elfhood, insofar as it has become selfhood, is, once again, *ecclesiastically* constituted.[32]

This brief survey, supplementing and in some important ways correcting MacIntyre's account of Augustine, is meant to establish several main features of Augustine's theology in preparation for our later use of it. We have seen, first, that Augustine has a full account of the virtues, which are constituted precisely as *our* virtues only because they are actualized by God's grace; second, this means that Augustine has a non-competitive account of the interaction between divine and human "agents"; third, this implies that Augustine does not have a Cartesian notion of the "self"[33];

---

32. Hanby, *Augustine*, 100.

33. See Hauerwas's response to Taylor's account of the Augustinian self (Hauerwas, "Sources,") expanded by Hanby (*Augustine*, 8–12). Taylor argued that, for Augustine, the road from the lower to the higher (the divine) passes from the outer to the inner. Thus God is not just "out there" illuminating the world of ideas, as the Good is for Plato, but is the inner light of the soul itself. We can thus find God when we take up a stance of radical reflexivity, where we try to experience our experiencing. This turn makes the language of inwardness irresistible. This does not get us all the way to Descartes, but it does establish the first person stance. For Augustine, the development of the will is twofold: (1) He takes up the development made by the Stoics that humans have the same perceptions as animals do but that we have *prohairesis*, "moral choice." (2) But Augustine goes beyond Plato's and Aristotle's explanations of evil in humans. Augustine's two loves introduce the fact that our stance could be radically perverse: we might see the good and turn our back on it anyway, because of Adam's sin. We must first be healed through grace. The tricky part is putting *prohairesis* together with the will. The former is strong or weak, the latter good or evil. What this means is that for the first time it might be the will that determines what we are in a position to know. So we discover that we are dependent upon God most in those powers that are most our own (will and intellect). Both Hauerwas and Hanby show that properly contextualizing Augustine as *theologian* and not just philosopher makes such a reading deeply problematic.

fourth, Augustine's theology of grace and nature is not abstracted from the concrete practices that make up the church; they are, rather, the necessary ways of talking about God for those who take part in them.

The depth of our account of Augustine has been necessitated by the fact that a critical reading of MacIntyre in light of the work of Hanby, Herdt, and others reveals that an abandonment of a notion of virtue and a competitive conception of divine and human agency go hand in hand. This will become clearer below, but it is enough to say that without a notion of virtue as truly one's own disposition toward God as the ultimate good we are led to assert constantly a competitive overriding of our own actions by God's grace to explain the performance of good acts.

Thomas Aquinas

St. Thomas is the hero of MacIntyre's later works. He is so because, for MacIntyre, he was able to plausibly (which is not to say always convincingly) overcome the conflict between the two great traditions of moral description we have treated so far: Augustine and Aristotle. The former was the canonical extra-canonical text in the Middle Ages, and the later had been recently revived in the form of an Arabic translation of the *Nichomachean Ethics*.[34] Augustine represented the deepening, and triumph of, Platonism and parts of the Ciceronean tradition even as he rejected the latter's Stoic elements and the implicit nihilism of Plotinus. Thomas brought the newly revived Aristotelianism (as well as a keen knowledge of the Eastern Fathers and Gregory the Great) to bear on all of this. Thomas represents, in other words, a focal point where all these various traditions of virtue converged.

Thomas' account includes both acquired and infused virtues. The former are attained by the habituation of practice, the latter by the habituation of the Spirit. The acquired virtues direct us toward the proximate end of happiness in this life, while the infused direct us to our final end in the enjoyment of God. Even the infused virtues, however, are habits that must be retained by practice: "Aquinas is concerned to make clear that the gifts dispose rather than displace human agency. Grace heals and elevates human character, but always in ways that stand in an organic relation to human agency."[35]

More specifically, *caritas* is the (Aristotelian) "form" of all virtue. Without it the other virtues lack the kind of directedness they require.

34. For a full account see *WJWR*, 165–82 and *TRV*, 127–48.
35. Herdt, *Virtue*, 73.

Charity itself, however, is the gift of the Holy Spirit, not to be acquired by moral education.[36] And the virtues are, as for Augustine, necessary for salvation:

> Salvation is made possible through the bestowal of infused virtues, dispositions to act. Human beings must act to increase these virtues and bring them to perfection, and only through this process will they become persons capable of enjoying God, capable of their own ultimate good. It is true that, since they are infused rather than acquired through human action, these virtues are most basically divine gift rather than human accomplishment... At the same time, it is important to recall Aquinas' insistence that the infused virtues are indeed virtues, that they transform the person's own will such that she herself is intrinsically ordered to God, rather than being shoved mechanically ... The infused virtues, rather than functioning as an excuse for passivity, are a disposition to act and are therefore fulfilled only through action.[37]

MacIntyre notes that this means that, for Aquinas, it takes *practice* to understand what we say about the good (natural or supernatural). So practical reason (*prudentia*) is a way of responding to the various questions that confront us about what is best to do when.[38] Prudence has the form of premises and subordinate conclusions, but we do not, like Euclidian geometry, grasp the whole once we grasp the premises. Rather, we don't grasp the principles until we understand the conclusions.[39] In other words, *prudentia* is supremely practical in that it arises from the "experience" of trying to live justly. This notion, MacIntyre rightly sees, is at odds with the way the modern world has sought to talk about morality in the first place. Specifically, this account diverges in the sharpest way with what Charles Pinches calls the "ethical principle monism" of Kant (categorical imperative), Hume (consensus about the passions) and Bentham (utility), and more recently Rawls (the fairness principle).[40] None of these regard the moral life as a journey towards conceiving the first principle as an end, and none of these authors require the virtues in Aquinas' sense for the coherence of their program.

36. *WJWR*, 204.
37. Herdt, *Virtue*, 89.
38. *WJWR*, 196–97.
39. Ibid., 254.
40. Pinches, *Theology and Action*, 40–44.

For Aquinas, on the other hand, without the virtues *there can be no right moral action*. A wicked woman cannot perform a just action in the same way that a just woman can. A child begins with rules intended to direct the will by providing a standard of right direction (*rectitudo*). But the right kind of rule following is not possible without education into the moral virtues.[41] Every situation has aspects that fall under rules and aspects that do not. In some cases rules that do apply are very important and sometimes not: knowing which and how to act is the role of *prudentia*, which is the counterpart of God's ordering all things to their end by his *providentia*. *Prudentia* is the ability to see and act with the grain of the universe.

MacIntyre says that while Augustine used the grammar of the "will" to accuse his Roman counterparts of only a semblance of virtue, Aquinas integrated Paul and Augustine's doctrine of the defective human will with Aristotle's account of practical reasoning to form a "single, unified, complex account of human action as such."[42] MacIntyre goes on to illustrate just how complex the "self" is for Thomas. First, the intellect judges some end good, with its virtue of prudence. An act of the will towards that end is elicited, an *intentio*, which may be directed towards immediate ends, distant ends, or a variety of ends. (*Intentio* distinguishes a genuine act of the will from a mere wish.) Will consents to the means judged appropriate by the intellect in the process of deliberation. This terminates in *electio* (note how different the grammar is from our "choice"), and the will then consents to the means, and commands an act that completes the action, implementing the *electio*.[43]

It is important to see that this is at once a picture of human action and a picture of the "soul." As such, this is an outline of what we would usually call the "self" that is quite different from a modern "self." The latter, as we will see, is often reducible to brute will-power. This means necessarily that, as with Augustine, Aquinas' picture of God's interaction with the human agent will be necessarily different than those with different psychologies. But, most basically, this account is much more complex than the relatively punctiliar notion of the subject to which moderns are accustomed.[44] One

41. *WJWR*, 194.
42. Ibid., 184.
43. Ibid., 190.
44. Aquinas learned from Augustine that all action implies something that is desired. This is important because it means that the object of an action is necessary, and so intention of it necessary, for there to be any action at all, since otherwise there is no motivation for action. (Transposed into the Pelagian controversy, this means that

important fact for our purposes is that, relative to a modern account, a classical account of action in terms of the virtues simply has a greater variety of "points" at which divine-human interaction could take place. This is a further way in which the eclipse of the virtues is implicated in an inability to conceive of a non-competitive divine-human cooperation.[45]

MacIntyre's Synthetic Account of Human Action

From this account of the classical tradition of the virtues MacIntyre develops his own. It is noteworthy, however, that he is not simply offering a historical "survey" of virtue from which he picks and chooses the best pieces and discards the rest. This would give the impression that one stood outside such a tradition in order to look at it "objectively" without changing anything.[46] Rather, he takes his account to be a development of the

---

grace is simply the always-prior presence of God as the object necessary before any "move" can be made towards him. For Augustine there is no engine to human action in the will itself apart from desire. The will has no last say as "power of choice." To the extent, therefore, that any account of grace and nature absorbs these Kantian assumptions, it will necessarily be Pelagian. Hanby, *Augustine*, 100, comes close to making this point.) For reason always has to be appetitive (hence Augustine and Aquinas' *voluntas*) and so for them the Stoics are wrong precisely in their theory of action: they provide nothing that would *motivate* action. "Reason cannot cast out passion without dividing its own house," since reason would be unmotivated so to do. "We *are moved* to action by what is judged to be desirable . . . We are moved by delight in what attracts us, which is to say we are moved by what has the character of the beautiful" (Hanby, *Augustine*, 100). Indeed, on a Stoic account, we cannot even *desire* beatitude. So, for Augustine and Aquinas, "[c]hoice between alternatives is not a sign of the will's freedom to choose but its bondage to an internal division of desire . . . in a single-minded love for the good . . . the need for choice never arises" (Hanby, *Augustine*, 99–101). So "choice" is not the last moment, but rather merely "consent" that "denotes our acting at last with the continence of a unified desire toward that which supremely attracts us. And to the degree that the fact consented to accords with the good of doxology, it denotes the restoration of the Trinitarian image in us (Hanby, *Augustine*, 93). Again I take it that Hanby is making the claim that the form of free action is church practice, and that this is the only way to be formed in God's image. Thus the place of desire in an account of action is one of the sharpest ways that this classical account diverges from the post-Kantian. For the latter, there is a contrast between inclination and desire (*SHE*, 86–87). This point regarding Kant and Aquinas is similarly made by McCabe, *On Aquinas*, 101–3.

45. See here Reinhard Hütter, "Grace and Free Will," 521–53. He quotes Bernard Lonergan that "because [God] is a transcendent cause, there can be no incompatibility between terrestrial contingence and the causal certitude of providence" (546). The whole article is relevant.

46. See his earlier conceptualization of this in *SHE*, 1–4 and his more mature

rationality embodied in the tradition that he has outlined. This is another way of saying that the historical account he gives throughout his work, and which we have just inadequately sketched, is not an optional extra that could be added on to a purely theoretical and timeless account of the virtues.[47]

If this is the case, one of the first questions that MacIntyre has to answer is about the possible coherence of such an account given the existence of varying conceptions of the virtues in different societies. For Homer, virtues are the abilities to fill certain roles *qua* roles, while for Aristotle, they are the abilities to live the good life *qua* human being. The New Testament adds new virtues like humility and charity, which Aristotle would have rejected. Likewise Aristotle thought riches good, but in the NT the rich man is evil and the *slave* is good. Looking more broadly, things become even more complex. For Ben Franklin, virtues empower *utility*, while Jane Austin introduces the virtue of "constancy."[48] How are we ever to construct a concept of virtue out of all of this?

MacIntyre begins with the notion of a practice. A practice is a "coherent and complex form of socially established cooperative human behavior through which goods internal to that practice are realized in the course of trying to achieve excellence in that activity, with the result that the virtues and conceptions of the end and the goods are extended."[49] A practice, in other words, provides the arena for the exhibition of the virtues, and their definition. Examples include the maintenance of hospitals, painting, the science of chemistry, or the playing of chess.[50]

---

accounts in *WJWR*, 349–69 and virtually the whole of *TRV*.

47. A detached account is impossible for several related reasons. MacIntyre has learned from Wittgenstein that to understand a concept is not simply to have certain "ideas" about it; it also involves certain types of behavior and the ability to act in certain ways. So, "to possess a concept involves behaving or being able to behave in certain ways in certain circumstances, to alter concepts, whether by modifying existing concepts or by making new concepts available or by destroying old ones, is to alter behavior" (*SHE*, 3). Because concepts such as virtue or human action cannot be given without reference to human action, one cannot tell a history of ideas without reference to the concrete history in which that history of ideas takes place. And of course once you have said this, the notion of a history of ideas in the traditional sense has already been abandoned. This claim against the possibility of a pure history of moral ideas is for MacIntyre simply another part of his claim that morality is not a sphere that can be theorized about apart from the lived practices of a specific society.

48. *AV*, 184–87.

49. Ibid., 187.

50. Ibid.

So there can be no true "goods" in the classical sense without the notion of a practice. But equally there can be no practices without the distinction between goods internal and external. So in chess, while making the right move achieves an objective good internal to the game, impressing onlookers by making that right move achieves an external good: "To judge someone good in some role or at discharging some function within some socially established practice is to judge that agent good insofar as there are goods internal to that activity that are genuine goods, goods that are to be valued as ends worth pursuing for their own sake, if they are to be pursued at all."[51]

But such delimited spheres of practice must give way to conceiving all of life in such teleological terms. For when we make judgments about the best way for individuals or communities to order their lives to the good *per se*, we commit ourselves to a stance on the good not just for this or that human practice and so this or that role, but for human beings in general.[52] This is to take a stance on what it is for a human to flourish. At the same time what

> it is for human beings to flourish does of course vary from context to context, but in every context it is as someone exercises in a relevant way the capacities of an independent practical reasoner that her or his potentialities for flourishing in a specifically human way are developed. So if we want to understand how it is good for humans to live, we need to know what it is to be excellent as an independent practical reasoner, that is, what the virtues of independent practical reasoning are. But we need to know more than this . . . having raised the question of what specifically human flourishing consists in, we find almost immediately, just as Aristotle did, that it has become the question of what the virtues are and of what it is to live the kind of life that the exercise of the virtues requires.[53]

---

51. *DRA*, 66.

52. Ibid., 67.

53. Ibid., 77. It is important to stress that MacIntyre does not mean "independent" in any absolute sense, for practical reasoning is always within a community. "By independence I mean both the ability and the willingness to evaluate the reasons for action advanced to one by others, so that one makes oneself accountable for one's endorsements of the practical conclusions of others as well as for one's own conclusions" (ibid., 105).

In other words, one only finds out what the good is in the midst of practical experience.[54]

With the notion of goods internal and external to practices in place, MacIntyre offers the definition of a virtue as a quality which tends towards achieving goods internal to a practice and the lack of which prevents us from attaining such goods.[55] But we can contextualize this account further. In *Dependent Rational Animals* MacIntyre gives an explanation of the virtues by showing their (necessary) place in an account of the development of a human being.

The difference between human beings and other animals is not that we have language while dogs do not but that we are able to reflect upon our reasons for action and ask if the reasons are good while dogs simply have reasons for action.[56] In this way babies and small children are the same as dogs. But while we say that dogs can live well or flourish as such, this is not the case with babies or small children. In order to flourish *qua* human, human beings have to develop the capacity for reflecting upon their reasons for acting.[57] Children act in the first instance simply for the satisfaction of bodily pleasures and desires. A significant part of development comes as they slowly learn to distance themselves from those desires and to ask if such fulfillment is what is *best*. This involves not just the development of reason but also of the slow training of the desires themselves so that now in fact the child desires that good which was better in the first place.[58]

First, the child learns that pleasing its parents rather than crying is to be chosen in order to get food or praise. From this intermediate stage the parents will have to teach the child not to act so to please them but to act for what is truly better. Once the child has become sufficiently detached from both its own desires and the influence of others it becomes slowly and for the first time a mature practical reasoner. The qualities that are cultivated in this transformation of desire, motivation, and action, are called virtues, and so a lack of virtue names the reason that one fails to attain what is good and best.

---

54. Ibid., 113. Even in Christian variations of the classical account wherein the good is given by revelation, the true character of that good is only apprehended successively as one journeys towards it.

55. Ibid., 191.

56. Ibid., 54.

57. Ibid., 64–65.

58. See ibid., 76.

But what is needed for any such development to take place is unconditional acceptance and a situation of trust and security. This is usually provided by the parents, who teach the child that their commitment to it is not threatened by the child's failure or by circumstance. In such an atmosphere the child is free to playfully test his experience and explore his world, knowledge of which is necessary for practical reasoning. The child is also free to take her first actions toward distancing herself from her desires and choosing a higher good for its own sake and so form the virtues. Absent such a situation of "trust based on experience", however, the process will be significantly stunted.[59] The child may become isolated from both parents and others, since the former does not provide support and the latter are a threat. As a result, of course, the child is unable to develop the virtues necessary to judge and attain the good.

In this connection, MacIntyre notes that, contrary to popular modern opinion, desire is not a sufficient condition for action, in that a desire can never by itself be the major premise in a practical syllogism. The practical syllogism has the form: X is good (major premise), doing Y will attain X (minor premise), and the conclusion is an action. But the major premise can never be "I desire X" because it is always possible and reasonable to ask why at this time I should act on this desire rather than another.[60] There is, in other words, internal to the logic of a practical syllogism, an ordering of goods. My reason for acting will always have to be that I want such and such *and* that I judge fulfilling this desire the best alternative.[61]

The virtues always develop in a relation of mutual dependence. We can see this as MacIntyre makes his own short-list of cardinal virtues. The three central virtues of almost all practices, which unite the history from Homer to Austin, MacIntyre proposes in *After Virtue*, are justice, courage and honesty. Justice is the quality of giving to each what is owed and it requires the virtue of prudence for its application (it is curious therefore that it is not listed). Honesty or truthfulness is the virtue of self-submission to others and critique of oneself and others. Courage is the ability to execute

---

59. Ibid., 85.

60. On the practical syllogism: *SHE*, 71–73; *AV*, 161–62; *WJWR*, 138–40.

61. What this means is that the virtues are necessarily going to have an "objective" quality to them in the sense that they cannot be reducible to what is desired or what is generally approved of or useful, since the virtues are specifically the training of the desires. "Just because our degree of success or failure in first acquiring and then practicing the virtues determines in significant measure what it is we find agreeable and useful, the characterization of the virtues, in Humean terms, as qualities that are generally and naturally agreeable and useful is misleading" (*DRA*, 87).

justice and honesty. Elsewhere MacIntyre treats variously numerous other virtues, notably temperance and generosity. But already we can see how it is that, whatever ordering and importance we give to our catalogue, by their nature the virtues cannot be treated individually. A virtue is cultivated with the help of virtues, while a lack in one area often will be to the detriment of several others.

Because such virtues are always part of a community practice, they will always be *political*, as for Aristotle the virtues were what was required for the good of the *polis*. The good of the community, in other words, will be the external structure that defines the nature of the virtues so that, without such a communal structure with common ends and roles, any determinate account of the virtues will be impossible. In other words, "we need to act for common goods in order to achieve our flourishing as rational animals."[62] And "common goods," of course, presuppose a community of people with shared goals. Every step of the way this involves dependence on others. Morality is not something that we *could* do on our own, as it is for Kant; human action is not accidently but essentially sociopolitical. "In the context of particular practices we generally have no one else to rely on but those who are our expert coworkers, to make us aware both of our particular mistakes in this or that practical activity and of the sources of those mistakes in our failures in respect of the virtues and skills."[63] Thus for any achievement of the good for a person to be possible that person will have to have pursued goods that are truly common.[64]

MacIntyre goes on to suggest that a concept of virtue implies that a human life has the character of a narrative. For to hold an account of the virtues, whatever it may be, is to describe human life as progress through harms and dangers to some end, wherein virtues and vices are those abilities that allow or hinder the attainment of that end. In other words, in order to know what the virtues are we will have to know some things about what the specific dangers are and how progress is to be measured.[65] MacIntyre notes that we cannot characterize action apart from intentions and beliefs and we cannot understand intentions and beliefs apart from a setting and its changes through time (a story). Every action has and presumes for its intelligibility a history, a narrative. Without these the question, "What is he doing?" will be unanswerable, and action will

---

62. DRA, 119.
63. Ibid., 96–97, see also 99.
64. Ibid., 109, 113, 119.
65. AV, 204–12.

be unintelligible. Thus, there is no such thing as 'behavior' in itself, apart from these things. Rather, we order intentions causally and temporally in relation to the agent's history and the history of the setting. This means that narrative history is the basic genre of human action.[66]

That there is a narrative quality internal to all human action that constitutes its particularity means two significant things. First, human action is inexpressible in terms of strict causality, and this turns out to constitute another objection to a view of divine agency as construed on the analogy of physical causality. For action so construed is not sufficiently explicable.[67] This is because any account of the divine comingling with human action has to take account of the continued existence of human intentionality in order to avoid not only the evacuation of free will but also the ultimate lapse of human action into incoherence.[68] To say that something is caused

---

66. In this way it becomes clear that because the virtues involve the training of desire and thus a different view of the good from someone who does not have them, it is also true that the virtues are only recognizable as such by those who have them. Others, indeed, may see the same virtuous actions as harmful. What this means, however, though I do not find MacIntyre making this point, is that to the extent that one lacks the virtues necessary to recognize virtuous action as such one may also misconstrue the story in which those actions make sense. So it turns out that moral development will significantly influence our ability to understand and rightly characterize actions and their stories, including our own.

67. See MacIntyre "Hegel," 81–83: "A particular historical event cannot on Hegel's view be dissolved into a set of properties. One reason for this is that such a situation has to be characterized in terms of relations to earlier particular events and situations. There is an internal reference to the events and situations that constitute its history ... To respond to a particular situation, event or state of affairs is not to respond to any situation, event, or state of affairs with the same or similar properties; it is to respond to *that* situation conceived by both the agents who respond to it and those whose actions constitute it as the particular that it is.... Just because this concreteness is not constituted by a mere collection of properties, *it evades causal generalizations and so makes causal explanation*, whether phrenological or neurophysiological, inapplicable" (my italics). In other words, "a certain kind of causal explanation will not give us the understanding that we require of self-conscious rational activity" (82). This constitutes a significant difference then, between psychology and social sciences on the one hand, and the natural sciences on the other, however much this would be denied by the former. "For what we can observe in nature is, so to speak, all that there is to discover; but what we can observe in human beings is the expression of rational activity, which cannot be understood as merely the sum of the movements that we observe" (83). The question then of course becomes whether MacIntyre is right that there is no "intention" internal to nature.

68. In other words, for our purposes, there may be buried into either or both of the views of Paul that I will be opposing a sort of anachronistic physicalism wherein neurochemistry is the "cause" of behavior and so God would need to act directly on

by God, in other words, is not to deny the internal "human" narrative that gives that action intelligibility. To be sure, there are times when it seems that the divine and human agent have come together in such a way that the human narrative breaks off and that an action or set of actions lack sufficient continuity with a human narrative. We call these miracles. But so to name them is to say that this is not the normal mode of divine interaction with human agents.

Second, the narrative quality of human action brings us to the heart of MacIntyre's positive proposal, namely, that we simply cannot make sense out of our lives without something like the classical tradition of the virtues. This is the argument he makes at the close of *After Virtue*. Because human beings tell stories and only understand themselves and their world as such, the first question of life is not "what am I to do?" but "what kind of stories do I find myself in?" Without the latter we would have no roles with which to respond to the former. We would have no way to characterize our own actions and would have no idea what to expect from others. Thus the unity of life consists in the unity of a narrative in a single life. To ask 'What is the good life for me?' is to ask how best to bring that narrative to completion.

Thus far narrative. But the virtues are a necessary part of the unity of life, since these are the abilities that allow us to sustain practices necessary to achieve internal goods, overcome obstacles, and come to a greater knowledge of the good. Without virtues we would have no practices—only, for example, utilitarian emotivism. MacIntyre names a common history of practice or practices over time that constitutes a continuous argument as to the nature of the good for that practice a "tradition."

What happened so that we no longer talk about our actions this way?

The Breakdown of the Classical Synthesis in Modernity

MacIntyre's work is perhaps most poignant in its narration of the incoherence of the culture of modernity, including American society. Such incoherence arises for him to a significant extent because of the breakup of a

---

something physical in a manner that makes us think of God's cause and effect in the same way as that between physical objects. So MacIntyre ("Hegel," 78) says that "[B]uried in [the] dubious contentions [of the old science of phrenology], is one that is less obviously dubious, that is indeed familiar and widely accepted. I mean of course the thesis that there are biochemical or neural states of affairs, processes and events, the occurrence and the nature of which are the sufficient causes of human action."

classical account of human action. What our society currently is, and what it continues to try to go on living with, are incompatible bits and pieces of different accounts of action that were never designed to fit together in the first place.[69] That is, the language in which we moderns describe our actions is an incoherent jumble of fragments taken from their proper place in the classical model and haphazardly assembled in a new, nonsensical arrangement. The modern attempt to make sense out of and guide our lives, for MacIntyre, is therefore futile apart from a revival of virtue.

MacIntyre thinks that the current bureaucratic, emotivist cultural situation is a failure of *both* philosophy and society (since the two are never separable) to find a rational alternative to what he sees as a broadly Aristotelian framework that hitherto dominated. "Emotivism," as he uses the term, names that broad family of moral theory and practice wherein "all moral judgments are *nothing but* expressions of preference, expressions of attitude or feeling."[70]

In this section I want to press MacIntyre's narration of this development into the service of three interrelated points. First, MacIntyre's work suggests, most obviously, that a radical change in the concept of "the self" (the soul) has happened, especially in the last three hundred or so years. In fact, the very development of our grammar of the word "self" goes hand in hand with this change. Second, this means a necessary change in the way that we talk about the human body. Ours is a world that does not have bodies in the same way it used to. Finally and correlatively, the way that we talk about the interaction of divine and human agency has changed. These three points all arise as a result of a culture that has suffered the loss of the notion of virtue. What are the characteristics of such a culture and how did we get here?

MacIntyre thinks he can date one of the most important turning points in our cultural history to the years around 1780. This date suggests itself because the two last works of the classical view of human agency, Hume's *Treatise of Human Understanding*, and Smith's *Theory of Moral Sentiments*, were published in 1759 and 1740, while two significant works that *break from* that tradition, Kant's *Fundamental Principals of the Metaphysics of Morals* and Reid's *Essays on the Active Power of the Human Mind* were published in 1785 and 1788 respectively. Hume and Smith represented a minimum necessary to be classified as classical theorists since they took the passions—though in truncated form—to be central to the moral life.[71]

---

69. So begins *AV*, 1–2.
70. *AV*, 12.
71. See MacIntyre, "How Moral Agents Became Ghosts," 295–312.

The result is that for Hume practical reasoning and morality, with the classical tradition, is a matter of *fact*: the good for Hume can be objectively specified in terms of desires and so an evaluation of an action as movement towards or away from that good is possible. Action is explicable and rational to that extent. Hume is thus the last major philosopher who integrated philosophy of mind and moral philosophy. Kant, on the other hand, and Reid with him in his own way, both assume that the passions are one sort of thing and that the moral life is another. The self has ceased, with Kant, to be an agent that acts within the context of unified life of virtues and vices progressing or failing to progress towards a telos.[72]

In other words, while the identity of the Humean actor is circumscribed and constituted by the dynamics inherent in a "practice," the Kantian agent does not stretch out towards a goal dictated by a place in a story in which one responds to obstacles on the way more or less successfully. Kant's self is neither stretched-out, nor storied, nor capable, nor incapable. Rather, the agent simply acts or does not act to fulfill the demands of the categorical imperative.[73] This is a major change. But such a radical modification does not only touch the realm of moral theory. Rather, people who try to embody something like a Kantian doctrine are going to understand themselves quite differently than their classical counterparts. With Kant the concept of a "person" has lost much of its former content. This is a fundamental change in what we think of as the notion of the "self." The simplicity of Kant's human actor compared with the classical counterpart, the complexity of the latter having been stripped away, prepares the way for the understanding of the self as a relatively extensionless, immutable point of pure will wherein one's "identity" lies.[74]

MacIntyre observes, and I think actually understates, the extent that this move was prepared for by certain strands of the Reformation that reject any knowledge of a natural telos, and at the same time reject any power of human beings to move toward an end, even one that has been *revealed* to them. In the context of a particular theological construal of "grace," Christian ethics become radically transformed. Now for perhaps the first time obedience does not *achieve* anything—Christian ethics are deontological full stop. Only God can move us toward any sort of goal, and that goal is increasingly defined non-temporally.[75]

---

72. Ibid., 298.
73. *SHE*, 193.
74. See ibid., 196–99.
75. So, for Herdt, Luther rejected traditional Christian virtue and promoted a

The consequences for traditional Christian theology of a hyper-Augustinianism (Herdt's term) coupled with the decay of virtue can be seen especially in a figure like Luther. For him, according to Herdt, no human action can lead to the cultivation of virtue. Action is merely "exterior", and the starting point of the Christian life must be entirely passive in order to avoid falling into pride and hypocrisy. Moreover, for Luther the "works of the soul are no better than the works of the body, for we should not be working at all. A special sort of self-emptying must be the starting point, not something toward which we gradually advance."[76] Luther himself says that the Exodus from Egypt should not be understood, as it usually was in patristic and medieval commentary, as "one of faults to virtues. But it would be better to understand it as an exodus *from virtues* to the grace of Christ."[77] Virtue, in any classical sense of the notion, has been cast off. This means not just that we have to "cease from our own labor and trade but much more—that we let God alone work in us and that in all our powers we do nothing of our own."[78]

On Herdt's reading of Luther, therefore, justification is not a process, united with sanctification, wherein God makes sinners habitually lead lives that are just and holy. Rather, justification is entirely invisible and forensic, as Christ's merits are imputed to us. *In this life we remain in the same state as we were without Christ.* We look different only to God. We have put on Christ's mask, he takes on ours, "and God applauds the disguises."[79] This is of course Luther's doctrine *simul iustus et peccator*. Indeed it is the constant confession of our lack of ability to be anything more than a sinner that makes sure Christ's merits count for us.[80] The truthful admission of our own worthlessness is the only thing that makes us worth saving. Thus

> what we encounter in Luther is an exaggerated insistence on passivity arising out of a competitive understanding of human

---

notion of grace that can be called hyper-Augustinian. But I think Luther's rejection of virtue and his own distinctly modern version of predestination as God's immanent causality is unintelligible except as a move away from a full-fledged classical notion of virtue.

76. Herdt, *Virtue*, 174–75.
77. Ibid., 176.
78. Ibid.
79. Ibid., 179.
80. Ibid., 186, notes that Luther is not altogether consistent on this point. At times he speaks as though there is a minimal amount of effort that is required for salvation. His theology of grace and works, however, makes it difficult to see how this might be possible.

and divine agency. This makes it difficult for him to develop anything but a paradoxical account of growth in Christian virtue. The exercise of human agency is for Luther inherently an attempt to displace divine agency. Hence, it must itself be displaced.[81]

We see in Luther, I would suggest, nothing short of a radical reinterpretation of classical Christianity. Broadly speaking, the classical tradition seeks to explain how the Triune God saves humanity by restoring in it the image of God which had been wholly or partially lost. Christ brings about such a restoration as both sacrifice for sins and model for imitative, participatory growth towards that divine image. Thus the Christian life involves irreducibly the manifold means of grace whereby we participate in the active reformation of the divine image by remaking our actions, tendencies and desires. Baptism, Eucharist, Scripture study, fasting, almsgiving, serving the poor, confession, marriage, penance, and the like all serve to remake us by grace in God's image and represent the practical content of Christianity. But Luther, ultimately, has exchanged all this content for a simple affirmation that we can do nothing of ourselves. This is more important than all the sacraments and all the prayers in the world. Pride and humility assume now an unprecedented place of importance in the soteriological schema. Affirmation of one's depravity and weakness replaces the irreducible variety of ecclesial practice as the *sine qua non* of Christian practice.

MacIntyre rightly notes that, with Luther "[w]e could not be further away from Aristotle; he is, said Luther, 'that buffoon who has misled the church.'"[82] I might add that we are equally far from Plato, Augustine, Aquinas or Erasmus. Far from a classical understanding of salvation as the progressive remaking of the whole person in her actions, desires, will, intellect, and body, for Luther "[t]he true transformation of the individual is entirely internal; to be before God in fear and trembling as a justified sinner is what matters . . . [T]he events that matter all occur in the psychological transformation of the faithful individual."[83]

So, allowing MacIntyre, Herdt and Hanby to push and pull on one another, we see that the break up of the classical model of human action goes hand in hand with the inability to conceive of a non-competitive human action. After the classical breakup, virtue as the "external" practice of

81. Herdt, *Virtue*, 188.
82. *SHE*, 122.
83. Ibid.

the good can find very little place in the Christian life, and any such action always threatens to be prideful sin. These two major factors are regular theological complements of each other.[84]

These twin notions, I suggest, collude to produce the hyper-Augustinian agent. This individual stands before God alone in the utter perversity of her desires. The most she can hope for in terms of any "progress" is that she become humble enough to accept that she is and will always remain utterly a justified *sinner* before God and his commands.[85] The other option—one that is sometimes deployed—is for *God* to make the sinner holy through something like instant theosis. In neither case can there be effectual human striving. Nevertheless, the individual's agency is conceived largely in terms of one's ability—or inability—to follow the strictures of an arbitrary law that simply involves her running back and forth between the cold impenetrable divine law and the gracious offer of salvation "by faith alone," which has nothing to do with "works." The motor that keeps this law-grace piston running is unruly desire coupled with reason corrupted by original sin.

This gives us a clearer picture why, with Kant, whatever sort of floating, unreachable telos the Reformers had left has dropped completely from view with the rejection of *both* Aristotelian and revealed ends. For MacIntyre, the trio of Kant, Reid, and Luther collude to create for the first time the human actor who journeys nowhere, from nowhere, and is simply implored to observe the Golden Rule (or the categorical imperative).[86] This is a significant narrowing of the concept of a person because it is a narrowing of the concept of the actor.

More specifically, Kant jettisons the traditional notion of the virtuous person as defined by the tendency to pursue the good *consonant with* their inclinations, desires and passions precisely in his insistence that morality is the doing of one's duty *in spite of* the way one tends.[87] An action that *is* done because of one's inclination to do so is not properly speaking a moral action at all, and certainly is not as praiseworthy as one done against one's own wants and for the sake of duty itself.[88] But such an opposition

---

84. Though this is not the place make the case, I think Charles Taylor's *Secular Age* contains an extended and complex account of the rise of a competitive account of divine-human interaction that is the necessary entailment of a loss of a full notion of transcendence.

85. See *SHE*, 122.

86. MacIntyre, "How Moral Agents Became Ghosts," 305–7.

87. *SHE*, 192.

88. Ibid.; Herdt, *Virtue*, 324.

between passions and duty cannot but make impossible any notion of the moral life conceived of as a journey. So much less then can the moral life be a journey enabled by God:

> Kant can conceive of human and divine agency only as competing or [zero-sum] cooperating with one another; he cannot grasp human agency as utterly enabled by and participating in divine agency. If Luther's pure foundational starting point is one of relinquishing agency and recognizing absolute dependence on God, then Kant's pure foundational moment is one of perfect autonomy and independence, of self-determined agency. Neither can he make sense of a fundamental transformation of being through doing, of character through action, proceeding gradually through external practices to fundamental inner transformation, which is at the same time a transformation wholly dependent upon grace . . . If it is God who makes us good, it is not we who are good. Grace is permitted only to assist us, to give us an extra surge of energy, but not to redirect our own moral energy. Were it to do the latter, it would destroy our moral agency which is the heart of our identity. Kant must conceive of autonomy as independence from God, since he is unable to conceive of how an action could be fully my own while at the same time being an act of God.[89]

Herdt points out, in other words, that something can be "moral" only by being a purely rational act of the individual alone, and so there can be no such thing as genuine human agency that is at the same time graced. The same is true, however, of the notion of virtue. Virtue is a tendency to act in one way that derives at least in part from a desire that has been habituated to delight in the good. But for Kant, exactly contrary to the classical tradition, such a desire cannot but *detract* from the worth of an action. This shows, in other words, that Kant is no virtue ethicist, despite the claims of some: his "good will" that is necessary for an action to be morally good is not *voluntas*, habituated in the classical sense, but the very exclusion of it. Kant, in many ways by being Luther's more secular disciple, has become an ultimate irony: a hyper-Augustinian Pelagian.[90]

89. Herdt, *Virtue*, 332, 337.
90. I suspect that such a Kantian account shapes much contemporary inability to conceive of divine and human agency in noncompetitive terms. Most of us would unreflectively and at an implicit level agree with Kant's position that "allowed that all events and experiences in time are subject to strict causal determination, while requiring a strong indeterminism for freedom and moral responsibility" (Herdt, *Virtue*, 338). We then find that we can protect freedom only by making it non-temporal. But

MacIntyrian Challenges to the Modern Study of Paul

One of MacIntyre's central points is that the birth of the new, truncated human subject required the production of a new rational justification for the regulation of behavior. I say the regulation of "behavior" and not "morality" because the grammar of the latter is in fact the product of the new situation of having to speak about action in this particularly modern way.[91] If it was indeed the case that murder, adultery, robbery and the like were still to be prohibited, there would need to be a way to ground that prohibition without referring to the recently-jettisoned traditional canon of ends.[92] And so out of the devolution of classical modes of describing human action was born the modern project of creating a rational basis of morality for a human subject who had never hitherto existed, a pure "self" stripped of its goals and character, who now needed reasons to "be moral."

Put another way, MacIntyre suggests that the classical agent had three components: (1) a conception of human nature as it is, (2) a conception of human nature as it could be, and (3) imperatives coupled with virtues enabling one to get from the former to the latter. With figures like Luther (or at least on one particularly influential read of him), however, we loose any notion of a *telos* to be attained. Therefore what was once practical reason becomes purely calculative reason: it can only track means, only calculate effectiveness, not discover ends.[93] With the secular rejection of Protestant

---

this makes it difficult to speak about human agency that effects any change at all, much less change associated with a moral life conceived as journey.

91. For this insight see *AV*, 51–61 and "How Moral Agents Became Ghosts," 309–12.

92. *AV*, 36–49.

93. Charles Taylor elucidates MacIntyre's point about practical reasoning in a slightly different light in his *Sources*, 143–76. To paraphrase: On the classical view the cosmos is the embodiment of the Ideas, and all Ideas point to the Good, to know the world is always to gain a better knowledge of the telos of human activity. Descartes and Locke, on the other hand, reject any such teleological mode of reasoning in preference for a mechanistic one. With the latter comes the necessity of understanding the external world as mere extension, disengaging the "self" from it, including our bodies, in order to see it as an outside observer would. We demystify the cosmos and make it only a domain of possible means—of instrumental control. We want to render ourselves "masters and possessors of nature." To be free from the illusion that mingles mind with matter is to stand in a relation of control to the latter. The "enchanted" world is cast off for a mechanistic one. Taylor explains further that the former "no longer sets norms for us—or at least it does not set norms in the traditional way. Nor was this simply a side effect of a move prompted by purely epistemological considerations. On the contrary, *part of the impetus for the new science came from an anti-teleological morality*. The source was theological: the nominalist revolt against Aristotelian realism, by figures like William of Occam, was motivated by a sense that propounding an ethic founded on the supposed bent of nature was attempting to set limits to the sovereignty

35

and Catholic theology and the scientific and philosophical rejection of Aristotelianism a rejection of perfected human nature takes place. What is left of the three-part classical scheme is the two residual parts (1 and 3) whose original connection has been severed.[94]

> Since the moral injunctions were originally at home in a scheme in which their purpose was to correct, improve and educate that human nature, they are clearly not going to be such as could be deduced from true statements about human nature or justified in some other way by appealing to its characteristics. The injunctions of morality, thus understood, are likely to be ones that human nature, thus understood, has strong tendencies to disobey. Hence eighteenth-century moral philosophers engaged in what was an inevitably unsuccessful project; for they did indeed attempt to find a rational basis for their moral beliefs in a particular understanding of human nature, while inheriting a set of moral injunctions on the one hand and a conception of human nature on the other which had been expressly designed to be discrepant with each other. This discrepancy was not removed by their revised beliefs about human nature. They inherited incoherent fragments of a once coherent scheme of thought and action, since they did not recognize their own peculiar

---

of God. God must preserve the fullest freedom to establish good and bad by fiat . . . In the end, a mechanistic universe was the only one compatible with a God whose sovereignty was defined in terms of the endless freedom of fiat" (169). Thus freedom comes to be defining, and is passed on to humans in the face of this mechanistic world. Instrumental control can then even become a criterion of scientific truth. The same is true of the passions: we must get them under instrumental control, since God has placed them in the soul as a means of our survival. The function of the passions is to make us desire those things which nature tells us are of use. Reason controls the passions when it can hold them to this normal instrumental use. (That this is perhaps a quite obvious way of understanding the passions shows how influenced we are by Descartes.) Rationality is defined procedurally in deference to certain canons. This brings us, Taylor shows, to a difference within the concept of reason itself. On a classical model to be reasonable is to have one's soul ordered by the Good which presides over the cosmic order. Reason, in some sense, is always practical reason. But with Descartes reason is simply instrumental: the power of thought is to construct orders which meet the standards demanded by certainty. Reason does not track the Good which orders our passions to the proper end or gets rid of them; rather, it presides over body, world, and passions, allowing us to use them all as we like to get some good. "Reason" is now defined as mind dominating a disenchanted world of matter. The "good life" can then be defined for the first time as a life with this sort of control. And modern ethical and political writing names this control man's "dignity" and with it the closely allied virtues of instrumental reason—"responsibility" and "control."

94. *AV*, 54–55.

historical and cultural situation, they could not recognize the impossible and quixotic character of their self-appointed task.[95]

Thus, the deontological character of contemporary moral judgments is the ghost of divine law alien to the metaphysics of modernity, and their utilitarian character is the ghost of concepts of human nature equally alien. So philosophical puzzlement will continue: "good," "right," "choice," "moral," "obligatory," and the like are words that we have forgotten how to use. They are used only as fragments, having lost their proper grammar as part of a practice.

In this connection, MacIntyre notes that the marginality of practices has had important consequences for the way we perceive human action. He says that Aristotle's *Ethics, Politics* and *On the Soul*, were as much explanations of human action as they were about "morality."[96] But now, this side of modernity, talk about human action becomes talk of physiology and psychology, detached from language about the good or virtue.[97] Why is this so?

For Aristotle a human is functional to established good, end, and hierarchy, so that the good is factual. The human being's action, in other words, can be evaluated as good or bad *objectively*, in the sense that a move in chess or the functioning of a clock can be so evaluated. In these latter arenas, there are established goals for the game (to win) or for the machine (to keep accurate time) so that, e.g., a move in chess can be called good or bad as a matter of fact with reference to the goal of winning (so we see that "practices" inherently define morality functionally). We can now see that the reason that human action is no longer like this is that the telos has been lost. So it is impossible for moral judgments to be factual because human nature has ceased to be functional. There is nothing against which to measure an action. Another way of saying this is to say that now we think that we can state the "facts" of human action apart from making a claim on their "moral value."[98]

As Pinches shows, it is only in words like "murder" that we get a glimpse of what action-language would be like in a functional context.[99] If action can no longer be evaluated as good or bad in any objective sense, it is left to be characterized in the "purely descriptive" terms of "science":

95. Ibid., 55.
96. Ibid., 82.
97. "How Moral Agents Became Ghosts," 295–96; "Hegel," 78.
98. *AV*, 58–60.
99. Pinches, *Theology and Action*, 43, 77.

physiology and psychology.[100] It is simply intuitive to us that human actions are describable in these scientific terms. We have, in other words, come to think of human action as simply "movement" of the human body, to be supervened by "moral judgments," of course, but never embodying them necessarily. "Action," once a full-fledged moral concept, has come to name discrete movements of the body, divorced from any broader context and open to "value free" explanation in terms of the laws of biology, chemistry and neuroscience.[101]

In our partitioned "moral" realm, the central action is something called "choice." But this concept is far from what *prohairesis* or *electio* names for the classical human subject. In the latter case the subject has a particular history that determine her virtues and vices that in turn define the limits of what the human subject is "free" to choose.[102] For Aristotle, a courageous man is simply not free, under normal circumstances, to choose to be cowardly. The emotivist moral agent, however, is free to choose any and all moral positions and can criticize any other, since she has no stable and (ultimately) rational telos toward which she has moved and whose action is therefore at least partially determined by such movement. This self can evade any and all historical contingency and in fact this becomes the essence of the "self." "Choice" comes close to naming the full extent of a person's fundamental action: "life" is but an endless series of choices.

Thus, regardless of contingencies, the ability to choose remains the *sine qua non* of modern subjectivity and of moral action. This is not least because "moral" action is defined as that which we do when we could have done otherwise. The "self" can only so choose, however, because it has freed itself from a classical account of human agency in which one's character puts severe restraints upon what actions one is capable of performing. It is no surprise that the principal metaphor for classical models of action is the journey. Therein, one is only able to act consonant with whatever "moral land" one is traveling through at that point with whatever tools and materials one has. Saint Francis simply cannot commit murder. But such a statement is hard for us to understand: we always want to say "but he might." This is so precisely because we do not think people are on a journey. Rather, for us character is always relatively unstable, and unrestricted choice might result at any time in any number of actions.

100. *AV*, 82–83; "Hegel," 83; also see "What is a Human Body?"
101. See MacIntyre, "Hegel."
102. "How Moral Agents Became Ghosts," 295–97; McCabe, *On Aquinas*, 67–68.

Compared with the journeyman, for post-Kantian ethics the essence of a person has become a dimensionless dot; or, as MacIntyre has it, a ghost.

Throughout this explication of MacIntyre's nuanced account of our present cultural situation I have been pointing out the changes in the concept of the human agent involved in the eclipse of virtue. We have seen that the person becomes a dimensionless dot, or a ghost, whose only action is to "choose" and who is only responsive to commands, but who never develops moral proclivities that might do away with the need for such demands. We are, in other words, a historical oddity: we are "selves." A "self" is the "core" of an "individual" who has no telos, no virtues, no vices, no character, no practices, no communities, no emotions, no hierarchy, no authority, and no story. We are, in other words, a shadow of what we once were. We live in a way that our classical forefathers, if MacIntyre is right, could hardly have recognized as human.

Human Agency in Contemporary Pauline Scholarship

This account of classical human agency and the account of Pauline agency that I develop below through a reading of Romans is in many ways at odds with the most influential alternative schemes available in contemporary scholarship. I now turn to survey several major figures in Pauline scholarship. I hope to show that, while each of these authors (and often their respective "schools") has contributed significantly to our understanding of Paul, we actually still remain in the grip of what is normally called the Lutheran—but more accurately probably just the "Reformation"—reading of Paul. We remain this way because we fail to situate Paul within a classical understanding of human action, and we therefore fall prey to many of the difficulties MacIntyre chronicles.

A few caveats are in order. First, in what follows I look at the way that *human agency* is treated in Pauline scholarship. I will not, therefore, be entering directly into debates about *justification* and *salvation*. This is important to remember since most accounts of human agency in Paul are found *within* discussions of justification, sanctification, and soteriology more generally. In other words, we are not concerned here with debates about the nature of the law, of the character of "Judaism," "covenant," "nomism," etc., but rather in showing that a good number of important trends in Pauline scholarship are captive to concerns that are raised precisely by the breakup of the classical model of human action. My concern is to show that we normally approach Paul with the inadequate resources available to us in a post-classical model. This does not preclude, of course, that in turn our study will have implications for justification and soteriology. We will see below that this is exactly the case. Second, this is by nature a limited survey, but one that tries to cover a representative sample. I must be limited in part simply by the nature of our subject: because human agency touches closely on so many aspects of Pauline theology it is impossible to survey all the literature in which its treatment might be relevant.[103]

E. P. Sanders Warned Us

In a significant way, but in different terms, Sanders saw the conflict in Pauline studies regarding human and divine agency over thirty years ago. Sanders noted that for Paul the church is not perfect but is certainly holy. "In their present life the Christians have been *sanctified* in the sense of *cleansed*."[104] After saying this he quotes many Pauline exhortations to this effect, and at the same time notes the tension regarding *whose* work such sanctification is: "While Paul's principal view thus seems to be that Christians *have been cleansed* and *established in the faith*, and that they should *remain so*, so as to be found blameless on the day of the Lord, he can also urge them to cleanse themselves."[105] Here Sanders is highlighting the fact that sometimes Pauline agents are spoken of as passive and sometimes active. Paul has a "soteriology of cleansing, awaiting the coming salvation in a pure state, possession of the Spirit as the guarantee of future salvation and the provision of repentance for the repair of relapses."[106] Sanders himself appears to think that for Paul Christians have at least *some* active part to play in their own salvation.

Elsewhere Sanders is on guard against a view which marginalizes human action. He sees the possibility for such a reading especially in those

---

103. There are of course many figures whose work is relevant but do not diverge significantly from the typologies of the figures treated here. I interact with these in the footnotes of the exegetical chapters to follow. These include classical studies like Hays, *Moral Vision*, 16–46; Furnish, *Theology and Ethics*; idem, *Moral Teaching*; Barclay, *Obeying the Truth*; Jewett, *Anthropological Terms*. More recently, and often with an eye, sometimes explicitly, to contemporary culture, see Horrell, *Solidarity and Difference*; Engberg-Petersen, *Paul and the Stoics*; Lewis, *Paul's Religion*. See the relevant collection of essays too in Harink, *Paul*.

104. Sanders, *Paul*, 450–51.

105. Ibid., 452, italics original.

106. Ibid.

Pauline texts that speak of what he calls "participation and union," where the Christian[107] appears all but already perfected. Sanders comments that

> the "discoverers" of [this] view, such as Deissmann and Schweitzer, may justly be accused of giving it too much prominence as a unique, creative and ultimately (to modern man) incomprehensible view. In reaction, there has been some tendency to de-emphasize the view, almost to the point of eliminating it from Paul's thought. Thus Bultmann . . . insisted that these various conceptions [of holiness, union with Christ, etc.] must be interpreted in terms of Paul's "real" view : there is "no magical or mysterious transformation of man; rather, a new understanding of one's self takes the place of the old." Bultmann, Conzelmann and, to a lesser degree, Bornkamm, have been . . . concerned to deny that Paul held a view which implies more than a change in self-understanding.[108]

I think Sanders is pointing to something significant here, but that its importance has not usually been recognized. He is telling a story of two alternatives to understanding Paul.

The first consists of those like Bultmann, who fall basically into a Reformation pattern. The significant contours of that reading are consonant with the hyper-Augustinian theology already sketched: the utter depravity of human beings before God, justification understood as forensic decree of God the judge, the continuing primacy of our sinful nature after justification (*simul iustus et peccator*) and the futile and indeed sinful nature of human striving toward the good.[109] As Sanders notes, the principal transformation of the Christian concerns the way she *understands* herself. Transformation of habits and dispositions is not what salvation is about.

The other major alternative follows Schweitzer in stressing that for Paul a real transformation of the Christian has taken place. Sanders associates this view, as we have seen, with a divine-human interaction in which the Christian is primarily *acted upon*. As Sanders notes, however, those who hold such a view have often stressed that they cannot explain how such a transformation takes place, or how Paul thought such a change happened. Sanders is at the same time not immune to his own critique, as

---

107. I use "Christian" and "Christians" in this book to refer to Paul's converts in full knowledge of the fact that, historically, this is something of an anachronism. I name nothing more by it than members of Paul's churches.

108. Sanders, *Paul*, 453–54.

109. See Campbell, *Deliverance*, 21–25. For Bultmann's interpretation of Paul see below, chapter 2.

he himself acknowledges, since he is going to come down (after a bit of hedging) with Schweitzer:

> It seems to me best to understand Paul to be saying what he meant and meaning what he said: Christians really are one body and one Spirit with Christ, the form of the present world really is passing away, Christians really are being changed from one state of glory to another, the end will really come and those who are in Christ will really be transformed. But what does this mean? How are we to understand it? We seem to lack a category of "reality"—a real participation in Christ, real possession of the Spirit, which lies between naïve cosmological speculation and belief in magical transference on the one hand and a revised self-understanding on the other. . . . That does not, however, mean that the more easily appropriated language of trust, obedience, renunciation of one's own striving, and the like, is the real and exhaustive interpretation of what Paul meant. What he really thought was just what he said: that Christ was appointed Lord by God for the salvation of all who believe, that those who believe belong to the Lord and become one with him, and that in virtue of their incorporation in the Lord they will be saved on the Day of the Lord.[110]

I suggest that Sanders's two ways for interpreting Paul, specifically with reference to human agency, are still more or less accurately descriptive of the lines that Pauline scholarship has moved in since him: either what has been effected is a new understanding of our situation or a real but inexplicable transformation has occurred (the two types of agency mentioned above). I suggest that the former description is more or less descriptive of interpreters such as Dunn and (to a lesser extent) Wright, while the latter is roughly applicable to interpreters such as Martyn and Gorman. While Sanders rightly pointed to these trends and their problems, what he could not diagnose is that each of these readings of Paul falls prey to a

---

110. Sanders, *Paul*, 518. "Participation" so understood has the unfortunate effect of meaning something like "ontological" participation that has nothing or very little to do with what Christians do: it is not a matter primarily of behavior but of a simple "status," however real. It is also, however, not entirely clear how this would fit with "covenantal nomism." Sanders himself thinks that the phrase does not ultimately fit (precisely because of the participatory language). Covenantal nomism does not help us make sense out of the fact that these people not only obey (which is true, and this is the virtue of covenantal nomist) but that they have been and continue to be *transformed*.

hyper-Augustinianism that arises because we fail to situate Paul within a classical model of human action.[111]

James D. G. Dunn

In 1983 Dunn gave a famous lecture heralding a "new perspective" on Paul that attempted to cast off the yoke of centuries-old Lutheran readings.[112] We have seen that this Lutheran view involved a rather minimal place for, as well as evaluation of, human agency. But Dunn's reading of Paul does not seem to offer much substantially different on this front. Indeed, it is rather amazing how closely he voluntarily aligns himself with Luther himself in this regard. He is explicit that Paul affirms that "human effort cannot achieve righteousness. The message of justification is entirely to the contrary: that God justifies the nonworker, the ungodly, those with nothing in their favour and everything calling for their condemnation."[113] What is fascinating in light of the different options we have surveyed for construing human agency in the scheme of grace, is that Dunn seems to totally align the possibility of "having something in their favour" with "human effort." It appears that the only way that Dunn can conceive these two standing together in a soteriology is one that is essentially Pelagian, wherein one looks to earn merit in a pre-graced state in order to gain grace in the first place. But this is of course simply to put the baby down the drain with the water. For this but one of many different ways of retaining human effort and something like prevenient grace. We need only think back to Aquinas' infused virtues that imply required actions for salvation, and yet that action is itself entirely gift. It does not appear that Dunn has moved beyond his Lutheran predecessors.

Elsewhere Dunn writes that "[f]undamental to Paul's conception of the process of salvation . . . is the conviction that the believer has not

---

111. In the end, I am going to suggest below that Sanders and Schweitzer are right that the language of participation has to do with radical transformation but wrong that this has to do with something essentially mystical and transcendent that we can no longer understand and which excludes human agency. Such language is explicable precisely in a classical model of the virtues.

112. Published as Dunn, "New Perspective", 95–122. See especially 98, 111. Dunn is especially concerned to spell out the fact that the Lutheran polemic against the "works of the law" was not the same thing Paul meant by the same, the latter being the performance of the Torah. It is ironic given this central focus, as I show below, just how much Dunn's interpretation of Paul retains the substance of a Lutheran critique of human agency.

113. Dunn, *Theology*, 366.

yet arrived, is not yet perfect, is always *in via*, in transit. It is this which determines the experience of 'being saved' as a process of 'eschatological tension...'"[114] We note that Dunn sees the human being as essentially passive, as entirely determined by where she stands in salvation history. The time is an inter-time, and this appears to mean for Dunn that the agent is necessarily also divided between and dominated by two worlds.

Dunn's comments point us to the fact that the common characterization of Paul's ethics in terms of partially-realized eschatology has the potential to sit alongside an essentially passive, Reformation view of agency. Often, in the latter, as we have seen, human striving, even simply to actively participate in the divine will, is characterized as prideful, since such striving can only be construed in terms of trying to merit grace from a pre-graced position. A partially-realized eschatology can also affirm the passive nature of the agent by placing her in the midst of cosmic forces wholly determinative of that person's nature and action. Such a view is itself derivative of the Lutheran position in that being in the "old age" (or "this present age") seems to mean that one is only able to do evil. Indeed to hold otherwise is to lose the force of such an anthropological application.[115] Dunn is explicit about the connection between a Lutheran view of agency and the "already but not yet":

> it is equally important to emphasize that what has begun (by God's grace) is an ongoing relationship. In that relationship it is the righteousness of God which sustains the sinner within that relationship [sic]... This recognition of the "not yet" dimension of justification by faith gives added force to Luther's *simul peccator et iustus*... In terms of Paul's theology of justification, the decisive beginning has to be worked out until the final verdict of acquittal. The relationship with God must be sustained by God to the end. Luther's *simul iustus et peccator* is also *semper iustus et peccator* until God's final summons.[116]

That the various elements of Paul's theology need not be arranged in such a hyper-Augustinian manner is clear since we saw in Augustine himself a theology of the two ages in which the agent remains an active contender with the cosmic powers, striving to develop the virtues necessary to

---

114. Dunn, *Theology*, 465.

115. Ibid., 476: "Since the present age is characterized as being under the power of sin and death, that continues to be its character as long as it endures. And those who still are part of the present evil age, in any degree, are, to that extent, still caught in the nexus of sin and death."

116. Ibid., 467.

continue the battle. But, far from actively battling, for Dunn, "in terms of the eschatological tension, *the believer is the battleground* for the forces of the present age and the age to come, or the prize over which sin and Spirit wage war against each other."[117]

Having set things up in these terms, Dunn's subsequent attempts to talk about what part Christians do play in their transformation cannot but be an inconsistent undertaking. He recognizes "what may be regarded as Paul's most basic conception of the salvation process as one of personal transformation, that is, in particular, as transformation to become like Christ."[118] The language of "process," however—of the journey of MacIntyre's classical model—has no place to rest in Dunn's account. It has already been undercut by the adoption of a Reformation model opposed to the virtues and genuine human progress. "Process" and "transformation" are fragments of an earlier theological system incommensurate with the terms in which Dunn has described Paul.

When he does come to actually describe such a process, we find, predictably, typically *modern* words (also fragments of the earlier system) rather haphazardly applied to Paul. In spite of the fact that he uses none of these terms or concepts, in terms of human action we find an Apostle that talks about "morality" like a post-Kantian Liberal (Protestant): Paul affirms a tension "between God's saving righteousness and his wrath, between the grace/faith nexus of salvation and the moral outworkings of human choice and mind-set." Some human actions are invested, for Paul, with a "moral significance . . . A moral choice has moral consequences whose outcome will usually be uncontrollable by the chooser."[119] Notice here too the division of the world into moral actions that have special significance and that much broader class of actions that do not. We see this division made precisely between things that we can control and things we cannot, between things in which we have a choice and those in which we do not. Equally, however, Dunn has given us no way of understanding how someone might have such a choice, given that they do not themselves battle but are battled over.

Moreover, it is again notable how small a part human actions play in Dunn's schema. They show up as an afterthought—to be tidied up in the last judgment—and they are characterized by imprecise and rather awkward modern language. Nevertheless, Dunn rightly senses that Paul

---

117. Ibid., 481, my italics.
118. Ibid., 468.
119. Ibid., 490.

wants more than this, even if Dunn expresses it in Kantian language: "in every moral decision there was a choice to be made, for the flesh or for the Spirit. Conversion is every day."[120] Nevertheless, in spite of his emphasis on the process of being transformed into Christ *every day*, at other times it does not really appear that there is *any* place for progress all. For instance, he even goes so far as to say that the Spirit does not bring freedom, but rather is what allows for tension, and for bondage to be perceived as such.

At this point we suspect that Dunn has simply fallen into the incoherence MacIntyre cites. He is using various fragments of a vocabulary for human action to describe a figure's theology whom MacIntyre predicts (and I will below show) would have construed these terms in very different ways.

N. T. Wright

N. T. Wright is often associated with Dunn and the New Perspective, but he himself disavows such an identification and in fact differs considerably from Dunn, not least on the topic of human agency.[121] For Wright, God in Christ brings the covenant of Israel to its climax and this issues in God opening up the covenant to all nations now no longer through the covenant badge of circumcision, food laws, et cetera, but through belief in Jesus. Like Sanders, Wright is much clearer than Dunn about the status of the Christian as *holy*:

> What happens between the moment when pagans, and indeed Jews, come to worship the true God revealed in Jesus Christ, and the moment when they find themselves transformed in the life of the resurrection? . . . Holiness is a complex and difficult topic. I simply want to stress, under this heading, that Paul sees holiness not as an optional extra, not something to which some Christians are called while others are allowed to stay in a state of semi-paganism, but as something which necessarily characterizes all those who are renewed in Christ. At the same time, he is a realist. He does not suppose . . . that Christians are able to live a hundred-per-cent holy life all the time. For him, the life-renewed humanity is held in the tension between the "now" and the "not yet."[122]

---

120. Ibid., 477.
121. See Wright, *Paul*, 13–20; more recently see his *Justification*, 27–29.
122. Wright, *Paul*, 143.

We should note here both the way holiness is conceived and how this conception is explained. First, that Wright can describe it the way he does might suggest that the Christian life is one made up primarily of discrete "moral actions" or "choices" which we could count and quantify as holy or not, apart from one's character. Such a view of a never-ending stream of "choices" to be made is of course part and parcel of what MacIntyre characterizes as a modern account of human action. Moreover, Wright wants to say that the Christian life is more holy than the pagan, but also to allow for Christian moral failure. This is explained not by reference to the fact that the Christian has not progressed far enough but by reference to partially-realized eschatology.[123]

Elsewhere, however, Wright does speak of the Christian life as a journey.[124] Approvingly taking up the contemporary revival of virtue ethics he says rightly that "[t]he virtues are the particular 'strengths' (that is the meaning of the Latin word *virtus*) that allow us to grow into . . . the highest activity of which human beings are capable . . . to advance toward that eventual goal."[125] Throughout this essay he maintains a strong sense of the Christian life for Paul as a voyage toward a goal.[126] The question, however, is if a virtue ethic really does any work in Wright's construal of Paul, or if this is just a helpful heuristic device to illuminate things otherwise describable at "holiness" or "sanctification."

Specifically, I'm not quite sure that Wright has moved outside Reformed categories, in spite of his laudable level of awareness of them.[127] He says that what we need is a virtue ethic that is "generated and sustained by grace . . . ruling out from the start any suggestion that the 'virtue' we are going to talk about is something that 'we do' through self-effort."[128] Or again: "our journey is not one of achievement but of implementation, not of unaided goodness but of unmerited grace."[129] But that this is so obvious to Wright is simply indicative of how much his construal of Paul is influenced by hyper-Augustinian theology: meriting grace has been essential

---

123. See this also in his *Paul*, 147–48.

124. What we have said about Dunn also suggests that it may not be clear that Wright can hold these two ways of understanding Paul's theology together coherently, much less exegetically.

125. Wright, "Journey," 476.

126. Ibid.

127. So Wright, *Paul*, 11–14, 243–45.

128. Wright, "Journey," 473.

129. Ibid., 478.

to major writers in the classical tradition across the board. In other words, as we have seen, in a classical account of human agency, it is certainly proper, and theologically so, to name our actions precisely as *our* actions. Without a notion of virtue as a cultivated habit, there is a significant sense in which our actions cannot be so claimed. As we have seen, only in a world in which the classical model of human action has disappeared do we have to worry in this way about virtue being Pelagian.

Wright's worry in this regard is strange, for elsewhere in the same essay he is happy to talk about Christian "moral effort," "will" and "moral self-discipline." On the one hand, these are hardly unambiguous terms and Wright's use of them could be characterized as the misplacement of fragments of an earlier system. On the other hand, in part motivated by his Anglican heritage, we see the courage to move beyond the Reformed fear of human effort—talking at several points of acquiring habits slowly and arduously through time on the way towards a telos for which we were created.[130]

Elsewhere we see a similar ambiguity. Wright characterizes virtue, somewhat ambiguously, as formed by "choices."[131] The ambiguity lies in the fact that, as we have seen, for a virtue ethic "choice" is but one part in the long chain of practical reasoning that leads to action, and which forms habits. Yet Wright writes as if habits could be formed by the exercise of choice alone. And at the very least he has implied that choice is the principal moment in this sequence. Wright appears here to want an ancient model of virtue made up of very modern moral machinery.

This intuition is substantiated when Wright's account of the Christian moral life turns out to be a version of a Kantian ethic MacIntyre described in *After Virtue* as the ability to consistently follow the rules. Wright says that "we can actually *become the kind of people* who are more likely to obey than not, and that this will come as we cultivate the habits of mind, heart, body and life—in short, the virtues—that will dispose us to obey."[132] Similarly, Wright says that the gift of virtue is that of a "more responsible humanness; authenticity includes the choice to make an act of will despite desire, not simply bringing desire and will into line."[133] But once we have gotten this far, as we have seen, Kant has already won the battle. Wright's account must remain a hybrid of two different models of human action.

130. Ibid., 479, 488, 495.
131. Ibid., 489.
132. Ibid., 480.
133. Ibid., 489.

J. Louis Martyn

We have already met Martyn as perhaps the main figure in the "apocalyptic" reading of Paul's letters.[134] Through countless articles and especially his commentary on Galatians, he has skillfully developed a nuanced reading of some of Paul's central texts. The account of Paul's theology that has emerged is compelling and at times breathtakingly incisive. In the Introduction I noted his positive contributions in the area of Christology, and that he is beginning to reveal a more developed account of agency. Here, however, I claim that he has not yet gone far enough and that, as such, his account of agency remains problematic.

The central points of interest for us surround the account of agency that arises from his particular construal of Pauline soteriology. The latter is marked by the one, punctiliar, salvific fact of the death and resurrection of Jesus. For Martyn this event is the turning point, or rather, the end (or the beginning of the end) of history. God calls individuals out of the evil world and into the kingdom of his Son by sending the Spirit of his Son into their hearts. The Spirit thus *invades* the hearts of unbelievers and calls them into community with one another in the body of Christ. Pre-call unbelievers have no power of their own to choose the life of the Spirit, but are completely dependent upon the grace and calling of God's Spirit itself to enter the community of the New Creation. Once called, individuals live in the community by the Spirit, which always "leads" them and, taking each step before them, prompts them into deeds that are consonant with the fruit of the Spirit. By living in the Spirit, Paul's converts participate in the cosmic battle with the Flesh, the Power that rules this present age. Any step *back* into this present evil age (for instance, by taking on the Torah), *from* the new creation to which they have been transferred by the Spirit, can only mean a return to the bondage to Sin out of which they were plucked. Called to live by the Spirit they have left the old age behind and now live in freedom and newness of life in the community of the body of Christ.

This is Martyn's account in broad outline, and we will see it substantiated below in his own words. My account of Paul below will largely concur with what Martyn clams about the Pauline account of the *initium fidei*. The central question for us regards the nature of the Christian life once

---

134. I let Martyn stand as a representative for the "apocalyptic" school of interpreting Paul primarily because he writes much that is relevant for our purposes but also because he has been active in recent debates precisely on our topic. The other major representative is of course Beker. See his *Apocalyptic Gospel* and *Triumph*.

called by the Spirit. As I have indicated, I suggest that Martyn's account of Paul does not yet have a robust enough ecclesiology and that this issues primarily in a further failure to give any coherent account of progress in the Christian life. To illustrate this, I focus on Martyn's treatment of the imperatives in Galatians 5. MacIntyre's account of human action helps us see that Martyn has trouble with these passages because he has nothing but a passing account of the church as the place of progress in the virtues. Martyn leaves little room for any sort of progressive sanctification or the cultivation of virtues and seems to posit a more or less instantaneous "theosis" of the believer at the time of the Spirit's invasion of her heart. Martyn tries, at times, to give an account of genuine Christian agency, but is profoundly hindered by prior commitments.

Repeatedly, Martyn stresses the motif of the cosmic, apocalyptic war currently taking place. This is how he reads Gal 5, (re)describing Paul's theology there by subsuming it within such language. He emphasizes what he thinks of as

> the weighty role Paul has given in prior sections of Galatians to the motif of divine invasion. That motif is also central to 5:13–24. As we have noted, the Spirit to which Paul refers here is not an inherent component of the human being, comparable, let us say, to an individual's heart. It is the Spirit of God's Son, the Spirit that God has sent invasively into the human orb (4:6). In a significant sense, peace is a result of that invasion, for the Spirit bears its fruit of love, joy, and peace in the community of God's church (Gal 5:22; contrast 5:15). In another sense, however, the divine invasion has certainly not happened peacefully. Indeed it has been necessitated by the fact that the human orb has been subject to an alien, occupying power, the Flesh. With the sending of the Spirit, then, God has invaded the territory of the Flesh (cf. Gal 1:4), inaugurating a war against that monster.[135]

Martyn wants us to see Paul's theology as envisioning some sort of "military invasion" in which "God has commenced his invasive and ultimately victorious war against the Flesh."[136] Moreover, this "war was declared by God when he sent his Son and the Spirit of his Son into the territory of the Flesh," engaging a three-actor stage made up of God, humans, and evil apocalyptic forces.[137] "This war, then, is the new-creational struggle,

---

135. Martyn, "Daily Life," 258.
136. Ibid., 265.
137. On the three actors see his "De-Apocalypticizing Paul," 61–102.

the apocalyptic war of the end-time, the war in which God's forces are the ones on the march."[138]

The consequences of reading Paul, and especially his passages on what have traditionally been called "ethics" (i.e., Gal 5-6), in light of this cosmic war theology, we will see, are exensive. God sends the Spirit to invade the hearts of individuals and change them into those who now walk—exclusively—in the Spirit. But, I will show, in so emphasizing the *divine agency* involved in the apocalyptic war, and in describing the work of Spirit as he does, Martyn has completely ruled out the notion of progress in the Christian life and subsumed everything that might normally fall under such a notion (including the church) to a charismatic moment that looks a lot like, so to speak, instant theosis. So Eastman writes that a central difficulty in Martyn's reading of Galatians is "his emphatic distinction between divine and human activity."[139]

Martyn does not see Gal 5:13-26, which is introduced by the "love command" ("through love be slaves to one another"; v. 13) and the imperative πνεύματι περιπατεῖτε καὶ ἐπιθυμίαν σαρκὸς οὐ μὴ τελέσητε (v. 16), after which follow the lists of τὰ ἔργα τῆς σαρκός (vv. 19-21) and ὁ καρπὸς τοῦ πνεύματός (vv. 22-24), as hortatory in any normal way. Rather, he holds, these verses are *descriptive* of the character of a whole way of life that was *given by God* when he invaded the Galatians' hearts with his Spirit. About this section Martyn comments:

> Paul does not lay the Spirit before the Galatians as a new possibility, a mere alternative to the Flesh. He does not exhort them, therefore, to make a sovereign choice between them, as though the Spirit and the Flesh were two paths, both of which lay equally open before them. On the contrary, with his imperative, Paul calls on the Galatians steadily to be what they already are.[140]

---

138. Martyn, "Daily Life," 259.

139. Eastman, *Mother Tongue*, 16. She continues: "The question remains whether it is necessary to maintain a complete separation between divine and human activity in order to maintain the centrality of God's gracious initiative in the gospel."

140. Martyn, "Daily Life," 264. In his "Epilogue," 174-83, Martyn draws from Paul's culture, a picture of the "self limiting divine agent and the human agent who is competent to choose. For in numerous regards that was an era of individual 'choice'. And texts—both Jewish and pagan—in which the divine agent urges the human agent to choose life, virtue, happiness, etc. presume not only the self-limitation of God, but also the competence of the human agent to choose" (177). Earlier he has asked: "Is the Hellenistic era not marked in general by two major images of the human agent, the competent and the incompetent, and do these not correspond to two dominant forms of the moral drama?" (176) He says that for this sort of culture that has a "competent agent," God puts the two ways before the agent and then "goes into a sort of retirement"

The Practice of the Body of Christ

While rightly rejecting a Kantian notion of "free choice," Martyn's characterization of the passage as non-hortatory *description* is equally puzzling. But the reason for it is clear. Martyn has so emphasized the agency of the Spirit and the incompetence of the Galatians, he *cannot* read the imperative in 5:16 as a true imperative that commands *either* each deed or virtue separately *or* an imperative to a particular way of life so characterized. Indeed, even less can he admit this second view—that the *exhortation* is to a whole way of life—for only God's invasive Spirit is supposed to be able to reorient. Martyn is clear that this is not something someone could be commended or commanded to do.

But it is not just salvation that is initiated and carried through by God, but each person's actions considered piecemeal are products of the Spirit.

> Thus, the Spirit is and remains the primary actor in the military engagement. The Galatians are soldiers already enrolled in *the Spirit's* army [emphasis original], not contestants in a struggle that is theirs, and in which they are merely free to call on the Spirit for aid. Their deeds are first of all the acts of the Spirit (5:22; cf. 4:6), and secondly the acts of themselves [*sic*] as persons into whose hearts the Spirit has made its entrance (5:24).[141]

---

(178). The human being then has "autonomous choice" without God "taking measures to improve that agents' formation." He stands "*alone*" (emphasis original) at the fork in the road, and it is the human being who provides the "*movement*" (emphasis original) (178). First, to say that this picture of "*the* ancient world" is tenuous is an understatement. From where does Martyn draw the conclusion that the ancient world was primarily about "choice"? The extent that MacIntyre's work is an accurate depiction of the ancient world would be prima facie evidence that Martyn's contention is false. Second, is Martyn suggesting that Paul differs so much from these other thinkers? As I will argue below, this argument seems to be another form of the Lutheran caricature of Judaism as concerned with "works," now transposed into a slightly different ethical mode. Third, when Martyn talks about the incapacity of the human agent and then looks for references in Paul, what he cites are undeniably instances of the un-saved, those not in the church (cf. 179: Rom 1, 3, unbelieving Israel, etc). *Of course* these are not able to act competently. But this must fundamentally mis-describe the agent in Paul as well as in other these Hellenistic (Jewish) texts. For Paul and for the others there is always the community, the church or the Law, or the practices of philosophy, the gift of virtue (see Barclay "Grace," 143–46) etc., that are God- or Logos- driven and which provides the context even for the agent's *first* act.

141. Martyn, "Daily Life," 265.

What Martyn means that agency belongs "first" to God and only "then" to people is unclear.¹⁴² It looks, however, as if in some way the Spirit is over-riding genuine human action.

A corollary to this position is that Martyn does not see in Paul's lists any exhortation to the vice and virtue lists to which they bear such a strong resemblance. This is significant for my argument below that Paul has a classical model of human action. Martyn writes:

> At least a number of the Galatians will have sensed that Paul draws the lists of vv. 9–21a and vv. 22–23a from the widespread philosophic and religious tradition of compiling catalogues of vices and virtues. Momentarily, then, they may have thought that, having identified them as soldiers, Paul now lists in vv. 19–23 the "vices soldiers should avoid" and the "virtues they *should cultivate* [emphasis original]" . . . [But] Paul paints a picture far removed from that given in the traditional catalogues. He does not introduce the list in vv. 19–21a by identifying "fornication . . . the worship of idols . . . outbursts of rage, etc." as vices with which individuals can be charged, and from which, alternatively, they can abstain. On the contrary, for him this first list presents "*the effects of* the flesh," [emphasis original—translating τὰ ἔργα τῆς σαρκός] deeds accomplished in a significant sense *by* the Flesh as an apocalyptic power. Similarly, for Paul, the list of vv. 22–23a, "love, joy, peace, etc." is not a catalogue of virtues, but rather "*the fruit borne by* the Spirit," communal evidence of the Spirit's own activity. Thus, none of the things in either list is an autonomous act of a human being that could be correctly called that individual's vice or virtue.¹⁴³

In this paragraph Martyn lays out his exegetical moves quite clearly. First, he does not deny that these lists are look a lot like normal Hellenistic lists of virtues and vices. So he admits that the Galatians might have "momentarily" identified them as such. In a strange comment however, he appears to think it likely that this identification would give way to the realization that Paul is actually referring to something else. Are we to assume that

---

142. Barclay, "Grace," 155–56, is similarly puzzled, as is Engberg-Petersen (see esp. his essay in that same volume "Divine and Human Agency" 126–39). I must confess to some puzzlement with Engberg-Petersen's entire approach to Paul, and centrally his assumptions about what we can and cannot understand today. However, does conclude rightly that there can be no competition between God and human agency (139), but beyond such a conclusion offers very little substance for understanding how this might be the case or what it might mean to make the progression in the moral life he is so fond of pointing to.

143. Martyn, "Daily Life," 261.

The Practice of the Body of Christ

Paul has here invented a genre of list that looks like exhortations to virtue but functions completely differently?

Additionally, Martyn does not address the significant fact that the introduction to the lists seems to support their nature as hortatory lists of vices and virtues, for the language is consistent with that of a classical account of human agency in which we might expect such lists. The classic language of desire, perfection, willing and doing is evident in vv. 16–17: Λέγω δέ, πνεύματι περιπατεῖτε καὶ ἐπιθυμίαν σαρκὸς οὐ μὴ τελέσητε. ἡ γὰρ σὰρξ ἐπιθυμεῖ κατὰ τοῦ πνεύματος, τὸ δὲ πνεῦμα κατὰ τῆς σαρκός, ταῦτα γὰρ ἀλλήλοις ἀντίκειται, ἵνα μὴ ἃ ἐὰν θέλητε ταῦτα ποιῆτε.

I suggest that, at least at this point in his thinking, Martyn is working with something like a strict contrast between acts that humans perform autonomously and those done to and through the human by the sole agency of the Spirit.[144] We saw that, recently, he has begun to think in terms of dual agency. But at this point—1997—he does not appear to have countenanced such. This means that his reading of Galatians threatens to fall into the hyper-Augustinian trap of competing agencies. Though Martyn says that "the profound radicality of Paul's apocalyptic picture is seriously domesticated when one credits him with speaking of vices and virtues," my suggestion below is that an apocalyptic reading of Paul actually needs such an account, both theologically and exegetically.[145]

Martyn's account of Gal 5 would be significantly aided by a fuller ecclesiology. This becomes apparent in his treatment of the hortatory nature of v. 16:

> Does not the promise of 5:16 show, after all, that Paul thinks of the Flesh and the Spirit as two alternatives placed before a human being who is competent to decide for the one or for the other? In fact, this interpretation reflects a failure to see the centrality of the metaphor of warfare . . . and presents a false reading of Paul's imperative in Gal 5:16 (and a consequent misreading of the hortatory dimensions of 5:25—6:10) . . . it is easy to misunderstand the thrust of the promissory sentence of 5:16, as though Paul intended it to be the equivalent of a simple

---

144. Though Martyn elsewhere denies this either-or, he gives no way of understanding how this is possible in his schema. Barclay, "Grace," 155, writes in critique of Martyn that "non-contrasting" agency is "a condition still requiring some conceptual apparatus to explain their mutual relationship." I think that Martyn has so construed divine agency as exclusive of human agency that there can be no solution to this problem.

145. Martyn, "Daily Life," 262.

condition, focused on the inception of a relationship with the Spirit: if you will commence a life with the Spirit, then I can promise you that you will not carry out the Impulsive Desire of the Flesh. It is true that the promise of the second clause is predicated on the imperative given in the first. That imperative itself, however, is predicated on three major factors that precede it, reflecting Paul's awareness that, in formulating his promise, he is not speaking to humanity in general.[146]

A couple of items can be noted here. First, Martyn has aimed at the wrong target several times. No one is claiming that Paul here exhorts the Galatians to *begin* a relationship with the Spirit. It is quite clear that they already have one (cf. 3:2). No one is making *that* mistake. Paul is addressing his own Galatian church which he founded, to which he thinks he has special claim, and which (presumably) is in the midst of trying to figure out how to be faithful to the risen Jesus. There is no reason that the church cannot have morally competent agents.

What he really needs to aim at is the place of imperatives (normally conceived) in Paul's ethics at all. Martyn has said repeatedly that the list of the fruits borne by the Spirit pertain to the characterization of the community that lives in the Spirit. So the imperatives of 5:16 and especially 6:1–10 appear to be superfluous. What need for exhortation is there in a community that is already divinely constituted by good fruit? This is a question I do not think Martyn can answer. If as the community of the Spirit the Galatians do not practice the vices of 5:20–21, what does Paul mean when he says εἰ ζῶμεν πνεύματι, πνεύματι καὶ στοιχῶμεν. μὴ γινώμεθα κενόδοξοι, ἀλλήλους προκαλούμενοι, ἀλλήλοις φθονοῦντες (vv. 25–26)?

His answer in various places is that by the Spirit God has formed *addressable* communities.[147] Thus, he gestures toward the fact that the church

---

146. Martyn, "Daily Life," 263.

147. Martyn, "De-Apocalypticizing Paul," 91; idem, "Daily Life," 264. From "Epilogue," 181–82: "When, being the newly addressable agent, *and being confidently exhorted to do so* (emphasis mine), one of Paul's churches corporately follows the lead of the Spirit—infused by God into their hearts and thus *already active* among them (e.g., Gal 5:16–26)—it is indeed taking a second step after God's first step. But in Paul's theology it is emphatically *not a separate step* (emphasis original), one that is separate from the continuing causative (!) activity of the divine agent in the daily life of the community. . . . this invasive God *consistently participates in human morality itself* . . . Lead by the Spirit, this communally competent agent is neither alone nor passive, being literally inspirited and collectively called by God to vigorous, world-wide activity; for forming Christ in their communities, God places this communal agent in the

is essential for Pauline agency, but his prior commitment to a contrastive account of divine and human action makes such an ecclesiological move difficult. In other words, it is certainly right that Paul thinks his communities are addressable, but there is absolutely no place for this notion in Martyn's theological schema. Human beings cannot rightly appear as agents at all, but must remain puppets tossed about by super-human powers. If the communities are in fact addressable, why cannot Paul's lists be regular hortatory lists of vices and virtues?

From the perspective of a classical account of human action we can characterize the problem even more fully. For not only do Martyn's problems stem from a hyper-Augustinian duality of agency, but, as we should expect in a post-classical model, this duality is coupled with the sort of truncated account of human development to which MacIntyre points. MacIntyre has taught us that any account of human action involving imperatives is going to be incoherent without the necessary twin complements of (1) a conception of human nature as to some degree untutored but capable of advancement, and (2) a conception of perfected human nature toward which the imperatives drive. Martyn's apocalyptic reading has developed neither.

Clearly, then, Martyn needs to move toward a fuller ecclesiology. The place to start is his recognition that the *community* as a whole is formed by Paul's address in Gal 5 and that the Spirit has formed not just addressable individuals but addressable *communities*. In the account we surveyed here, it is unclear such statements make any substantial difference in his reading of Paul beyond these bare affirmations. Throughout his work, the Spirit interacts with individuals and brings them into a community that appears only a secondary and soteriologically accidental fellowship of the Spirit-invaded. This non-essential ecclesiology is one more misplaced fragment of a once coherent classical grammar.

Michael J. Gorman

Recently, Michael Gorman has made a noteworthy contribution to this discussion, and to the discussion of Paul's theology and soteriology in general, with his book *Inhabiting the Cruciform God*. The subtitle, *Kenosis, Justification and Theosis in Paul's Narrative Soteriology* encapsulates his

---

front trenches of his war for cosmic liberation *for all*." But we simply needn't accept as the only alternative this Reformed narrative about the *utter* inability of the unsaved and (within the church) unperfected humanity to give even a half-hearted "response" to God.

main thesis. Justice for Paul is a matter of theosis—being drawn into the life of God by becoming like Christ on the cross. This kenosis is paradoxically the way through death to resurrection life, which means that Paul redefines justification and faith in terms of co-crucifixion.[148] Justification itself has four aspects: theological (God is just), covenantal (God requires justice), legal (God is judge), and eschatological (God will judge).[149] The task of justification is a matter of God establishing his people in a "right covenant relationship."[150] This means that justification is not just legal, as in some construals, but that holiness is necessarily involved, defined in terms of participation in God (theosis) by means of co-crucifixion.[151] In other words, the major move Gorman is pushing in this book is to make sanctification internal to justification.[152] So "there can be no separation of [justifying] faith from love, or faith from action."[153] This is a big step in the right direction. Formally, I could not agree more.

But in terms of specifics, I'm not sure that Gorman has made this move altogether coherently, either theologically or exegetically, and especially in terms of his account of human action. Because he argues that Pauline sanctification is part of justification, he is overly guarded against charges of Pelagianism in way that unnecessarily skews his picture of Paul. He writes that this account of "justification is not in any sense a self-generated activity. The passive voice . . . implies an external agent, a divinely initiated action . . . we must rule out any semi-Pelagian or Pelagian interpretation . . . "[154] He also notes the "many passive participles and main verbs Paul uses to describe the salvation event. This important

---

148. Gorman, *Inhabiting*, 67.

149. Ibid., 54.

150. Ibid., 53.

151. At the same time he does not seem to make what to me is the obvious connection that being "justified" means actually being given the habit of acting justly. So *Inhabiting*, 99: "Should the justified continue to practice injustice . . . their fate will be that of those who have never experienced the justifying justice of God." But my reading below shows that those whom God has made just are defined as those who do not do injustice.

152. Gorman, *Inhabiting*, 54. But his division of justification into three "moments" of Christ's death, subjective response, and substantive content (56) is wholly untenable and actually out of keeping with what he says elsewhere. His statement that Rom 5–8 is constitutive of salvation (73) and not a separate step is more to the point. I will argue this case below in chapter 3 differently.

153. Gorman, *Inhabiting*, 81.

154. Ibid., 69.

grammatical phenomenon suggests a salvific source outside the self, even an 'alien' righteousness."[155]

With MacIntyre's help we can see that the mistake Gorman has made in his disavowal of Pelagianism is to accept a hyper-Augustinian Reformation (mis)construal thereof in the first place. In such a misunderstanding of Pelagianism, we must disavow as heretical *any* affirmation of genuine human action that is part of the soteriological process. This means that one thing Gorman shies away from saying is perhaps what would help him most. His implicit claim is that for Paul salvation is always going to look a certain way, it is always going to involve particular behavior. In other words Gorman should affirm that, *in this sense*, salvation is indeed by works. But that we have forgotten that there is a non-Pelagian way to say this explains why Gorman feels he must repeatedly affirm that even action that looks like "our" action must really be God's. Why does Gorman fall into this dynamic?

The short answer is that he doesn't have an account of the virtues. This is especially striking since all of the Fathers who used the language of theosis did so in the classical framework and theosis therein simply means the transformation of one's habits to be like the habits of Christ.[156] So the biggest question to be asked was put to him by Stanley Hauerwas in a lecture Gorman gave on this book at Duke Divinity school: "What does theosis do to my body?"[157] Hauerwas's worry was that, in spite of a good bit of courageous work in challenging the normal reconfiguration of Pauline theology and doing so precisely by rehabilitating terms that were utilized to describe the Christian life within the classical model of human action, Gorman's account remains very thin in terms of habituation.[158] As such, I suggest, theosis has actually become one more fragment of a displaced account of human action—this time specifically Christian. The Fathers were able both to keep sanctification internal to justification and to hold that those acts that make up the "good works" of the former were genuinely

---

155. Ibid., 79.

156. See esp. the primary sources cited by the recently flowering literature on theosis and deification, notably Lenz, "Deification of the Philosopher," 47–67. The whole volume is significant, esp. the piece McGucken, "Cappadocians," 95–114. Also in this connection see Russell, *Deification*; Finlan, *Theosis*, esp. 104–42.

157. The lecture was on April 15, 2009 and the discussion was moderated by Dr. Campbell.

158. It is amazing that Gorman does not seize on the potential to talk about habits of the body in a text that he treats at length, namely Rom 6:1—7:6. See my exegesis in chapter 3 below.

human acts precisely because they could characterize those acts as infused habits that genuinely made us different people whom God has *graced* to act virtuously "all on their own." In other words, theosis names the process by which God really does transform people's habits. A hyper-Augustinian soteriology of theosis that lacks the virtues, however, must conceive of God "causing" each good act to avoid the charge of Pelagianism, but thereby end up giving a docetic account of human transformation. Absent an account of the virtues, in other words, one is left with a competitive account of human-divine cooperation wherein genuine good works can *only* be attributed to the *divine* if the (correct) charge of Pelagianism is to be avoided.

Another significant omission in a book on theosis is Gorman's lack of an account of the church for Paul. Again, for the Fathers, and as Gorman affirms, theosis is not an individual experience but a corporate one.[159] But Gorman does not include even one section devoted to how such an account of salvation includes the church in any substantial way. He talks about the church from time to time, but his grammar of church is of that which aids the individual's justification and holiness and not of something by which the individual is defined.[160] On the other hand, the Fathers' answer to Hauerwas's question about what happens to my body in an account of theosis is more or less that "the church happened to my body." For the Fathers, and I will argue below for Paul as well, church practices (which are always communal) are constitutive of and not accidental to the cultivation of virtue in which salvation consists. There is no salvation outside the church for Paul for a reason that MacIntyre has already pointed us towards: it is not so much individuals as it is the whole church that cultivates virtue, because each member requires the whole and the whole requires each member in order to achieve her individual and the common good. But this means that a passing reference to the church will not suffice to sustain a classical account of human action. The church in Gorman's account, as it was in Martyn's, is but one more misplaced fragment.

---

159. Gorman, *Inhabiting*, 91.

160. Gorman's account of the concrete practices and dynamics that make up holiness for Paul ranges across community, contemplation, the Spirit, the "praxis of justice," peacemaking, ethical and political practices. He also says a lot about "cruciformity" and "love" and "our neighbor," but it is unclear whether this is all ecclesiological or not and, if so, how this all fits together.

Conclusion

I have argued that significant voices in contemporary Pauline scholarship describe his theology using the categories of a truncated and fragmented account of human action. This often involves lack of a telos towards which a Christian life is moving and so the lack of an account of the virtues as the abilities necessary to attain those goals. Part and parcel of this account is a competitive account of divine and human action in which to affirm that my action is really *mine* is to make the Pelagian error of denying the grace of God.

We have seen that this configuration, and specifically the perception that this is the only possible configuration of divine and human agency, owes much to the dynamics and polemics of the Protestant Reformation (a true, if hopelessly oversimplified claim) and of its secular heirs. But I have suggested that the deeper explanation for this is that this theology and philosophy is itself necessitated by the breakup of a classical model of human action.

I argue, therefore, and the following chapters are dedicated to showing, that it is well worth trying to read Paul within a classical model. To so situate Paul is not to predetermine what must be true of him, for this is a broad tradition and it will take precisely some situating to see where he fits and why. This is, on the one hand, to take seriously MacIntyre's challenge to the hegemony of modern construals of human action and to seek to discipline our reading of Paul thereby. On the other hand, this is more specifically to take up Sanders's insight about two radically divergent accounts of Pauline theology. We must begin to push through such an impasse.

2

Gifted Obedience

Rereading Romans 5:12–21

Introduction

A NECESSARY FIRST STEP TOWARD READING PAUL WITHIN A CLASSICAL model of human action is to establish that human action matters for him in the first place. This is the burden of the present chapter. I suggest that the church for Paul is constituted by lives that are visibly recognizable by their obedient actions. This is traditionally called the holiness of the church. For Paul such obedience is genuine human action that is at the same time entirely a gift. This is the substance of my account of Pauline agency.

More specifically, the argument below is that the grace of God in Rom 5:12–21 does not effect an abstract forensic declaration, nor result in the imputed status of "righteous" or "justified", as it were only "before God," such that no one else sees what has been done. Romans 5:12–21 is not Paul's statement of how Christ saved us through a judicial accounting system in which we come to stand before God in an imputed state of righteousness, regardless of what happens to, and what we do with, our bodies. This reading, which enjoys almost universal consensus, comes from reading Paul for too long through forensic categories. Even if such metaphors are present in Romans at places like 2:13 and 3:21–26 (and this itself is debatable), I argue below that Rom 5:12–21 depicts a fundamentally different aspect of whatever soteriological picture he has painted so far.[1]

I suggest that in Rom 5 Paul argues that Christ makes possible for the church a *just practice*. Christ's obedience unto death, his "just act"

---

1. A good summary of the various types of forensic judgments is available in Campbell, *Deliverance*, 659–62. My interpretation of 5:12–21 is fundamentally non-forensic in that Paul is concerned with human actions and not with their judicial evaluation in a court of law (at least not until the very end of the section, see below).

(δικαίωμα) is what makes an obedient life possible. This act, however, comes to the world entirely as God's gift (ἡ χάρις, ἡ δωρεὰ) of a new Adam that reverses the trend of the first Adam's sin and for the first time since the fall creates a community of just practice (δικαίωμα). God's grace, in other words, is a way of life, a particular obedient practice, which is also a gifted practice (χαρίσμα) that leads to eternal life, as opposed to the practice of sin that leads to death.[2] This reading reconfigures the usual assumption of Pauline scholars regarding the relationship of divine and human in this passage, since the just practice in which the church actively participates is always already a gifted obedience.

I make this argument in three steps. First, I survey some major figures in contemporary academic exegesis of Romans 5:12–21 in order to demonstrate the nearly universal consensus that I argue against. Next, I argue in detail for my reading. Finally, in order to show just how overdetermined the contemporary consensus is, as well as further establish my reading, I show that the proposed reading is supported by Origen and Irenaeus, the two earliest exegetes of this passage that have come down to us. Both offer a similar construal of this passage consistant with a classical account of human agency.

Grace and Human Agency in Rom 5:12–21 in Modern Scholarship

The usual reading of this passage in contemporary scholarship presumes that, while humans acted in the fall, there is absolutely *no* active human participation necessary in the grace of God that brings justification and salvation. Even if there is human agency involved in salvation for Paul, I can find no one who thinks it is discussed in the present passage. There may be ethical *implications* for the church in this passage, but the passage itself is not about what the church does. This view is represented nicely by Bultmann:

> As sin led to death, so righteousness leads to life (Rom. 5:17, 21; 8:10). The goal ahead of him who has righteousness is the gaining of life (Phil. 3:9f.); God's rightwising act is followed by His

---

2. The reading presented here is not necessarily parasitic upon a similar interpretation of the earlier chapters of Romans. Take, for example, Rom 3:21–26: one could hold either (1) a traditional forensic interpretation or (2) Campbell's (*Deliverance*, 662) purely "performative" interpretation or (3) an interpretation similar to the one I offer of 5:12–21, and still maintain that Rom 5:12–21 is about practice of justice.

> glorifying act . . . At this point it is of basic importance to comprehend that by his thesis that righteousness is a present reality Paul, nevertheless, does not rob it of its forensic eschatological meaning. The paradoxality of his assertion is this: God already pronounces His eschatological verdict (over the man of faith) in the present; the eschatological event is already present reality, or, rather, is beginning in the present. Therefore, the righteousness which God adjudicates to the man of faith is not "sinlessness" in the sense of ethical perfection, but is "sinlessness" in the sense that God does not *count* [emphasis original] man's sin against him (II Cor. 5:19). What *consequences* [my emphasis] this has for his ethical conduct will be considered later . . .[3]

The implications for agency are clear. Bultmann names it a "misunderstanding" to suggest that "'righteousness' denotes the ethical quality of a man, whereas in truth it means his relation to God."[4]

So, slightly later we have C. H. Dodd contending that "what has actually been effected by the work of Christ" is not anything that we can see, but rather that "the root of that corporate wrongness which underlies the individual transgresses" has been "cut out. In Him men are lifted into a new order in which goodness is as powerful and dominant as was sin in the order of Adam." This means that "[w]hile justfication, or aquittal, is to be accepted as a present fact, without which the process of salvation is not even begun, the full attainment of actual righteousness lies in the future."[5]

On this reading everything that Rom 5:12–21 sets out happens, as it were, "behind the scenes." In this passage is described a sort of secret financial transaction that has taken place to secure our salvation. Insofar as the Adam-Christ contrasts set out the root of salvation it is a salvation the nature of which has been and remains essentially hidden. This hyper-Augustinianism is apparent in the early Barth's commentary when he says that

> we must not think of sin as an event or as the sum of a series of events or as a particular status . . . we must not regard it as sharing in the contingency of moral or of actual happenings. Rather, we must think of it as the presupposition which underlies every human event and conditions every human status. Sin

---

3. Bultmann, *Theology*, 1:157–58. Also important here, taking a similar line in more detail is his "Adam und Christ," 424–44.

4. Bultmann, *Theology*, 1:277. See also Scroggs, *Last Adam*, 77, for a similar view.

5. Dodd, *Romans*, 82–83.

> is the characteristic mark of human nature as such, it is not a lapse or a series of lapses in a man's life.[6]

Therefore, as sin is invisible, so, for Barth, is grace, and this means "that the identification of the old with the new man has yet to be fulfilled (ii. 13, iii. 20, v. 20); we have as yet only been *declared* free [my italics] and our actual redemption cannot be identified with any concrete happening in history."[7] In other words, there is no visible change. We are

> *appointed as* [my italics] righteous before God, as seen and known by God, as established in God, as taken unto Himself by God. All are renewed and clothed with righteousness, all become a new subject, and are therefore set at liberty and placed under the affirmation of God. But, as what we are, Thou and I can think of this positive relation with God only in terms of hope, as we are reminded by the words: They shall be accounted righteous. We stand only at the threshold.[8]

Käsemann, in a big step in the right direction, famously tried to take the apocalypticism of Barth and transpose it out of the individualism of Bultmann and onto the cosmic scale. He thus rightly reads the Adam-Christ contrast not basically in terms of anthropology but as Paul's language of new creation. This means that, at least in theory, sanctification "is integrated into the event of justification."[9] But the problem is that this meant for Käsemann that Paul's notion of "justification" is really *invisible*, for it requires "sanctification" in order to be visible. Despite the cosmic nature of "justification," the righteousness Paul names in Rom 5:12–21 remains God's righteousness that will be *accounted* as such at the eschatological judgment.[10]

So stood things earlier last century. Yet still today, in spite of all the subsequent vexation regarding Paul and the question of justification, it remains really impossible to find a fundamentally different reading of our passage. Wright, interpreting this section in his commentary says that "what Christ accomplished on the cross will be effected at the final

---

6. Ibid., 280.
7. Ibid., 281.
8. Ibid., 282. See his later, and slightly less ephemeral *Adam and Christ*, esp. 33–35.
9. Käsemann, *Romans*, 156.
10. Ibid., 157–58. So typically in this vein Cranfield, *Romans*, 118: "By 'the gift *which has come* by the grace of the one man Jesus Christ' we should probably understand God's gift of a status of righteousness before himself."

Gifted Obedience

judgment."[11] Thus, with almost all others, he perceives a particular dissimilarity between the disciples of Adam and the disciples of Christ:

> To be a "sinner" is, to be sure, more than a mere status. It involves committing actual sins. But it is the status that interests Paul here. Likewise, to be "righteous" . . . is more than simply status, but again it is the status that matters here. Justification, rooted in the cross and anticipating the verdict of the last day, gives people a new status, ahead of the performance of appropriate deeds.[12]

Here Wright gives an exposition of the basic position outlined by Bultmann. Justification is something that happens only "before God." It does not have deeds that are internal to it—constituative of it—other than the deed that Jesus did for us. Further, Wright says that justification has deeds that are *appropriate to it*, not that justification itself is the production of just deeds. So, while Wright is surely trying to keep justification close to a certain church practice, his very language suggests that such practice is necessarily external to justification itself. For him deeds are a *consequence* of what is fundamentally a soteriological *status*.

A final example of this forensic theology shows up in the recently published commentary by Robert Jewett in the Hermeneia Series. Again the assumption is that in this passage for Paul to say "justification" is to say nothing at all about the involvement of the human agent. For Jewett, Paul's soteriology is the common forensic sort that involves a simple schema wherein the believers "accept the gospel" and are so granted a new "status": "The gift of righteousness is the new status of honor granted to believers through the sacrifice of Christ . . . God makes believers "right" through their acceptance of the gospel of Christ crucified and resurrected."[13] The grace that effects justification is only concerned with one's state at the "last judgment."[14] It does not treat any sort of enacted righteous deeds, since at this last judgment, this state "does not take human qualifications or performance into account in any way."[15]

We should notice that such a judgment, like those others that we chronicled, is not required by what Paul says. Interpreters consistently find it necessary to comment about terms such as "status," "performance,"

11. Wright, "Romans," 529.
12. Ibid.
13. Jewett, *Romans*, 384.
14. Ibid., 386.
15. Ibid.

"appropriate deeds," "accounting," and the like, but they are nowhere in Paul's discussion. A certain hyper-Augustinianism has found its way into the minutiae of biblical exegesis.

Modern Roman Catholic interpreters tend to present substantially the same picture. Fitzmyer has an entirely forensic account in which justification is defined as a gracious action that "cleared human beings of guilt but also granted them a share in 'life.'"[16] Nowhere does his reading of our passage ever touch the ground—at the level of the character or practice of the church—between such a decree of "acquittal" and the eschatological granting of eternal life. Christ "won lawful and theological significance for the humanity of the eschatological period.... The formal effect of Christ's obedience has been to make humanity upright *in the sight of God* at the judgment seat... The many will be constituted as righteous... because God has in Christ identified himself with sinners and taken upon himself the burden of their sin; hence they will receive as a free gift from God that *status of uprightness* which Christ's perfect obedience alone has merited."[17] Paul says nothing, in other words, about ecclesial acts in this passage.

Byrne's account at first looks more promising in this respect when he says that "Paul in no way wishes to suggest that human beings become helpless tools of a power somehow separate from themselves," but this does not seem to carry over to the side of "justification."[18] Rather, Christ has created a "positive situation with respect to the righteousness required at the judgment."[19] Once again "justification" has nothing to do with anything visible, but with "being found righteous at the judgment [as] the necessary condition for the gaining of life."[20] Justification as such cannot directly involve church practice but only have "implications" for it: "Until the judgment is finally given, believers have to live within and '*live out*' the favorable *verdict* they have already received."[21]

A sort of middle case is given by Simon Légasse, who sees justification as a present reality, but ends up "hiding" it in the concepts of "faith" and "the Gospel," so that one wonders what bearing the notion has on the church at all: "L'objet de ce don est la justice. Ce don est actuel pour ceux que ont donné leur foi à Dieu agissant par le Christ : le participe

---

16. Fitzmyer, *Romans*, 421.
17. Ibid., 421–22, my italics.
18. Byrne, *Romans*, 175.
19. Ibid., 181.
20. Ibid., 185.
21. Ibid., my italics.

présent *lambanontes* ne peut guère être ici pour un future . . . car Paul n'envisage pas la justification comme une réalité projetée dans l'avenir eschatologique; elle est acquise par quiconque accueille dans la foi et fait sien le message de l'Evangile."[22] This is, in other words, possibly a step in the direction I would want to move, but Légasse says nothing else about what la foi and le message de l'Evangile have to do with justification. One suspects their content has been emptied out into other theological terms which themselves are rather vacuous.

In the end, I am unable to find an interpreter of Romans that sees Rom 5:12–21 as having anything to do with the practice of the church. Rather, interpreters find here almost universally a hyper-Augustinian eschatology in which human agents stand idly by and watch as various levers in the cosmic judicial machinery are manipulated. In the rest of this chapter I show just how over-determined this reading actually is at the level of exegesis. I turn first to two key points of vocabulary that suggest that Paul writes of a certain symphony of divine and human agency in producing people who actually *do* behave and perform differently.

Two Interpretive Anchors

The Just Action

My interpretation of our passage begins by focusing on two different but interrelated issues. The first is the meaning of the word δικαίωμα, especially in v. 16. The usual rendering of this word is something like "righteousness" or "acquittal." This rendering has seemed right since we have assumed that Christ's gift must be literally or exactly be the *opposite* of what it is contrasted with, condemnation. Thus the NRSV is typical: "For the judgment following one trespass brought condemnation, but the free gift following many trespasses brings justification." "Justification" is likewise the translation given by the ASV, KJV, NKJV, NET, RSV, NIV and most commentaries.[23] This has been a tradition at least as far back as the Vulgate's *iustificationem*.[24] Similarly, others read "acquittal," making a forensic dynamic even more forceful.[25]

22. Légasse, *Romains*, 481.

23. E.g., Byrne, *Romans*, 173; Wright, "Romans," 528; Käsemann, *Romans*, 153; Dunn, *Romans*, 1:270.

24. Rom 5:16 in the Vulgate: *et non sicut per unum peccantem ita et donum nam iudicium ex uno in condemnationem gratia autem ex multis delictis in iustificationem*.

25. So even Stowers, *Romans*, 254.

But such a meaning would be uncommon. It certainly would be the only one of its kind in Paul, and a scan of extra-biblical Greek literature points in the same direction.[26] In fact, *BAGD* lists our very text, Rom 5:16, as the only attested such use in the extant Greek corpus.[27] As noted, it has long been supposed that this translation is *required* on exegetical grounds, so that "condemnation" can be contrasted with its opposite.[28] But this is simply not the case, for not every contrast is a simple opposition. What if Paul did not mean to contrast *opposites*, but simply things that are different in some aspect? To assume that condemnation must be contrasted with "justification" is to claim we know what Paul is saying ahead of time.[29]

A much more common meaning (i.e, one that is not freighted with so much hyper-Augustinian baggage) is simply "just deed," or, as the primary definition of *LSJ* has it, an "act of right."[30] Greek speakers could say things like:

> An orator must be ready with propositions dealing with greatness and smallness, and the greater and the less, both universally and in particular; for instance, which is the greater or less good, or act of injustice (ἀδίκημα) or justice (δικαίωμα).[31]

Elsewhere Aristotle makes this explicit:

> There is a difference between τὸ ἀδίκημα and τὸ ἄδικον and between τὸ δικαίωμα and τὸ δίκαιον. Nature or ordinance pronounces a thing ἄδικον, when that thing is done (πραχθῇ), it is ἀδίκημα, until it is done, it is ἄδικον. And similarly with δικαίωμα, more commonly called a δικαιοπράγημα.[32]

This passage establishes two things. First, a common meaning of δικαίωμα is "just deed." Second, even if Aristotle is creating a technical distinction between words that are usually synonymous, this does not detract from

---

26. See the survey in Kirk, "Dikaioma in Romans 5:16," 787–92.

27. *BAGD*, δικαίωμα, 249–50.

28. So, see Schrenk, "δίκη δίκαιος, κτλ," in in *TDNT* 221.

29. Kirk, ""Reconsidering Dikaioma," 788.

30. Liddell, Scott, and Jones, "δικαίωμα," in *A Greek-English Lexicon*, 429. Interestingly also, this is the translation of Barth, *Christ and Adam*, 31, but it does very little work for him in any sort of ethical direction. Also noted by Byrne, *Romans*, 184.

31. Aristotle, *Rhetoric* I.III.9. Unless otherwise noted, all translations and text of extra-biblical classical Greek and Latin texts are taken from *LCL* (as listed in the bibliography), with modifications.

32. Aristotle, *N.E.* V.VII.7.

the point that δικαίωμα falls into the grammatical realm of words used to talk about just and unjust actions.

We see this also in the LXX: "Now then, listen to their voice nevertheless, since you shall testify to them, and announce to them the just way (δικαίωμα) of the king who shall reign over them."[33] At other times it is used simply to refer to the "duties" of the priests in the temple.[34] So, in the same way, Philo of Alexandria writes, squarely in the context of a discussion of good or just works, that

> they who have thought that beyond behaving justly to their fellow men (ἔξω τῶν πρὸς ἀνθρώπους δικαιωμάτων) there was no such thing as goodness, have clung solely to their fellowship with and to the society of men, and, being wholly occupied by a love of the society of men, have invited all men to an equal participation in all their good things, laboring at the same time to the best of their power to alleviate all their disasters.[35]

By extension, δικαίωμα was used simply as "practice," "custom," or even "habit."[36] When it means this, however, it never appears to quite lose the nuance of "*just* practice," or "*just* habit." Thus "all Israel heard of this judgment that the king had rendered; and they stood in awe of the king, because they perceived that the wisdom of God was in him, to execute justice (ποιεῖν δικαίωμα)."[37] In Revelation 15:4 the word is used to refer to the "just deeds" of God that have been revealed (τὰ δικαιώματά σου ἐφανερώθησαν), and likewise in 19:8 in reference to the just deeds of the saints (τὰ δικαιώματα τῶν ἁγίων).

Significantly, in Rom 5 Paul himself gives us good reason to prefer this translation. He uses the term twice in the verses that immediately follow 5:16. From this we are able to get a good grasp on how Paul uses this term. In v. 18a he speaks of the "one δικαίωμα" of Jesus which leads for all to δικαίωσις (we treat this latter term below). The next verse (v. 19), *explaining* v. 18 (cf. ὥσπερ γάρ), makes it apparent that it is Jesus' *obedience*

---

33. 1 Sam 8:9.

34. 1 Sam 2:13: καὶ τὸ δικαίωμα τοῦ ἱερέως παρὰ τοῦ λαοῦ παντὸς τοῦ θύοντος καὶ ἤρχετο τὸ παιδάριον τοῦ ἱερέως ὡς ἂν ἡψήθη τὸ κρέας καὶ κρεάγρα τριόδους ἐν τῇ χειρὶ αὐτοῦ.

35. Philo, *Deca* 1:109.

36. 1 Sam 27:11: ἄνδρα καὶ γυναῖκα οὐκ ἐζωογόνησεν τοῦ εἰσαγαγεῖν εἰς Γεθ λέγων μὴ ἀναγγείλωσιν εἰς Γεθ καθ' ἡμῶν λέγοντες τάδε Δαυιδ ποιεῖ καὶ τόδε τὸ δικαίωμα αὐτοῦ πάσας τὰς ἡμέρας ἃς ἐκάθητο Δαυιδ ἐν ἀγρῷ τῶν ἀλλοφύλων.

37. 1 Kgs 3:28.

that is the referent of the "one δικαίωμα" in v. 18a: ὥσπερ γὰρ διὰ τῆς παρακοῆς τοῦ ἑνὸς ἀνθρώπου ἁμαρτωλοὶ κατεστάθησαν οἱ πολλοί, οὕτως καὶ διὰ τῆς ὑπακοῆς τοῦ ἑνὸς δίκαιοι κατασταθήσονται οἱ πολλοί. The context of the passage suggests that Jesus' δικαίωμα is not his obedience in general, but specifically his obedience *unto death*:

5:6	Χριστὸς ὑπὲρ ἀσεβῶν ἀπέθανεν
5:8	Χριστὸς ὑπὲρ ἡμῶν ἀπέθανεν
5:9	δικαιωθέντες νῦν ἐν τῷ αἵματι αὐτοῦ
5:10	κατηλλάγημεν τῷ θεῷ διὰ τοῦ θανάτου τοῦ υἱοῦ αὐτοῦ

So rendering δικαίωμα "just deed" in this passage fits well with the fact that Paul seems to use it in reference to Jesus' act of obedience unto death. Paul gives no indication here that he is talking about a forensic status of "justified" or "righteous" before God. Rather it is precisely the *work* of Christ on the cross that is in view. Vv. 18 and 19, taken together, make any other reading impossible. On these grounds we can render 16b: "For the judgment from one man led to execution, but the gift that arose from many transgressions led to a just act."[38]

Moreover, if "just action" is the sense of δικαίωμα in this context, then not only is Paul saying something about *Christ's* action but also about the *church's*. We can see this if we look at vv. 16b and 18 together.

16b	18
τὸ μὲν γὰρ κρίμα	Ἄρα οὖν ὡς
ἐξ ἑνὸς	δι' ἑνὸς παραπτώματος
εἰς κατάκριμα,	εἰς πάντας ἀνθρώπους εἰς κατάκριμα,
τὸ δὲ χάρισμα	οὕτως καὶ
ἐκ πολλῶν παραπτωμάτων	δι' ἑνὸς δικαιώματος
εἰς δικαίωμα.	εἰς πάντας ἀνθρώπους εἰς δικαίωσιν ζωῆς

What emerges from such parallel structure is that v. 18a repeats and fleshes-out v. 16ba, which treats the transgression of Adam that led everyone who followed to execution. The next section (v. 18b) then concretizes v. 16b's "gift that followed on the many sins" by saying that the gift is none other than Christ's just deed of obedience unto death.

We then come to the rare word δικαίωσις. Although it does in some places appear to mean "legal demand" or "claim," it can also simply be a

---

38. What this translation means, of course, is that the parallel Paul is making is not yet complete, and he is simply not yet making the parallel we have usually supposed he is. See below for more comment on parallelism.

substitute for δίκη.³⁹ Thus while δικαίωμα is *a* just act, δικαίωσις is the *process* of *doing* a just act. This accords well with the first definition given by *TDNT*, the "act of executing the δίκαιον" which is slightly extended in the meaning "to make just."⁴⁰ The two words are so closely related that Schenk can even add that we see from "a comparison of the meanings of δικαίωσις and δικαίωμα that the two are interchangeable . . . in relation to the sense of the just act."⁴¹ This parity is of course that of many Greek words that share a common root: the -ωμα suffix suggests a discrete act, in this case a just act, while -ωσις suggests an ongoing performance.⁴² The parallelism further suggests that Paul might be using these words synonymously.

So we should consider a translation as follows: "Now if through the one trespass [of Adam] condemnation came to all people, in the same way through a just action the practice of justice that leads to life comes to all people." This translation is fully in accord with the lexical constraints of Paul's grammar—in fact more so than the usual translations. I suggest, in other words, that Paul is explicating how the deed of one man leads to similar just deeds *of others*: Christ's good work leads others to similar good works. This reading is supported in the broader context of Rom 5:12–21 by the true parallelism it allows between Christ and Adam: Adam's one deed led to disobedience for all and so Christ, untying the knot as the true second Adam, does the one deed that led to obedience for all.

So, with Stowers, I do not think Paul sets out the traditional notion of original sin in this passage; although, against Stowers and most who hold a position like his, I do think Paul leaves plenty of room for it.⁴³ This is because it is certainly plausible to read the infamous ἐφ' ᾧ (5:12) as

---

39. Schrenk, *TDNT* 2:223–24.

40. Ibid., 2:223. Though we cannot treat Rom 4:25 in detail here, the use of δικαίωσις there can also fit with our argument, and in fact it solves a problem in that text of the difference between v. 25a and v. 25b. Christ was raised not for our "justification" in the forensic sense, since that would be the same, on that reading, as dying for our transgressions. Rather, Christ is raised "to make us just" (διὰ τὴν δικαίωσιν ἡμῶν).

41. Schrenk, *TDNT* 2:222.

42. So in Paul cf. esp. Rom 11:25 πώρωσις; 2 Cor 4:10 νέκρωσις.

43. Stowers, *Rereading*, 254. For good survey's of the extensive literature on this topic see, besides the commentaries, the two articles by Lyonnet, "Le sens de *eph' hoi*," 436–56; "Le péché originel," 63–84. Fitzmyer, "Romans 5:12," 321–28; Kirby, "Romans 5.12," 283–86. The central mistake in the literature is to presume that if the later church notion of "original sin" is not found in these passages it follows that his theology has no room for such a notion. See, thus, Scroggs, *Last Adam*, 78.

indicating some sort of quasi-biological explanation for the passing on of sin, but the particular aspect of that sin that Paul pulls to the fore in this passage is its *performance*.⁴⁴ Paul cites Adam because, following his trespass, all simply *did* sin: πάντες ἥμαρτον (5:12, cf. 14b).⁴⁵ The Apostle is concerned here about particular types of *behavior*, not in an anthropological "state of sin" or "status as sinner." Those in Adam are sinful because of visible sinful *action*. In the same way, it is beginning to become clear that Christ's obedient and just act did not bring some sort of generalized *condition* of "justification" or "acquittal," but, as the use of the word here necessitates, it brought about another just act, the just action of those "in Christ"—the church. Christ's just act of obedience unto death made it possible for the church to "execute the just."

But this is not the only possible non-forensic meaning of δικαίωσις that fits our passage. We noted above that at times it means "make just." In accordance with the particulars of Greek morphology noted above δικαίωσις often meant "being made just" (just as, e.g., θεώσις means "being made divine," etc.).⁴⁶ So another possible understanding of the phrase in 18b is that by Christ's just act *he makes* the church just. Thus, Christ's just action does not, on this reading, lead to other just *acts* of the church, but leads to the action of making the church just. This interpretation takes δικαίωσιν, perfectly plausibly, as a noun signifying an action and the εἰς of εἰς πάντας ἀνθρώπους to indicate the object of the action named in the noun. The central difference from rendering δικαίωσις "just act," as we did above is that here Jesus' act leads to a *divine* remaking of sinners into people who act justly, while the former reading emphasizes the divine remaking of sinners into people who *act* justly. Both renderings, as will be further reestablished below, presume that the church in engaged in a just *practice*, not that they are merely "declared" just. The difference is in point of emphasis, not in ecclesial practice.

This second possible rendering of δικαίωσις also points out that a non-forensic reading of the passage is possible, however, even on the most traditional translation. We can follow, e.g., the NRSV: "Therefore just as one man's trespass led to condemnation for all, so one man's act of righteousness leads to justification and life for all." There is no reason that

---

44. Elsewhere, notably Gal 3:8, 29, Paul is clearly making arguments from something like biological succession.

45. So Scroggs, *Last Adam*, 78: "The point is that men actually became sinners . . . Whether or not there is a forensic level of meaning here."

46. Schrenk, *TDNT* 2:222.

we have to construe "justification" here in terms of a status "before God," much less than to understand it as being essentially at odds with a true description of their present actions in terms of *simul iustus et peccator*. So, if there were not so much baggage associated with the term, *justification* would be not be a bad rendering of this second interpretive option, since philologically the English suffix *-ication* corresponds to the Greek -ωσις. Both words can be used to designate the process of "making just."[47]

So far I have given two possible renderings of Rom 5:18, neither of which assumes that one is still essentially sinful while at the same time *in another way* one is just. The first sees Jesus' just act as producing a further just act on the part of the church. The second sees Jesus' just act as the act that makes the church just. Both readings presume that the church is made up of people who actually are obedient. I do not see a reason to artificially choose and champion one of these two options as more probable than the other. The purposes of my argument are well served by merely by establishing these as live interpretive options. As I will show in more detail below, there is no indication in vv. 16 and 18 that Paul is trying to name an invisible status known only to God. Paul's language is not *simul iustus et peccator* but *iustus et sic necessarie non peccator*, which is to say that Jesus makes possible the church's actual obedience to God—the visible just practice of the body of Christ.

The Gift

The second major interpretive anchor for my reading grounds itself in the language of gift that pervades this section. In v. 15 alone, where such language is first introduced, Paul uses "gift" language four times, using three different words, which appear *prima facie* synonymous: Ἀλλ' οὐχ ὡς τὸ παράπτωμα, οὕτως καὶ τὸ χάρισμα· εἰ γὰρ τῷ τοῦ ἑνὸς παραπτώματι οἱ πολλοὶ ἀπέθανον, πολλῷ μᾶλλον ἡ χάρις τοῦ θεοῦ καὶ ἡ δωρεὰ ἐν χάριτι τῇ τοῦ ἑνὸς ἀνθρώπου Ἰησοῦ Χριστοῦ εἰς τοὺς πολλοὺς ἐπερίσσευσεν.

---

47. The usual way an English speaker uses "justification" is to name the reasons, or tell the way, that one is in fact just. "A car wreck is a good justification for being late." "I had a good justification for that." "I did not behave wrongly—I was justified in what I did." The practice of naming the wreck is regarded as showing or trying to show that in this case being tardy is not unjust. In other words, in English, one of the uses of "justification" is to name the reason someone really is just. And this brings up how strange it is that only in certain theological contexts do we assume that "justification" names a process that counts people just who are really not.

This theme of gift is then strung through the rest of the section (v. 19 is the only verse in which the notion of gift does not appear).

We can take our cue concerning what Paul names by such language from the frequent use in his letters of the word χάρισμα. This word is unique among the others in that it is clearly defined elsewhere in relatively straightforward passages (Rom 12:6; 1 Cor 12:4, 9, etc.) where it names the practice that constitutes Christ's body. Each of Christ's body parts has a particular gift that serves the up-building of the body so that χαρίσματα name the "gifted things" that are the practices of Christ's body.[48] Nevertheless, we have become accustomed to calling these "*spiritual* gifts," and the picture we have of these is based, I suspect, more on an old-fashioned tent revival than on anything Paul says about them.

The χαρίσματα Paul names are more often than not utterly mundane things that a body does: it helps, it serves, it gives, it comforts, it forgives, it teaches (cf. Rom 12:7–8). This means that if a χάρισμα is something God gives, is at the same time something that can be practiced (ἐνεργέω: 1 Cor 12:6, 10–11; ποιέω: Eph 4:16) by humans.[49] Indeed it is only God's gift once we have received it by *using* it. For Paul the gift is given in its very operation, for the gift *is* the operation.[50] Contesting this claim would involve bringing forward evidence that shows Paul regarding χάρισμα as something like an ability which might be potentially put to use but which can theoretically subsist apart from its practice. I am unable to find texts to this effect.

This means that χάρισμα and δικαίωμα are quite closely related. The grammar of each seems to be that of things that are done within the body of Christ. We have seen at length that the latter is the "just action" that Christ makes possible for those in the second Adam. But the former is also an action, a "thing that is given" to each member of Christ to perform as a way of building up his body. Just as a δικαίωμα is not an abstract state, so a χάρισμα is not a potentiality waiting to be actualized, but the concrete act of some part of the body.

---

48. Cf. Eph 3:7-8, where the grace that Paul received from God is his diaconate to the gentiles: οὗ ἐγενήθην διάκονος κατὰ τὴν δωρεὰν τῆς χάριτος τοῦ θεοῦ τῆς δοθείσης μοι κατὰ τὴν ἐνέργειαν τῆς δυνάμεως αὐτοῦ. ἐμοὶ τῷ ἐλαχιστοτέρῳ πάντων ἁγίων ἐδόθη ἡ χάρις αὕτη, τοῖς ἔθνεσιν εὐαγγελίσασθαι τὸ ἀνεξιχνίαστον πλοῦτος τοῦ Χριστοῦ.

49. The element of human agency in the gifts is further shown by the fact that Paul can exhort "seek the better gifts" (1 Cor 12:31), as well as by the fact the verbs in each section on the gifts have human beings as their subject.

50. See Afanasiev, *Church*, 98–100.

This clarification brings us back to v. 15. The trespass and the gift contrast with each other precisely *as* discrete actions, and not (even in part) *because* one is a discrete act and one not. Moreover, v. 15b is shown to be anticipating the parallelism we already looked at between v. 16b and v. 18: the gift (ἡ χάρις, ἡ δωρεὰ) of the one human Jesus Christ abounds to many, and this gift is precisely the concrete act of his obedience unto death. So it appears that the three gift words in this section are synonymous in that they refer to a concrete, gifted practice.[51] In other words, Paul's basic associations in this passage are slightly drawn out but clear: the χάρισμα which we have from God *is* our δικαίωμα made possible for those in Christ because of his own δικαίωμα, which *is* his ὑπακοὴ μέχρι θανάτου.[52]

Rereading the Comparisons of Adam and Christ

We are now in a position to take a step back and view the passage as a whole. Rom 5:1-11 spells out the καταλλαγή that God has effected through the death of Christ, and then goes on to explicate exactly of what this reconciliation consists.[53] The Apostle does this by a number of contrasts and comparisons. The first that is important for us is, again, v. 12: Διὰ τοῦτο ὥσπερ δι' ἑνὸς ἀνθρώπου ἡ ἁμαρτία εἰς τὸν κόσμον εἰσῆλθεν καὶ διὰ τῆς ἁμαρτίας ὁ θάνατος, καὶ οὕτως εἰς πάντας ἀνθρώπους ὁ θάνατος διῆλθεν, ἐφ' ᾧ πάντες ἥμαρτον. Death entered the world as one of the

---

51. Stowers, *Rereading*, 254, *may* be after something like what I am suggesting in the two pages or so that he devotes to our passage: "Christ's obedience affects the many in a way analogous to the effect of Adam's disobedience in the period before the giving of the law. Adam disobeyed, and all until Moses subsequently shared in his tendency to sin, and all shared in his sentence of a limited life span merely because the punishment was passed on from Adam. The law permitted renewed possibilities for obedience and disobedience. Christ's obedience canceled the sentence of death and *produced the possibility of righteousness for all after him* [my emphasis]."

52. Cf. 2 Cor 5: 15: καὶ ὑπὲρ πάντων ἀπέθανεν, ἵνα οἱ ζῶντες μηκέτι ἑαυτοῖς ζῶσιν ἀλλὰ τῷ ὑπὲρ αὐτῶν ἀποθανόντι καὶ ἐγερθέντι. The connection between Rom 5 and Phil 2 was also made by Irenaeus; see Andia, *Homo vivens*, 119.

53. Thus, I see in 2 Cor 5:18-20 a condensed version of the extended argument in Rom 5: τὰ δὲ πάντα ἐκ τοῦ θεοῦ τοῦ καταλλάξαντος ἡμᾶς ἑαυτῷ διὰ Χριστοῦ καὶ δόντος ἡμῖν τὴν διακονίαν τῆς καταλλαγῆς, ὡς ὅτι θεὸς ἦν ἐν Χριστῷ κόσμον καταλλάσσων ἑαυτῷ, μὴ λογιζόμενος αὐτοῖς τὰ παραπτώματα αὐτῶν καὶ θέμενος ἐν ἡμῖν τὸν λόγον τῆς καταλλαγῆς. ὑπὲρ Χριστοῦ οὖν πρεσβεύομεν ὡς τοῦ θεοῦ παρακαλοῦντος δι' ἡμῶν· δεόμεθα ὑπὲρ Χριστοῦ, καταλλάγητε τῷ θεῷ τὸν μὴ γνόντα ἁμαρτίαν ὑπὲρ ἡμῶν ἁμαρτίαν ἐποίησεν, ἵνα ἡμεῖς γενώμεθα δικαιοσύνη θεοῦ ἐν αὐτῷ.

results or curses of sin when Adam sinned (Gen 3:19: γῆ εἶ καὶ εἰς γῆν ἀπελεύσῃ), and so in the same way, Paul says, *because* everyone else *sinned* who followed Adam, they all died too. The problem then—the real question at issue—is that of death and life. In Adam all have lived sinfully, all have committed acts of sin, and so all have died. This is further affirmed in v. 13 when Paul parenthetically comments on the Torah's role in this "history of sin": in the period from Adam to Moses death was victorious even over τοὺς μὴ ἁμαρτήσαντας ἐπὶ τῷ ὁμοιώματι τῆς παραβάσεως 'Αδάμ. This phrase further rules out a reading of sin in this passage as a "condition" or "state" that a person is in, since it implies two categories of people who sin: (1) those who sin, but not "in the same way as the transgression of Adam" and (2) those who do sin in the same way as Adam. Such a differentiation focuses on two types of sin precisely as sinful acts. "Sinner" names one who either *performs a sinful act* in an Adam-like way or in an un-Adam-like way. Either way, Paul is referring to *acts* of sin, because he names two kinds of people, differentiaed by their sorts of acts.[54] Sin is not one homogeneous category of those subject to an abstract power.

The problem Paul sees is death and a world of people sinning; or rather, death because there is a world of people sinning. So what is necessary for the reversal of death, for "life," is right living. What is needed, in other words, is another "one man" who would institute a new way of living that leads to life. And such a one—one who would change the behavior and thus destiny of humanity—could aptly be called a second Adam. Thus the first Adam is τύπος τοῦ μέλλοντος (5:14).

There are several things that must be re-read in v. 15 before we state the comparison that is being made. First, Paul says that God's gift *was* Jesus and that *this gift* abounded to many (v. 15). We are tempted by hyper-Augustinian theological systems to think that already in this verse Paul wants to make a complete comparison between the *effects* of Adam and Christ, so that since Paul says that Adam's sin resulted in death, "grace" must be the opposite of death, and so fundamentally causal—as sin is of death. In our dash to so read, however, we have assumed that "grace" must contain, in itself, the notion of "life."

But Paul does not yet make this connection. In v. 15b he states that Adam's trespass caused many to follow him and so many died. But v. 15c does not say that because of Christ's righteous act *eternal life* abounded to

---

54. So Stowers, *Rereading*, 253: "Only before Moses did everyone die merely as a result of the sentence passed on Adam for his disobedience (5:13–14). After the giving of the law, people became accountable for their own transgressions."

many. Rather, it says that just as Adam's trespass lead to death for many, so God made abound the gift *of another "one man"* to many: ἡ χάρις τοῦ θεοῦ καὶ ἡ δωρεὰ ἐν χάριτι τῇ τοῦ ἑνὸς ἀνθρώπου Ἰησοῦ Χριστοῦ εἰς τοὺς πολλοὺς ἐπερίσσευσεν. So the resumptive τῇ emphasizes that the χάρις is of another εἷς ἀνθρώπος and the genitive τοῦ Ἰησοῦ Χριστοῦ is epexegetic: the gift *is* the "one human" and the gift *is* Jesus Christ.

What Jesus has actually *done* is yet unstated. Paul has not brought Jesus' obedient deed into the conversation at this point. Rather, the focus is on the gift that God has given, the one man Jesus, in response to the fact that the one man's disobedience led to death for all. It does not seem, then, that Paul is saying that this grace could have been given by God for a deed performed by *any* one human. Paul does not portray God waiting around until someone finally got it right so that he could then save humanity. God specifically gave Jesus to be the new "one human" who was to deal with the old "one man's" failure.[55] Thus God's bounty was ἐν χάριτι τῇ τοῦ Ἰησοῦ Χριστου: "in the gift, namely that . . . of Jesus Christ." The uniqueness of Jesus as the second "one human" is clear, for at this point Paul has only said that God has *given* him. He has not yet said anything about what Jesus has done.

This reading concretizes the various "grace/gift/favor/bounty" language that begins this verse (ἡ χάρις τοῦ θεοῦ καὶ ἡ δωρεὰ ἐν χάριτι τῇ . . .), for the emphasis is specifically on the gift of the second "one man," and not on "grace" in the abstract. We might, therefore, gloss this καὶ as "explicative" in that what follows explains the foregoing: "The grace of God, *indeed* the gift in the favor . . ." At the same time, reading Ἰησοῦ Χριστοῦ as an epexegetic genitive removes the ambiguity regarding whether Paul refers to God's gift or Jesus'. The usual translation as "the grace of God and the gift in the grace of the one human Jesus Christ" is better rendered as "the gift of God and the bounty that is in that gift *which is* the one man . . ."

Paul then continues in v. 16a with another comparison, καὶ οὐχ ὡς δι' ἑνὸς ἁμαρτήσαντος τὸ δώρημα: "The gift is not like the one person who sinned." He then immediately sets out in nuce what he will later say in more detail in v. 18—that the sin of Adam resulted in condemnation or "execution" (κατάκριμα), by which he names the death that comes with sin. But,

---

55. This reading takes seriously the incarnation as more than *merely* a theological "outgrowth" of reflection upon salvation. Salvation was not effected by just anyone but by the new Adam whom God gave for the purpose of redeeming humanity. Adoptionism is firmly ruled out by the fact for Paul God *sends* his son as the Second Adam precisely for the *purpose* of redeeming humanity. Without God's gift of a second "one man" Adam's progeny and its lethal consequences would still rule.

as we saw in v. 18 above, the contrast in v. 16 is not between condemnation and "justification," as all the major translations suggest. The contrast is rather between "condemnation" and a righteous *act*. The χάρισμα means "gifted practice," and here appears to have the basic meaning of "gifted thing," that followed on many trespasses (ἐκ πολλῶν παραπτωμάτων) and led to a righteous act (εἰς δικαίωμα). So Paul is explicating the gift language that he emphasized in the previous verse. Moreover, at this point it is ambiguous whether the "just act" is Christ's just act on the cross or our just act that resulted from it. At this point Paul only tells us that the gift lead to a righteous act. He explicates this language presently in v. 18.

But first v. 17 finally gets to what we usually think must have already been said, namely, that the gift of God leads to life. Even so, Paul travels the road from gift to life differently than a forensic reading of the passage would expect. In the structure of the section, v. 17 is the conclusion of the contrast that he started making in v. 16 with the rhetorical question equating the gift and the sin of Adam. Paul says that just as death ruled through one person (v. 17a) so others will rule in life through that other one person, Jesus Christ (v. 17b). The language is that of eschatological life, the life that awaits them after the resurrection of their bodies, since Paul says not that they *do reign* in life but that they *will*. And, given what I have argued so far, I suggest further that Paul has at this point elided the middle terms of the contrast, namely the just and sinful practices.

So v. 17 does not occlude human agency. This is shown in the text itself, for the people who will rule are "those who receive the abundance of grace and of the gift of justice (δικαιοσύνης)." Because δικαιοσύνη refers in Rom 6, as we will see in the next chapter, to a quality of Christian action, I think it best, anticipating this, to retain that nuance here. In other words, δικαιοσύνη is simply the practice of justice: the gift that God has given through the one Jesus Christ is justice in contrast to the trespass of Adam.

This is supported by reference to Rom 5:7–8. There Paul denotes the sinful and the just in terms that certainly name a person's present actions and way of life: μόλις γὰρ ὑπὲρ δικαίου τις ἀποθανεῖται· ὑπὲρ γὰρ τοῦ ἀγαθοῦ τάχα τις καὶ τολμᾷ ἀποθανεῖν· συνίστησιν δὲ τὴν ἑαυτοῦ ἀγάπην εἰς ἡμᾶς ὁ θεός, ὅτι ἔτι ἁμαρτωλῶν ὄντων ἡμῶν Χριστὸς ὑπὲρ ἡμῶν ἀπέθανεν. For these verses to make any sense at all as a part of Paul's argument, they have to be about people who are actually performing righteous, good, or sinful deeds, for whom we would be more or less likely to expect someone to die. At no point following this does Paul give any indication that he has stopped talking about practices and ways of life and started talking about something else.[56]

Subsequently, this is confirmed by the two statements of 5:9–10:

> But how much more, therefore, now being made just (δικαιωθέντες) by his blood, shall we be saved (σωθησόμεθα) through him from wrath? For if while we were enemies we were reconciled (κατηλλάγημεν) to God by the death of his son, how much more, now that we are reconciled (καταλλαγέντες), shall we be saved (σωθησόμεθα) in his life?

In this passage the two parallel concepts of δικαιωθέντες and κατηλλάγημεν/καταλλαγέντες are set in relation to σωθησόμεθα. The former pair is something that happens, or has happened, *now*; the latter term will happen in the future. That δικαιωθέντες in v. 9 can semantically be assimilated to καταλλαγέντες in v. 10 strongly suggests that both name a changed manner of life worthy of future salvation. Hence the thrust of the passage is that if while we were sinful Christ died for us, how much more now that we are *not sinful*, now that we are *just*, will God save us from his wrath.[57]

But a strictly forensic reading has a difficult time giving an account of this passage at all. In the first instance it cannot give a satisfactory account of the difference between being "made just/reconciled" on the one hand and being "saved" on the other. Forensic readers must argue that God has done something invisibly now, called "reconciliation" or "justification," *so that* he can later count us worthy of salvation. But in both verses this destroys the rationale for Paul's πολλῷ μᾶλλον. For Paul is not just saying that if God acted for us once he will surely do it again. Rather, the point is that if God acted mercifully towards us while we were his enemies, even more so now can we count on his favor since we are his friends. God took the initiative while we were sinners, so we certainly will not be condemned now that we are just.

The church's just practice is obedience (cf. v. 19). Thus those who practice these gifted, just acts will rule in life at the resurrection, since they are no longer under the tyranny of death that comes when they sin (v. 17). This precisely balances the otherwise lopsided parts of v. 17. The story is that of Adam's disobedience causing death to rule because it spawned more disobedience (v. 17a). God, however, was able to bring humanity back to just practice through the one Jesus Christ, who bestowed

---

56. See the discussion in Westerholm, *Perspectives*, 261–84.
57. So see Breytenbach, *Versöhnung*, 153, for the parallelism. Typical, however, is Breytenbach's equivocation over what Paul actually *names* by "reconciliation."

a richly abundant gift of justice, which means the overthrow of the rule of death and the proper restoration of humanity to life (v. 17b).[58]

Since we have dealt with v. 18 in detail above, it remains simply to reiterate that Paul is not making the contrast we expect, and he is not making a contrast in terms of precise opposites: not between Adam-Sin-Death and Christ-Justification-Life, but between Adam-Sin-Death and Christ-Obedience-Life. Since δικαίωμα refers to a just act, the Apostle contrasts the judgment that comes from Adam's sin with the righteous act that makes possible further righteous acts that lead to life.

But a further nuance can now be perceived in the sense of δικαίωμα. In both cases in v. 16 it appears that Paul names as δικαίωμα not only a just act, but an act that *makes* right, or as *LSJ* puts it, "amends a wrong."[59] The problem Paul sees, I have argued, is a world of people sinning which results in their deaths (thus "death rules"). What is required then is for people to act justly, for this will lead to life. This problem began with the sin of the first "one human," Adam, and so God graciously saved humanity by sending another "one human", the second one, Jesus. V. 16c provides the soteriology that we were left without in v. 15: Jesus performed a just act that made it possible for others to do similar things: living righteously has once again, for the first time since the original trespass of Adam and Eve, entered onto the world-scene. Thus Jesus' act is a just act that makes right the first human's trespass, and our gifted acts are themselves just and *thereby* likewise make right disobedience subsequent to Adam.

We come to v.19, where, against the majority reading, I suggest that Paul (1) makes a claim he has *not yet made*, and that he (2) does not make exactly the same claim that most have understood. He writes that ὥσπερ γὰρ διὰ τῆς παρακοῆς τοῦ ἑνὸς ἀνθρώπου ἁμαρτωλοὶ κατεστάθησαν οἱ πολλοί, οὕτως καὶ διὰ τῆς ὑπακοῆς τοῦ ἑνὸς δίκαιοι κατασταθήσονται οἱ πολλοί. Usually, of course, this is taken to be just one more redundant

---

58. At another point, however, things are not so balanced, and this is obviously Paul's intention. The asymmetry between death ruling on the one hand and "those who receive the gift" ruling on the other hand brings to light just how closely Paul's thought is here intertwined with the Genesis story. There, of course, the humans are in charge: Gen 1:26–27: εἶπεν ὁ θεός ποιήσωμεν ἄνθρωπον... καὶ ἀρχέτωσαν... καὶ ηὐλόγησεν αὐτοὺς ὁ θεὸς λέγων... πληρώσατε τὴν γῆν καὶ κατακυριεύσατε αὐτῆς καὶ ἄρχετε. If humanity is supposed to rule over creation it cannot do so in disobedience, for this causes another to rule, death. But if this is the case what can the defeat of death by gifted obedience that brings life be but the reinstitution of the created intention for rulership to belong to humanity?

59. Liddell, Scott, and Jones, "δικαίωμα," in *A Greek-English Lexicon*, 429.

contrast between Adam's sin that resulted in death and Christ's death that results in justification. What is the problem with this?

First, the focus is not on the death of Christ as sacrifice, but on his *obedience*. Adam was disobedient, Christ was obedient. This establishes "many just people" (δίκαιοι οἱ πολλοί). We do get a view now of the eschaton, as the future passive κατασταθήσονται designates. But it is important to note that on my reading even this eschatological scenario does not fit into a *forensic* construal, though Paul is certainly thinking of God's judgment (and so may be named "judicial" *at this point*). He says that, on the one hand, in God's plan many *were* established sinners, but, on the other, after Christ's obedience to death many will be established as "just." So this *is* a view from "before God" appearing for the first time. At the eschaton the judgment God will make about the character of these "many" is that they are "just" (δίκαιοι). What does this tell us?

First, the fact that Paul in v. 19 uses the future tense to denote the time when many will be held to be just suggests strongly that the other past and present tense verbs in the section (ὑπερεπερίσσευεν, ἐπερίσσευσεν, λαμβάνοντες, and ἔστιν understood in 15a, 16c, 18b) presume that the results of God's gift of Christ are not confined to the future judgment. These *non-future* verbs indicate that Paul sees many as being just *presently*, in the time of the church, between Christ's resurrection and second coming.

Second, there is no reason to think that these "many" are "just" in anything other than the usual sense of the word, i.e., in their practices. They are just because they act justly. This raises another awkward point for the forensic reading. It would be strange for Paul to give throughout the section a perspective on the many as invisibly "justified before God," and then in v. 19 to repeat the same thing in terms of what will be true before God.

The final two verses (vv. 20–21) of the section again make reference to the place of the Torah in this history of redemption, and present no difficulty for the proposed rereading, though some explanation is in order. Paul writes that οὗ δὲ ἐπλεόνασεν ἡ ἁμαρτία, ὑπερεπερίσσευσεν ἡ χάρις. The abstractness of the language, or at least of the conventional translations of these two verses, has added fuel to the supposition that we are dealing with abstract "powers" or "states before God." But the forgoing exegesis has shown, and the next chapter will continue to argue, that this is not what Paul is saying. Rather, these final two verses are the concluding summary of the forgoing argument. "Sin abounded, but the gift abounded even more" is merely a summary of the twin contrasts drawn out above.

Thus "sin ruled in death" (ἐβασίλευσεν ἡ ἁμαρτία ἐν τῷ θανάτῳ) because of the death that Adam and his heirs' disobedience brought upon the world, and "the gift rules through justice to eternal life" (ἡ χάρις βασιλεύσῃ διὰ δικαιοσύνης εἰς ζωὴν αἰώνιον) because of God's gift of Christ who performed a just deed that led to the church living justly and so entering eternal life.

The Hortatory Context

Further support for the reading I have proposed is found in the hortatory context in which Roman 5 as a whole falls. If Paul is talking about a gift from God that can be practiced we should should not be surprised to find exhortation to that practice. This is especially true—as I have intimated, and will argue below, regarding Rom 12:3-8—if it is a gift that is only received by being practiced, for the gift is the practice itself. The loss of the practices of the church from the reading of Rom 5 has both sustained and been sustained by the traditional forensic narrative of grace and justification being exclusively a matter for God's hands. The context is hortatory in several ways.

First, there is the material from Rom 6. We will come to that chapter as a whole below, but it is important to note that there Paul is commanding the church repeatedly to do away with any sinful practice (cf. esp. 6:1, 11, 12, 13). He is certainly not telling them to do away with the abstract "power" of sin in their lives (what would that mean?). Rather he is requiring of them (in the language of Rom 5) obedient practice as the antidote to their sin. He is telling them to *do* something about their sin. In the language of *our* inquiry, he is telling them to exercise their agency and practice the grace that they have been given.

Second, Rom 5 itself is introduced with exhortation. The rhetorical flare of 5:1–5 is no doubt meant to inspire as much as describe such phenomena as endurance, character, hope and love. This fact commends the alternative reading of the text critical issue in 5:1: Δικαιωθέντες οὖν ἐκ πίστεως εἰρήνην ἔχωμεν πρὸς τὸν θεὸν διὰ τοῦ κυρίου ἡμῶν Ἰησοῦ Χριστοῦ. Though nearly every nuance of this sentence is debatable, the only issue that need concern us here is the reading ἔχωμεν in place of the almost universally printed and translated ἔχομεν. Reading the indicative, I suggest, is heavily over-determined by the theological narrative in which we are first justified in Rom 1–4 and then sanctified in Rom 5–8. On this schema we must *already* "have peace towards God" by the time we get to

Gifted Obedience

5:1, and so we could not possibly be so exhorted. In this case ἔχομεν is clearly preferable, despite the fact that the textual tradition stands rather strongly in favor of ἔχωμεν. The first hand of ℵ, A, B, C, D, K, and other derivative witnesses, all read the subjunctive, while the indicative is present only in the first correction of ℵ, the second correction of B, in F, G, P, and other derivatives. On the textual witness alone, therefore, the subjunctive is preferable. Moreover, it is perhaps also a more difficult reading since vv. 2–3 contain at least two, and maybe four indicatives (cf. ἐσχήκαμεν × 2; καυχώμεθα × 2). It is easy to see why a scribe would assimilate to the indicative but not to the subjunctive.[60]

In other words, there is at least a very early and strong tradition of reading the Adam-Christ narrative of 5:12–21 within the context of ethical exhortation. If this is the case, Rom 5 actually provides, not itself an exhortation, but rather an explanation of the surrounding hortatory, along the lines we have already spelled out. The just practice of the church, the life apart from sin, of endurance and character, hope and love, that Paul exhorts them to *is* the graced life that is the practice of Christ.

The Practice of Adam and Christ in the Early Catholic Fathers

This way of interpreting the passage is much closer to that of the earliest interpretations of it in the catholic Fathers. Of course the most famous exegete of this passage in the first two centuries is Irenaeus, with his theology of recapitulation centering on Adam and Christ. I begin, however, with Origen, since he, unlike Irenaeus, actually produced a commentary on Romans and so we are able to focus on his understanding of this passage with particular precision.

Origen of Alexandria on Rom 5:12–21

Origen presents rather directly the reading of the passage that I am advocating. For him, time and again we see that the "justification" that Christ brings is a visible and practicable justice. Justification names the event whereby Christ makes our actions, and the habits that determine them, just. This is the other side of his fairly well-known argument that Adam's

---

60. Not surprisingly Bultmann dismissively says that the "variant reading ἔχωμεν is not to be entertained" without giving any reasons (Bultmann, *Theology*, 1:274).

"original sin" is transmitted by *imitation*, not transmutation. So Christ's "original justification" is transmitted by imitation of him.

Commenting on Rom 5:16 Origen tackles head-on the question of whether what Paul is talking about happens with or without human striving (as a visible or invisible justice):

> You will perhaps say: If death passed through to all men because of one who sinned, and likewise by the righteousness of the one the *iustificationem* of life reached unto all men, then we have done nothing that we should die or that we should live, but indeed Adam is the cause of death, and Christ, the cause of life. But certainly we have already said above that parents not only produce sons but they also educate them. And those who are born become not only sons of their parents but also their pupils; and they are not prodded into the death of sin so much by nature as by instruction.[61]

Origen thus begins to develop his thesis that the righteousness secured by Christ takes place, not invisibly "before God" but as a matter of *training* and *discipline* in the practices of the church. It is not a matter of Adam and Christ merely having "produced sons," but each also trains them so they are formed in a particular way. He goes on and spells out just what this means for Adam and for Christ:

> Now do you wish to understand that it was not only by birth but also by teaching (*doctrinae*) that death exercised its dominion from Adam? This can be learned from the contraries. For when the Lord Jesus Christ had come to amend what had been done wrongly, in view of the fact that the first birth, which came from Adam, was born to death, he introduces a second birth, which he called not so much being born as being reborn . . . so also he replaced one teaching with another (*doctrinae substituit aliam doctrinam*) that the teaching of godliness might shut out the teaching of godlessness . . . Death exercised dominion in us, therefore, not without our own engagement in sin; just as, on the other hand, life will reign in us not by our being idle and not by our doing nothing. But indeed the beginning of life is given by Christ not to those who are unwilling, but to those who believe. It spreads to the perfection of life by means of the perfecting of the virtues, just as formerly a beginning of death had

---

61. Origen, *Comm. Rom.* 5.2.9. Translations made in comparison with Origen, *Romans* (here 332) are hereafter noted by page number in Scheck included in parentheses. The Latin text is as printed in PG 14.837–1290. For Origen's place in the history of debates about justification see Scheck, *Legacy*.

> spread by means of the imitation of transgression and by the carrying out of the vices (*non ergo nihil peccantibus nobis mors regnavit in nobis, sicut rersum non otiosis nobis, et nihil agentibus vita regnabit in nobis. Sed initium quidem vitae datur a Christo, non invitis, sed credentibus et pervenitur ad perfectionem vitae perfectione virtutum sicut et in mortem dudum praevaricationis similitudine et vitorum expletione perventum est.*).[62]

For Origen Paul says that what Christ has brought us is the road towards perfection by the cultivation of virtues, as opposed to the vices of those in Adam. *This* is the nature and significance of the contrast between Adam and Christ. Christ has not just done away with some sort of invisible "state" of sin, but actually teaches, through the church, a discipline that replaces that of Adam. And *this* is what leads to life. Just as death ruled because we were sinning, Christ gives life to those who practice Christ's teaching, "not by our being idle and not by our doing nothing":

> After all, even in the passage which we brought in on account of the similarity of its sayings, namely, "For just as in Adam all die," he has not said: so also in Christ all have been made alive, or: all are being made alive, but instead, "all will be made alive." He wanted to show by this that the present time is one of effort and work, in which merits may be procured through good conduct (*laboris et operis, in quo per bonam conversationem merita conquirantur*). The future, on the other hand, is the time when those who die together with Christ in the present "will be made alive."[63]

Elsewhere, Origen clearly reveals that he reads Paul's δικαιοσύνη as a state that is brought about through the practices of the church.

> Therefore sin did indeed begin to exercise dominion in this world from the one Adam. And it reigned in those who pursued the imitation (*similitudinem*) of Adam's transgression; and for that reason, "the judgment came from the one leading to condemnation." But on the other hand through our one Lord Jesus Christ grace (*gratia*) began to reign through justice (*per iustitiam*), which grace will reign in all who obey him and keep his words, and by this means they come from many transgressions to the justification (*iustificationem*) of life.[64]

---

62. Origen, *Comm. Rom.* 5.2.11–12 (Scheck 333).
63. Ibid., 5.1.5 (Scheck 305).
64. Ibid., 5.2.15 (Scheck 335).

The Practice of the Body of Christ

In this passage, therefore, *gratia* is something that rules, not just by *God's* agency, but the church also finds the life of grace, its dominion, in obedience and the guarding of his words. Once again *iustificationem* comes to the fore as a visible state of life that is the opposite of the commitment of many transgressions. But, I would suggest, this is not proto-Pelagianism, for Origen does not say that the gifts of God that come through the church's practice exclude prevenient grace to amend biological sin. Origen is elsewhere very clear that it was God who chose us and saved us "while we were still sinners."[65] Indeed, God was the one who saved us when he gave us this graced practice. Part of his point in commenting on this passage is to show us how to use the language of gift in a way that does not exclude, but rather demands, participation by the receiving agent. So he comments

> concerning "the abundance of grace and of the gift of righteousness": it needs to be known that someone does not enter this kingdom, which we said is being prepared by means of war, who has attained only a single grace, that is to say, who has pleased God in respect to only one work (*non venit aliquis qui unam gratiam solum consecutus, hoc est, qui in uno aliquo opere placuerit*). On the contrary an abundance of grace is required according to him who says, "But I labored more abundantly than all of them; but not I but the grace of God with me." . . . Therefore grace is multiplied and abounds if our speech is always seasoned in grace as with salt, and if our deeds are done with the grace of humility and sincerity, and if everything we do, we do for the glory of God. The gift of justice (*iustitia*) should be interpreted in a similar way. For one who is made just (*iustificatur*) by Christ should do nothing without justice (*iustitia*).[66]

This does not mean, however, that for Origen the just person never sins. His categories of "the sinner" and "the just" are remarkably reasonable and fluid, as is fitting given his teaching of the *progression* of the sinner towards the perfection of virtue. Those who follow the one man Jesus are not yet always completely just, but rather they try to practice justice and succeed in making it more or less habitual. For

> it is one thing to have sinned, another to be a sinner. One is called a sinner who, by committing many transgressions, has already reached the point of making sinning into a habit and, so

---

65. He thus notes that Paul "supersedes 'abundance' and uses 'superabundance.'" See Origen, *Comm. Rom.*5.6.5–6 (Scheck 344–45).

66. Ibid.,5.3.8 (Scheck 339).

to speak, a course of study (*in conuetudinem, et, ut ita dicam, in stadium peccandi*). Just as, on the other hand, one is not called just who has once or twice done some just act (*semel aut dis aliquid iustitiae fecerit*), but who continually behaves justly and keeps justice in use and makes it habitual (*sed ille qui simper juste agendo, in usu et consuetudine iustitiam habet*). For if someone is unjust in nearly all other matters but should carry out some just work (*justi operis egerit*) one or two times, he will indeed be said to have acted justly (*egisse iuste*) in that work in which he practiced justice (*iustitiam tenuit*); nevertheless he will not on that basis be called a just man (*iustus*). Similarly it will indeed be said that a just man (*iustus*) has sinned if he has at some time committed what is not lawful. But he will not on that account be labeled a sinner, since he does not hold fast to the practice and habit of sinning (*peccandi usum et consuetudinem*).[67]

This sort of interpretation of Rom 5 has the added benefit of pointing up just how rigid and artificial are models of justification that I am arguing against. Origen understands Paul to be saying that God will graciously give eternal life to those who make a habit of just practice, even if they are not yet perfect. Indeed, he does not even seem to consider the possible objection that is likely to come from certain forensic readers today who think Paul is saying that God demands *perfection* (visible or invisible) before he announces a sentence of justification. It is this premise that demands Paul hold a theology of *simul iustus et peccator* since the existence of any visible sin would annul that perfection. Justification in that case has to name an invisible state that is counted as such before God. But Origen knows none of this and he certainly does not find this in Paul.

What he does find is real, visible, just practices that take a real, visible church that is made possible and finds its model in Christ's obedience unto death. He thus finds *imitatio Christi* at the heart of Paul's doctrine of justification: "So then Adam gave sinners a form through his disobedience; but Christ, in contrast, gave the righteous a form by his obedience" (*dedit ergo Adam peccatoribus formam per inobedientiam, Christus vero econtrario iustis formam per obedientiam posuit*).[68] Following Christ's example in being obedient unto death is for Origen the heart of what it means to be just. And this is consonant with his theory of Christian virtue and the progression toward perfection. He thus reads Paul as saying that it is the practice of just deeds that makes a man just. In Origen's philosophi-

67. Ibid., 5.5.2–3 (Scheck 341–42).
68. Ibid., 5.5.7–9 (Scheck 344).

cal parlance, since the only way to become virtuous in general is to train oneself in the habit of doing virtuous acts by simply doing virtuous acts, so the only way to be made just (sc.: be justified) is to perform just acts. Thus Origen can speak of "being made just by justice itself."[69] And this justice, this practice of the just act, is imitation of Christ.

Irenaeus of Lyons on Rom 5:12–21

What I am suggesting in terms of human agency in Rom 5 is quite consonant with the theology of Irenaeus, and in fact the two theologians appear mutually illuminating. This is so not least because, with much recent scholarship, I take Irenaeus to be a deeply Pauline thinker, who, reading Paul in the midst of his battle against gnosticism, managed to see things in Paul that we cannot.[70]

Irenaeus is especially important not least since he is really the first writer after Paul "to provide us with a clear and comprehensive doctrine of the Atonement and redemption."[71] This is most true when we come to Adam and Christ in Irenaeus' famous doctrine of recapitulation. Recapitulation for Irenaeus names the fundamental way that God redeems humanity though Christ's undoing and making right what Adam and his progeny, those "in Adam", got wrong. We are used to reading Paul expecting a story of salvation proceeding on forensic, penal, economic or covenantal models which make heavy use of "states" or "statuses" that are variously achieved, ascribed or imputed "before God." But Irenaeus understood and interpreted Paul without those categories, and so reviewing his theology helps us to understand what Paul is saying in Rom 5.

Unfortunately, nowhere does Irenaeus actually consider our passage verse by verse in anything like an exegetical commentary. This means that, unlike Origen, for the most part, he is not much help in the precise rendering of individual terms. Still, there are plenty of hints at the way he read this passage, since his entire theology of recapitulation is a meditation on Paul's words about Adam and Christ in Rom 5 and 1 Cor 15. So in Irenaeus we see on a macro level the way that Paul's soteriology in Rom 5 was worked out just more than a century after he wrote.

---

69. Ibid.

70. So, recently Noormann, *Irenaeus als Paulusinterpret*. The classic study is Werner, *Der Paulinismus des Irenaeus*; see also Aulen, *Christus Victor*, esp. 16.

71. Aulen, *Christus Victor*, 17.

Gifted Obedience

Irenaean Soteriology as Interpretation of Rom 5:12–21

That Adam and Christ are central for Irenaeus is obvious. But it is also true that not just these two figures, but the text of Rom 5 itself is crucial for his theology. This is indicated by the fact that often, and at central points in his argument, Irenaeus paraphrases or summarizes verses from Rom 5, not so much quoting Paul word for word as summarizing salient features. At these points, therefore, Irenaeus gives us a glimpse of the way he understood these verses. He works out the basic contours of his soteriology by thinking and working through what Paul says about Adam and Christ. This gives us some license, then, to read back from his worked-out theology of recapitulation to what he understood Paul to be saying about Adam and Christ. And, in a way, this is even *more* helpful than a systematic commentary on Romans. For in Irenaeus we see not just one person's opinion on the meaning of this or that word but an embodied interpretation, a living example of how a bishop imagined that Paul's soteriology was to be mapped onto and guide the church. In other words he indicates what kind of Christian practice these verses assume.

For both Paul and Irenaeus salvation is effected because Christ is the second Adam.[72] The central issue is *how* salvation works. How does Christ, as one man, save all humanity by being the second Adam? At this point, as I've said, we are used to looking for a whole stock of metaphors that Irenaeus did not use. Instead, salvation occurs by fallen humanity's participation in the true human, Christ.[73] Christ lived and died as the true human, without sin, in communion with God by the Spirit, an ἄνθρωπος τέλειος (cf. Eph 4:13), and salvation occurs when we become part of that perfect man.[74] We are not perfect, and we can only so become by conformity to Christ. Only by being subsumed into him does perfection become a possibility.[75] How does this occur?

There are three central and mutually dependent ways of participation, which is to say that these are three aspects of the one inseparable process of salvation. First there is the Eucharist. By receiving the body and blood of the Lord the church and her members are nourished and grow

---

72. *A.H.* 3.23.1, 4.22.1, 5.1.3, 5.5.1, etc. All citations of *Against Heresies* use the format in *The Apostolic Fathers* and shared by *PG*. 7.433–1120. Translations are adaptations from the former and Greek and Latin texts from the latter.

73. *A.H.* 4.20.5–7, 5.1.1.

74. *A.H.* 3.23.1, 7.

75. Cf. Andia, *Homo Vivens*, 127–48.

into Christ.[76] They do this (secondly), by the Spirit, which is the animation of the body, giving it again the breath of life lost in Adam.[77] Finally and for us most importantly, is imitation. We have communion with God when we participate in Christ by heeding his words and mimicking his actions. But this is not something that happens "in addition to" our salvation. It rather is the beginning and end of it:

> we could have learned in no other way than by seeing our Teacher, and hearing his voice with our own ears, that, having become imitators of his works as well as doers of his words, we may have communion with Him (*quidem operum, factores autem sermonum eius facti, communionem habeamus cum ipso*), receiving increase (*augmentum accipientes*) from the Perfect One . . . the mighty Word, and very man, who, redeeming us by His own blood in a manner consonant to reason, gave Himself as a redemption for those who had been led into captivity.[78]

When we so imitate we are acting as a true human since Christ is the true human and indeed the only place that we can look to find such a practice. But the practice of imitating Christ comes entirely as gift, since, in our state of fallen captivity, there is no other way for us to learn, indeed, no other way for us to be redeemed. As we learn, we grow towards perfection, progressing to the human form that God created us to become. In this gifted practice we regain communion with the life that we had lost.[79] This life is the Holy Spirit and it is given to us now as we practice the imitation of Jesus. For Irenaeus someone outside the church and so without the Holy Spirit is not fully human, since we were created with the Spirit in us as the breath of life, but we lose it when we sin. Interpreting Paul's lists of the fruits of the flesh and the Spirit in Gal 5 as an interpretation of Paul's theology of the First and Second Adam in Rom 5:12-21, Irenaeus writes that Paul

---

76. Cf. *A.H.* 3.19.1, 4.18.4–5, 5.1.2.

77. Cf. *A.H.* 3.24.1, 5.20.2.

78. *A.H.* 5.1.1. The whole passage is important: *Neque rerus nos aliter discere poteramus, nisi magistrum nostrum videntes, et per auditum nostrum vocem eius percipients, uti imitatores quidem operum, factores autem sermonum eius facti, communionem habeamus cum ipso, a perfecto, et eo qui est ante omnem conditionem, augmentum accipientes . . . quoniam Verbum potens et homo verus, sanguine suo rationabiliter redimens nos, redemptionem semetipsum dedit pro his, qui in captivitatem ducti sunt.*

79. For this see *A.H.* 5.12.

points out to his hearers in a more explicit manner what he means by "flesh and blood shall not inherit the kingdom of God." For they who do these things, since they do indeed walk after the flesh, are not able to live unto God (*vivere Deo non possunt*). And then, again, he proceeds to tell us the spiritual actions which vivify a man (*spirituales actus vivificantes hominem*), which is the entrance of the Spirit (*insertionem Spiritus*); thus saying, "But the fruit of the Spirit is love, joy, peace, long-suffering, goodness, benignity, faith, meekness, continence, chastity: against these there is no law." As, therefore, he who has gone forward to the better things, and worked the fruit of the Spirit (*fructum operatus fuerit spiritus*), is saved in every way (*omnimodo salvatur*) because of the communion of the Spirit (*Spiritus communionem*); so also he who has continued in the aforesaid works of the flesh, being truly reckoned as carnal, because he did not receive the Spirit of God, shall not have power to inherit the kingdom of heaven . . . He shows in the clearest manner through what things it is that a person goes to destruction, if he has continued to live after the flesh; and then, on the other hand, through what things he is saved.[80]

The last line makes it clear that such a practice is soteriologically central. For "the Spirit is theirs alone who tread down earthly desires."[81] Thus Wingren can write that the "only possibility of transforming defeat into victory and freedom for man is that the tyranny of sin must be first be destroyed by man's resisting every temptation to do wrong—then death's hold over man can be broken."[82]

Broadly, then, Irenaeus did not believe in justification by grace through faith the way that Luther did. Salvation for Irenaeus demanded obedient practice. This is patent, since obedience is part and parcel of what

---

80. *A.H.* 5.11.1. The citations to this effect could be multiplied. Cf., e.g., 5.11.2, where he discusses 1 Cor 15 and the earthly and the heavenly man: "When, therefore, did we bear the image of him who is of the earth? Doubtless it was when those actions spoken of as "works of the flesh" used to be wrought in us. And then, again, when [do we bear] the image of the heavenly? Doubtless when he says, "Ye have been washed," believing in the name of the Lord, and receiving His Spirit. Now we have washed away, not the substance of our body, nor the image of our [primary] formation, but the former vain conversation. In these members, therefore, in which we were going to destruction by working the works of corruption, in these very members are we made alive by working the works of the Spirit."

81. *A.H.* 5.12.2.

82. Wingren, *Irenaeus*, 113.

it is to believe in the Father, for "to believe in Him is to do His will."[83] Irenaeus' grammar of the human agent's participation is complex. On the one hand, he assumes that obedience to God and a holy life involving much human discipline and striving are integral and necessary for salvation. On the other hand, he repeatedly stresses that this kind of life is entirely a gift from God. God in Christ has made possible this kind of life and no human could attain it without the church, the Holy Spirit, and the sacraments. This active practice, which is assumed to be internal to salvation, comes out in passage after passage.

> This, therefore, was the long-suffering of God, that man, passing through all things, and acquiring the knowledge of moral habits (*morum*; sc. τῶν ἠθῶν), then attaining to the resurrection from the dead, and learning in practice (*discens experimento*) what is the source of his deliverance . . . [and] continuing in his love and subjection, and giving of thanks (or: "the Eucharist"), shall also receive from him the greater glory of promotion, looking forward to the time when he shall become like him who died for him, for he, too, "was made in the likeness of sinful flesh," to condemn sin, and to cast it, as now a condemned thing, away beyond the flesh, that he might call man forth into His own likeness, assigning him an imitator to God, and imposing on him his Father's law, in order that he may see God, and granting him power to receive the Father; the Word of God who dwelt in mankind, and became the Son of Man, that He might accustom mankind to receive God, and God to dwell in mankind, according to the good pleasure of the Father.[84]

But, to say that Irenaeus did not believe in justification by grace through faith the way that Luther did is not to say that Irenaeus did not believe in justification by grace through faith. Instead of God's free gift of salvation amounting to the invisible transfer of one's "legal status before God" from "sinner" to "righteous," Irenaeus sees God's salvation as the actual transformation of the church from "disobedient sinners" to "the obedient righteous." But this is only through God's grace. Christ's salvific action achieved the deliverance of humanity from obedience to disobedience in a way that they could never have effected for themselves. "It was the Lord himself who saved them because they could not be saved by their own instrumentality."[85]

83. A.H. 4.6.5.
84. A.H. 3.20.2.
85. A.H. 4.20.3.

Gifted Obedience

Internal to Irenaeus' Adam-Christ soteriology is thus quite literally the practice of the Holy Spirit and the practice of Christ. For there is ultimately no separating the two. To have the Spirit, to be alive and human, is to imitate Christ, and *imitatio Christi* is likewise the life of the Spirit. He finds no way of separating the Adam-Christ typology from active participation in Christ by the active imitation of the just act of Christ. This does not happen as a *result of* the narrative of Christ himself overturning what has held humanity in bondage. Even less so can it be a matter of our obedience being *motivated* by any factor external to Christ's act as recapitulation of Adam (such as our thankfulness for that act, etc.): "Irenaeus strongly emphasizes that the suffering and obedience of Jesus means abolition of sin, *the destruction of the domination of disobedience* and the expulsion of evil from humanity . . . for the first time since man's defeat at the dawn of the human race man holds his ground before the attack which is made on him."[86] Establishing the church as obedient is *part of* Christ's salvific act of recapitulation. If this act does not contain with it the just practice of the church, then Christ died in vain.

Irenaeus' Use of Rom 5:12–21

The second major way that we can tell how Irenaeus interprets Rom 5 derives from those cases where he quotes, or very nearly epitomizes, Paul's sentences or phraseology from that section.[87] These passages remove any doubt that the bishop finds the biblical locus of his Adam-Christ soteriology in Rom 5, for these are exactly the texts he reproduces when expositing his most basic theology. Thus he writes, just having explicitly quoted Rom 5:14, in the language of Rom 5:16 and 18:

> For as by the disobedience of the one man who was originally molded from virgin soil, the many were made sinners, and forfeited life (ἀπόβαλον τὴν ζωήν), so was it necessary that, by the obedience of one man, who was originally born from a virgin, many should be made just (δικαιωθῆναι) and receive salvation (ἀπόλαβον τὴν σωτηρίαν).[88]

While there is nothing in these sentences themselves that gives us a firm handle on the kind of human agency involved in salvation, the context of

---

86. Aulen, *Christus Victor*, 114, my italics.
87. Cf. *A.H.* 3: 18.3, 7; 20.2; 21.10; 22.1, 4; 23.7; 23.1; *A.H.* 4: 22.1; *A.H.* 5: 1.3; 5.1; 11.2; 12.2–3.
88. *A.H.* 3.18.7.

the passage makes it abundantly clear. Immediately before this passage Irenaeus summarizes Paul's argument in Rom 5:12–21 in the context of speaking of the obedience of the church that Christ's action has brought about. Christ

> fought and conquered . . . doing away with disobedience completely through his obedience: for he bound the strong man, and set free the weak, and endowed his own handiwork with salvation, by destroying sin. For he is a most holy and merciful Lord, and loves the human race. Therefore, as I have already said, he caused man to cleave to and to become one with God. For unless man had overcome the enemy of man, the enemy would not have been legitimately vanquished. And again: unless it had been God who had freely given salvation, we could never have possessed it securely.[89]

Irenaeus toes a fine line in this passage in relation to the agency of God and humanity in salvation. He says very clearly that Christ's death has taken away disobedience. Thus, that he has "destroyed sin" means that he has destroyed the disobedient practice of sin for those in Christ's body, and this is what constitutes salvation. Certainly there is a further destruction of sin to happen when the church looks upon God face to face, but Irenaeus here refers to the present obedience of the church that Christ's death has made possible and which *constitutes* salvation, for "he endowed his own handiwork with salvation by destroying sin."

The very next section of Book Three demonstrates further that Irenaeus reads Paul as saying that Christ's obedience brought forth the obedience of the church:

> But again, those who assert that He was simply a mere man, begotten by Joseph, remaining in the bondage of the old disobedience, are in a state of death having been not as yet joined to the Word of God the Father, nor receiving liberty through the Son, as He does Himself declare: "If the Son shall make you free, ye shall be free indeed."[90]

"Liberty," for Irenaeus, over and over again names the present state of conformity with God's will that exists in the church. The freedom of the church is its lack of *bondage* to sin and its practice of righteous obedience. Thus after a brief excursus on the law, again in 3.19.1 he writes that

---

89. *A.H.* 3.18.6–7.
90. *A.H.* 3.19.1.

> the Word set free the soul, and taught that through it the body should be willingly purified. Which having been accomplished, it followed as of course, that the bonds of slavery should be removed, to which man had now become accustomed, and that he should follow God without fetters: moreover, that the laws of liberty should be extended, and subjection to the king increased, so that no one who is convened should appear unworthy to him who set him free, but that the piety and obedience due to the Master of the household should be equally rendered both by servants and children.

What this tells us, in other words, is that when Irenaeus in *A.H.* 3.18.7 reads Paul saying that through Jesus "many should be justified and receive salvation" he understands him to mean that Jesus really makes these people (visibly) just now, in the time of the church.

Slightly later Irenaeus writes: "For as by one man's disobedience sin entered, and death obtained through sin; so also by the obedience of one man, justice (*iustitia*) having been introduced, shall cause life to fructify in those persons who in times past were dead."[91] This is Irenaeus' gloss on what Paul says in Rom 5:12, 17 regarding Christ's work "recapitulating Adam in himself." Since we have seen that the process of salvation by recapitulation involves as an internal necessity the church's just practice, we have every reason again to believe that Irenaeus was reading Paul as saying that the "righteousness" here introduced is not imputed but actual. This is even more evident in 5.1.3 where the Ebionites

> remain in that Adam who had been conquered and was expelled from Paradise: not considering that as, at the beginning of our formation in Adam, that breath of life which proceeded from God, having been united to what had been fashioned, animated the man, and manifested him as a being endowed with reason; so also, in [the times of] the end, the Word of the Father and the Spirit of God, having become united with the ancient substance of Adam's formation, *rendered man living and perfect, receptive of the perfect Father*, in order that as in the natural [Adam] we all were dead, so in the spiritual we may all be made alive.

It is clear that Rom 5 and 1 Cor 15 are just below the surface of this text. For all intents and purposes this could be his commentary on those verses. What is helpful for our argument is that Irenaeus does not use the

---

91. *A.H.* 3.21.10.

language of justification here; he simply says that now the Word, Paul's second Adam or the other "one man", renders the human being "perfect."

A final determinate is Irenaeus' reading of the similar comparisons of Adam and Christ in 1 Cor 15.

> "And as we have borne the image of him who is of the earth, we shall also bear the image of Him who is from heaven. For this I say, brethren, that flesh and blood cannot inherit the kingdom of God." Now this which he says, "as we have borne the image of him who is of the earth," is analogous to what has been declared, "And such indeed ye were; but ye have been washed, but ye have been sanctified, but ye have been justified in the name of our Lord Jesus Christ, and in the Spirit of our God." When, therefore, did we bear the image of him who is of the earth? Doubtless it was when those actions spoken of as "works of the flesh" used to be wrought in us. And then, again, when [do we bear] the image of the heavenly? Doubtless when he says, "Ye have been washed," believing in the name of the Lord, and receiving his Spirit. Now we have washed away, not the substance of our body, nor the image of our [primary] formation, but the former vain conversation. In these members, therefore, in which we were going to destruction by working the works of corruption, in these very members are we made alive by working the works of the Spirit.

As he did with the passage above from Rom 5:18, so here does he link Adam and Christ with different sorts of behavior through Paul's parenesis. There is even a hint at the end of this passage of the same theology of the "practice of the Spirit" that we saw above when he says that the church is "made alive by working the works of the Spirit."

We see then that for Irenaeus the figures of Adam and Christ principally denote, not states before God, but modes of behavior. Because of Adam we all bore the image of the one of the earth and practiced the works of the flesh, but because of Christ we all were washed, sanctified and made just, which consists of "working the works of the Spirit."

Conclusion

I have argued that there are multiple reasons for recasting our understanding of Rom 5:12–21 in terms of the just practice of the church. When this is done, the whole concept of agency usually assumed to be present in this chapter disappears. Instead of the drama of salvation happening exclusively by the movement of invisible and rather abstract notions or powers of "sin" and "grace," it moves by God's concrete gift of a new Adam who performed a just act so that the church might actively live justly. In this way humans genuinely are agents participating in the drama of salvation by obediently living the new life that is theirs as gift. This means that there is *both* a place for relentless human striving *and* the recognition that this made possible and sustained by God's action.

I have shown my reading of Rom 5:12–21 is lexically more satisfying than the alternative, since it allows us to retain the normal, everyday use of several important terms. On the usual forensic reading of the passage these terms are forced to mean something that neither Paul nor other Greek speakers would normally say. Specifically, I have not had to import a foreign soteriological calculus and fit it in "behind" the text to try to explain what Paul is saying. On my reading Paul simply says what he means when he says that just as one man and his heirs sinned and died so also another one man and his heirs were obedient and so live. *This* is Paul's soteriological calculus, and it is right on the surface of the text. As such, that Paul holds no distinction between "justification" and "sanctification" eliminates an entire host of problems regarding how we get from the former to the latter. Paul's soteriological unity of the two is much to be preferred.

Finally, it is important to be precise about the account of agency advocated, especially regarding complex issues that Paul's account leaves open. There is much that will later become very important for the church that Paul simply does not take a position on in these ten short verses. There is much, for that matter, that is very important for Paul later in Romans that he does not take a position on here. This narrative about Adam and Christ gives a necessary but still incomplete account of human agency. It gives, as I have said, the "what"—a macrocosmic account of Adam's trespass and subsequent disobedience unto death for all that Christ's obedience undoes, giving to the church obedience unto life. Hence, to say that Christ makes possible for the church a just practice is not to suggest that Christ simply places obedience as "external grace" before the disobedient person's "neutral" human nature. Grace as the gift of obedient, just practice to sinners is certainly prevenient, but Paul nowhere casts this in anything like the detail that would be required to properly characterize it by the later categories of "internal" and "external" grace. Importantly, therefore, this construal, by emphasizing humanity's imitation of Adam and the church's of Christ, does not preclude the corruption and regeneration of human nature. It simply does not imply one position or another.

Hence, the interpretation I am urging for in this chapter, far from closing down theological debate, opens it up. So for instance Irenaeus' statement that the second Adam renders the Christian "perfect" is one direction in which the present interpretation of Paul's grammar could be developed, but I would submit that, in itself, this Irenaean interpretation is itself open to various interpretations.[92] This is patent in the biblical interpretation of the later Fathers (though it is impossible to explore this here): something like my reading of the passage is a baseline, from which further theological work must proceed to sort out whether this entails (e.g.) a perfectionism we see at points in Irenaeus and (in a very different way) Pelagius or a "softer" notion of holiness like that of the later Augustine.[93] We have seen a third possibility in Origen who sees some Christians as perfect and others on a journey towards perfection.

But the first to develop the theology of Rom 5:12–21 was Paul himself, and from this development we can gather the ensuing questions this basic posture leaves unanswered: In what way does Christ's just act gift a just practice? What specific actions make up this justice? Paul's ultimate answer is going to be "the body of Christ," as I argue in chapter 4. But the next question that Paul took up is "How does Christ's just act transform the church's practice?" His answer to this in Rom 6–8 is "participation," and it is to this topic that we now turn.

---

92. See p. 134 above.
93. So see De Bruyn, ed., *Pelagius on Romans*, 92–96.

3

Practicing Participation

The Virtues in Romans 6–8

Introduction: Apocalyptic Powers or Human Habits?

I HAVE ARGUED THAT IN ROM 5:12–21 PAUL SETS OUT A NEW WAY OF LIFE opened up by Christ's obedience unto death. The present chapter suggests that Paul develops the nature of that just life in more detail in Rom 6-8 in a manner consonant with a classical account of human action. This is a contentious suggestion, since a majority of contemporary interpretations of these chapters, jumping off most directly from Rom 6:1–11 and carrying a particular theology thence derived into the subsequent chapters, presumes that Paul is here concerned with cosmic powers that force human beings into various states (of sin, righteousness, bondage, freedom, etc.).¹ In fact, is difficult to find a study that does not see in Rom 6-8 human bodies overtaken by some sort of quasi-demonic or spiritual force that heavily determines them in way that makes them less than genuine actors.

Most of this theology builds on Käsemann's thesis that conversion involves a "change of masters" that deals with cosmic and not anthropological conditions.² This tends to especially affect the notion of "sin" that becomes a "cosmic power that rules the world outside of Christ."³ That "righteousness" is never hypostatized as well, as Stowers and others

---

1. See the review of scholarship just below.

2. So Boer, *Defeat of Death*, 166–67, says that herein Paul does *not* describe "willful human action" but the effects of the "twin cosmological powers of sin and death." For good bibliography, reviews, and some critique of this literature, which I will not repeat here, see Röhser, *Personifikation der Sünde*; Käsemann, *Romans*, 158–85; Wasserman, "Paul Among the Philosophers," 387–415; Kaye, *Argument of Romans*, 30–47; Carr, *Angels and Principalities*.

3. Jewett, *Romans*, 394.

have said, in fact constitutes one major inconsistency in such a reading.⁴ Nonetheless, "Sin" (frequently capitalized) is often interpreted as a "destructive force", a "realm" which has a "location."⁵ So Tannehill says that it is a "power" that acts as a "master over men," and that Paul is concerned in Rom 6 with a "change of lordship," which involves transfer a new "power field, a sphere in which a power is at work."⁶ When the human comes to be dominated by this realm he can be said to have a "body of sin," which, along with the "old man," refer to "a collective entity which is destroyed in the death of Christ."⁷ Thus, "Paul is not speaking of the death of individual believers one by one . . . he is talking of the destruction of the dominion of sin, of which all believers were a part."⁸

Coupled with such a view, and often but not always connected to it, is a particular view of the nature of participation with Christ that is supposed to be Paul's solution to the problem of sin and the mechanism of "righteousness" (however configured exactly). Here the interpretive options range from the notion of a realistic/mystical participation with Christ to a simple imitation of Christ's behavior.⁹ The former is a normal part of the "cosmic-powers" reading sketched above, since only by being united with Christ himself in some realistic way could one ever hope to defeat such formidable adversaries.

4. Stowers, *Rereading*, 179–89.
5. Jewett, *Romans*, 395–96.
6. Tannehill, *Dying*, 17–19.
7. Ibid., 24.
8. Ibid., 30.
9. So, e.g., see the study by Proudfoot, "Imitation," 140–60, who puts the question thus (143): "The basic problem in the interpretation of these passages is this: Are we dealing here with a realistic "Christ-mysticism" or with the milder concept of the imitation of Christ?" His is own study concludes (153) that participation is matter of a "realistic bond in the body of Christ and denotes a real sharing in which the distinction in time is somehow beside the point." In the same way for Bruce, "Mystic," 67, Paul is a "communal or corporate mystic," and all share a "charismatic experience of life and death with Christ." For Wedderburn, *Baptism and Resurrection*, 54–56, "baptized into Christ" points "metaphorically to a mystical and corporate reality of the new community 'in Christ.'" For critiques of the apocalyptic interpretation of Rom 6–8, see Stowers, *Romans*, 179–89, Kaye, *Argument of Romans*, 30–47. Alternatively, Betz and Jewett think that Paul viewed the death on the part of the converted as happening prior to baptism, and so baptism, far from being a mystical joining to Christ, is just a symbol for a new mode of behavior—imitatio Christi. See Dieter Betz, "Baptism in Romans 6," 111–12. Jewett, *Romans*, 398, says that to "be baptized into Christ's shameful death is to quit the life of sin." But he offers no way that this could be possible for a person to *decide* if sin is an apocalyptic power.

Because such theologies, as they are developed in the exegetical literature, tend to be rather imprecise, it is rarely clear that what is asserted to follow from them is carefully considered. For example, Dunn thinks that in these chapters "the possibility of the believer's *continuing* to serve sin is very real," while Jewett thinks conversely that for Paul "persisting in sin is a logical and relational contradiction for those in Christ," since they are "freed from bondage to the cosmic power of sin."[10] Both interpreters, of course, believe they base their statements on something they have established about the nature of Paul's theology in Rom 6–8, but neither point to any specifics.

Often the result of such phenomena is bald assertion. So Jewett goes on to explain that when Paul speaks of being obedient to the desires of the body (Rom 6:11) he names the "aspiration to relationships of domination" while Käsemann thinks that by "desires" Paul means "self-will and self-assertion."[11] Such *ad hoc* glosses are in fact twice removed from Paul, since they do not in the first place follow in any concrete way from their own exegesis, and that exegesis is itself questionable. In any case they raise the question of just what Paul does name by such bodily desires.

Recently this dominant interpretation of Paul has been questioned by Emma Wasserman, who argues in several pieces that the discourse of Rom 6–8 belongs to a broad genre of Hellenistic philosophy that she names Platonic moral-psychological discourse.[12] Directly opposing the consensus, she holds that

> Rom 6.1–11 construes baptism as an analogy for a moral-psychological transformation brought about by God's work in Christ and 6.12–23 explains how the transformation restores the capacity for self mastery, obedience to God, and the acquittal at the coming judgment. Rom 6.12–23 further develops the language of dying to sin and living to God in moral-psychological terms.... Rom 6 also warns that in spite of this new situation, sin's rule still threatens.[13]

---

10. Dunn, *Romans*, 1:320; Jewett, *Romans*, 404.

11. Käsemann, *Romans*, 177, Jewett, *Romans*, 405.

12. Wasserman, "Death of the Soul" [2007]; "Death of the Soul" [2005], 793–816; *Death of the Soul*. Wasserman's work is primarily focused on Rom 7, but she treats 6 and 8, the chapters about which we are most concerned, often in passing, and from this her view of our topic is gathered.

13. Wasserman, "Paul Among the Philosophers," 404.

She further argues that in Rom 8:1–13 a special type of πνεῦμα "dwells inside the mind and restores its capacity for reason and self-control" which is lacking in the *persona* of Rom 7:7–25. This is a restoration of the mind of 1:18–32 such that "... the pneuma enables a new mastery of the body ... that allows for ethical behavior and acquittal at the final judgment."[14]

Wasserman's work is in many ways agreeable with the reading I will offer, primarily because it reads these chapters as treating the topic of human action and a "transformation" that has or should happen in a person's way of life upon entering the church. I do have serious disagreements with her, however, and these will come out in the exegesis and be pointed up in the conclusion. It is sufficient for now to say that in her critique of the usual reading of these chapters she swings entirely and unsustainably in the other direction and ends up, actually, with no notion of "real" participation at all. Being baptized into Christ's death for her appears *only* to name a change in moral behavior. She thus rules out a competing reading at the price of abandoning any significant notion of participation completely.

Against the consensus reading, and against Wasserman, I argue in what follows that we find in Rom 6–8 a strong notion of human agency and a strong notion of realistic participation. I call this "participation by practice." This is, I take it, at base what Richard B. Hays is getting at in his recent article on Paul's notion of participation.[15] The church is baptized into Christ and so receives the Spirit with which it cooperates to put to death its passions which have their seat in the body. By killing the body in this way the bodies that make up the church die with Christ, and at the same time are made alive by his Spirit. Thus the Spirit is, *in a very specific*

---

14. Ibid., 409–10.

15. Hays, "'Real Participation,'" 336–51. Especially suggestive in this direction are Hays' latter two proposals for understanding participation, namely, church participation and narrative participation, which he thinks are primary (347). Hays notes that for Chrysostom participation names a "moral struggle to live a holy life" (342). As such, participation includes "identity-forming sacramental practices ... by receiving these sacramental elements, members of the community concretely experience participation in Christ" (344). Thus, as I will suggest below, such participation includes but is not exhausted by sacramental practice, which is nevertheless integral to the intelligibility of these broader actions. So (344): "*ecclesial participation ...* includes participation in a specific social group, participation in the community's sacramental life, and participation in Spirit-inspired charismatic worship. (Or, to put the matter in more theoretical terms, ecclesial participation has social, sacramental, and pneumatological components.)" In some ways my reading of Romans that follows can be seen as putting flesh on these claims. As we will see in the following chapter, I do not think this project incompatible with Stanley Stowers' conception of the Spirit in something like "material" terms.

way, the key term in participation: it cooperates with the church to put to death its evil deeds and at the same time vivifies those dying bodies and *ipso facto* makes them virtuous qua dead to passions and able to genuinely cooperate with God toward the good. The Spirit's part of the cooperation is to "infuse" sinful and in-themselves-sin-tending bodies with Christ's dying (since dead bodies cannot sin) and at the same time with the life of Christ's risen body as a foretaste of the new bodies church members are to fully receive in the resurrection. The church thus imitates Christ's death by the death of its own sin-tending bodies in a way that literally and physically connects it to (participates in) Christ.

I develop this "participation by practice" further in Chapters Four and Five of this dissertation, but we can see already how such a notion cuts across the usual "mystical," "realistic," "metaphorical," and "imitation" models (including Wasserman's) in order to provide a thick account of both what Paul says about human action and the way that this action is connected to Christ.

The basic exegetical move this chapter makes is to take the majority reading set out above and turn it on its head. Instead of subsuming all of the "imperative" sections under the "indicatives" and defining the latter as describing cosmic powers, I have roughly done the reverse and subsumed the indicative passages entirely into the imperative. The former reading is theologically problematic because one cannot explain the existence of hortatory passages if all is a matter of the motion of cosmic forces that preclude genuine human agency. One *can*, however, explain the opposite reading by arguing that Paul assumes a holy church in which his commands are and will be carried out. Thus the "indicative" sections describe the church's consistent behavior rather than its cosmic "state," but this consistently holy action is not unassailable. In other words, this move creates space for a classical account of human action.

The best way for me to demonstrate this thesis is to work exegetically through the relevant sections of Rom 6–8, arguing my case. I develop thereby a cumulative picture of Paul's soteriology and the sort of human agency involved therein. In the conclusion I set this account next to Wasserman's to bring it into sharper relief.

Rom 6:12–23 as Exhortation to Virtuous Practice

We are interested in human agency. So I begin with Rom 6:12–23, which is hortatory in nature and so *prima facie* expects some action on the part of the church.[16] Rom 6:1–11 on the other hand, is often read as involving those cosmic powers that override human agency. My strategy will simply be to allow the rather straightforward portion of text to enlighten our reading of the more opaque one.

Paul says not to let sin reign in the body (μὴ βασιλευέτω ἡ ἁμαρτία ἐν τῷ θνητῷ ὑμῶν σώματι) (6:12a). The rest of the verse shows that he does not mean "try to escape a cosmic demon!" Rather, Paul speaks in terms of a classical account of action. He glosses "don't let sin reign in your body" as meaning "obedience to passions/desires!" (τὸ ὑπακούειν ταῖς ἐπιθυμίαις αὐτοῦ) (6:12b)."[17] So, letting sin reign in your mortal body is equivalent to obeying the passions.[18] This gloss is a clue to understanding what follows in vv. 12–21 as well as the nature of vv. 1–11. Specifically, what this means is that by "sin" Paul is talking about particular actions, actions of obedience or disobedience to one's "emotions/passions/desires" that are the culprit in classical accounts of human action.[19] The church in

---

16. So, Wasserman, *Death of the Soul*, 133.

17. "Rule" as a metaphor for the mind's rule over the passions goes at least as far back as Plato's charioteer analogy (in *Phaedr.* 253–54); see notes below.

18. John Chrysostom, *Hom. Rom.* 13, is very clear that we are right in the middle of a classical action theory, since sin is not a power, but action that caters to the body's desires. All citations of Chrysostom use the format in *Chrysostom: Homilies*. Translations are from the latter, infrequently modified from PG 60.399–675. See the recent work on Chrysostom as a reader of Paul by Mitchell, *Heavenly Trumpet*, though this work does not focus on the way Chrysostom reads the parts of Paul that are most controversial for us.

19. So contemporary with Paul see, e.g., James 4:1–2: "Where do those wars and battles among you come from? Is it not from inside, from the desires making war in your body-parts (ἐκ τῶν ἡδονῶν στρατευομένων ἐν τοῖς μέλεσιν)?" Also Cicero, *Resp.* 1.38: "When you are angry, do you allow your anger to rule over your soul (*dominantum animi*)? ... anger, when it disagrees with reason, is a sort of rebellion of the soul (*seditionem animi*) ... take as further examples avarice, greed for power and glory, and the passions generally. If there is a kingly rule (*regale imperium*) in human souls, it must be the rule (*dominantum*) of a single element and this is reason (*consulii*) and if reason rules there is no place for the passions (*dominante nullum esse libidinibus*) ... if reason be dethroned, our innumerable passions would obtain complete rule ... the soul should be a kingdom (*regno*), and reason its king (*regi*)." Also *Resp.* 3.23: "God rules (*imperat*) over man, the soul (*animus*) over the body and reason over lust and anger and other baser parts of the soul ... for the soul is said to rule the body as a king rules over his subject. (*animus corpori dicitur imperare ut rex civibus suis*)."

Practicing Participation

Rome is not to obey the passions (note the imperative), which are part of the body, which means that they are not to act on their sinful impulses.[20] In Origen's terms, Paul has named the habit of sinning, "sin."[21] And I think this is exactly right.[22]

That Paul names these desires "sin" means that they are not simply a trouble to the one who obeys them, wreaking havoc and causing an inability for self-control as in other moral philosophers Paul might have known, but that this obedience is also somehow problematic in relation to God. This is an important piece of grammar to grasp: it is possible to speak of God and sin without speaking of the latter as we would a demon. There *is* a personal element involved because obeying the passions of the body offends God, but the passions themselves are not "beings" much less "personal beings."[23]

That the trouble concerns the human body is confirmed in v. 13. Using the common ancient metaphor of "weapons" to designate the use of the body in human action, Paul tells the church not to make its "body parts weapons of injustice for sin" (τὰ μέλη ὑμῶν ὅπλα ἀδικίας τῇ ἁμαρτίᾳ) but to make them "weapons of justice for God" (τὰ μέλη ὑμῶν ὅπλα δικαιοσύνης τῷ θεῷ).[24] He has just indicated that the nature of the sin that he is talking about is obedience to the body's passions. So what it means to present one's body parts as instruments of injustice for sin is to use one's body in the exercise of the passions of that body. Rather, our bodies are to be for God (τῷ θεῷ). Paul calls for striving, as one would in battle, against the passions of the body.[25]

---

20. Chrysostom, *Rom. Hom.* 11: "He does not say, let not the flesh live or act, but, "let not sin reign," for He came not to destroy our nature, but to set our choice aright (τὴν προαίρησιν διορθῶσαι)."

21. Origen, *Comm. Rom.* 6.9.8.

22. So, too Thomas Aquinas, *in Rom*, 6.3: *Obedire enim per consensum mentis concupiscentiis peccati est peccatum regnare in nobis. Eccli. XVIII*, 30: *post concupiscentias tuas non eas*. Unfortunately Thomas' *Lectures* are not yet translated into English, making the fuller use of this massive work difficult. The Latin text is from the above site and subsequent citations to Thomas' *in Rom* refer to this source. The *Lectures* remain yet another paradigm of the possibility of a cogent reading of Romans from a classical framework. Occasional citations in what follows are simply a reminder of this fact.

23. Thus Origen, *Comm. Rom.* 6.1.4: "In fact sin itself does not exist since its substance could never exist except in works and deeds."

24. E.g., Aristotle, *Pol.* 1253a30–40.

25. This is unanimously what readers in tune with such discourse understood. So Aquinas, *in Rom* 6:3; Origen, *Comm. Rom.* 6.1.4.

The Practice of the Body of Christ

It is important that Paul can say this in spite of the fact that "sin no longer rules" (6:14).[26] Wasserman has shown in detail that the language of "ruling" is very common in connection with the language of the passions and virtues.[27] What Paul is saying therefore, is not that there is some sort of evil cosmic force that no longer controls the church but rather that, for reasons we will get to below, the passions of the body no longer hold sway over it. There is nothing in this verse about Christ somehow winning a battle with the ontological forces of evil so that now the Christian is "free" to act. Rather, Paul says that they no longer behave the way that they once did. He names a visible change, not an invisible one that has gone on behind the scenes: the church behaves differently now. *We are not at this point told how this has come about.*

So Paul has set before us in this passage a visible change in behavior. He goes on to explain this in more detail, filling out the same thematic lines he has already begun to draw. First, he confirms that the dynamics he is talking about is within the sphere that permits of human striving: "you are slaves to whom you present yourselves for obedience, for you are slaves to the one you obey . . ." (v. 16). Thus he exhorts the church that it must continue to live the way that it has come to live. He has said that the passions of the body no longer rule them, and yet there is still a need to strive to remain this way.[28] Otherwise, Paul implies, it is possible that they would once again become slaves of their passions.

---

26. The verb is grammatically future, but most are agreed that this is a "logical" future meaning "sin shall no longer rule you, from now on."

27. Wasserman, "Paul Among the Philosophers," 396–97.

28. The language of slavery is common in classical discussions of the passions. See Cicero, *Resp.* 1.34: "What can be nobler than the government of the state by virtue? For then the man who rules (*imperat*) others is not himself a slave to any passion (*servit ipse nulli cupiditati*), but has already aquired for himself all those qualities to which he is training and summoning his fellows . . . Such a man imposes no laws on a state that he does not obey himself (*ipse non pareat*) . . ." Also 3.15: "The soul rules over the passions like a master his slaves (*imperat libidini ut dominus servis*), restraining it and breaking its power. So kings, commanders, magistrates . . . rule a city as the soul rules the body . . . over its lusts, anger, and other emotions. The parts of the body are ruled . . . on account of their regular obedience, but the evil parts of the mind are ruled like slaves . . ." Cf. Chrysostom, *Sac.* 6.8; Aquinas, *in Rom* 6.4. Likewise, Diogenes Laertius, *Lives*, 7.121–22: "Only the wise man is free, but the inferior are slaves. For freedom is the power of autonomous action, but slavery is lack of autonomous action . . . Besides being free the wise are also kings, since kingship is rule that is answerable to no one; and this can occur only among the wise . . . They are also, it is said, godlike, for they have something divine in them . . . furthermore, the wise are errorless, and are liable to be free of error." Also Philo, *Prob* 17–18, 22: "Slavery then is applied in one sense

Practicing Participation

Paul now reiterates that they *were* (ἦτε) slaves of sin but *now* they have become obedient from the heart (v. 17). Here we see that Paul is picking up on the themes of obedience and sin that he began to discuss in 5:12–21. The choice is between obedience to God (ὑπηκούσατε δὲ ἐκ καρδίας) and being ruled by the passions (δοῦλοι τῆς ἁμαρτίας). The life of just obedience laid down before now comes into clearer focus as the life that is free from the passions and that submits to a particular type of teaching that has been handed down (παρεδόθητε τύπον διδαχῆς). Paul casts the church in the mold of the philosophical school where there was certainly "doctrine," but only as a means to a certain way of life.[29] He thus simply exposits the fundamental shift in behavior that has occurred, so that those who were enslaved to their passions now are enslaved to God.

But we must not lose sight of the hortatory nature of the grammar involved, for this in fundamentally important for understanding what Paul is talking about. Because he is not talking about some sort of literal slavery to personal cosmic forces much stronger than one could ever escape from, and rather about particular practices of the church that are either in obedience to God or to the passions, the imperative mood is entirely understandable right alongside the indicative.[30] The former are necessary because it is always possible to let the passions creep back in and to once again become slaves to them. The latter are necessary because nevertheless Paul assumes that a drastic change of life has already taken place. What is left to do now is, at least, maintain, and hopefully, press on farther.

That mix between the so-called indicative and imperative is present sharply in v. 19. Paul says that their body-parts used to be bound

---

to bodies, in another to souls; bodies have men for their masters, souls their vices and passions. The same is true for freedom; one freedom produces security of body from men of superior strength, the other sets the mind at liberty from the domination of the passions. . . . For in very truth he who has God alone for his leader, he alone is free, though to my thinking he is also the leader of all others, having received the charge of earthly things from the great, the immortal King, whom he, the mortal, serves as a viceroy."

29. Chrysostom, *Hom. Rom.* 11: "But what is the form of doctrine? It is living aright, and in conformity with the best way of life." See Hadot, *Philosophy*, 49–70. See also the comprehensive work by Vegge, *Paulus*.

30. So, Wasserman, "Paul Among the Philosophers," 410, "Understanding the new life in Christ in chs. 6–8 as a new state of self-control also resolves a tension that scholars have found in Paul's thought between the 'already' and the 'not yet' or the so-called 'indicative' and the 'imperative. On my reading, the 'already' statements refer to the renewed capacities of reason and the 'not yet' warn that the passions and appetites continue to threaten." She notes the indicative as 6:1–11; 7:1–6; and 8:1–9, and the imperative: 6:12–23; 7:7–25; 8:10–30.

impurity and lawlessness with the result that they tended towards lawlessness as it end (παρεστήσατε τὰ μέλη ὑμῶν δοῦλα τῇ ἀκαθαρσίᾳ καὶ τῇ ἀνομίᾳ εἰς τὴν ἀνομίαν). Now (νῦν), however, they are exhorted, just as they were above, to make their bodies bound to righteousness which has holiness as its *telos* (τὰ μέλη ὑμῶν δοῦλα τῇ δικαιοσύνῃ εἰς ἁγιασμόν).[31] Lawlessness and holiness are the proximate ends of their respective lifestyles, and these in turn are the means to the final ends delineated in vv. 20-22. They were once slaves to sin and free from justice, so that they did things about which they are ashamed and whose telos is death (ἐφ' οἷς νῦν ἐπαισχύνεσθε, τὸ γὰρ τέλος ἐκείνων θάνατος) (v. 21). On the other hand they are now bound to justice so that they are free from the passions and this means that they are holy (this is apparently so important that this proximate end is repeated in v. 21) and that the telos of holiness is eternal life (v. 23).

Verses 20-21 are subsequent confirmation that Paul is expounding a particular sort of life free from the passions and not any sort of cosmic war in which God has conquered some abstract "powers" and so somehow "in principle" set the Christian free for obedience to God. There is no "free for obedience" in this passage, only slavery of one type or another, either to the passions or to God.[32] But all this, as we have seen, comes about through particular actions, not through the divine manipulation of cosmic states. This is seen in the "fruit" that Paul names (v. 22) as the proximate ends of the two different lives: "deeds of which you are now ashamed" (ἐφ' οἷς νῦν ἐπαισχύνεσθε) on the one hand, and "holiness" (ἁγιασμόν) on the other.

Finally we come to v. 23, which implies more about agency. Paul comments on the two final ends, death and eternal life, that he has already set out (v. 22) and says that death is the price (ὀψώνια) for sin.[33] There

---

31. Origen, *Comm. Rom.* 6.4.2 (Schenk, 12), on Rom 6:19 comments that "righteousness" is a virtue, and indeed one that stands for all the others: "It certainly seems that he has named righteousness here for all the virtues together, just as, on the other hand, he set down iniquity for all the vices together . . . .Moreover, observe how everywhere through these matters he notes the freedom of the will . . . This could not be done at all if one's nature were fighting against this, as some think, or if the course of the stars opposed it." Also 6.5.3 (Schenk 123): "Now when he speaks of someone becoming a slave of righteousness, understand that it is, at the same time, of wisdom, piety, chastity, and all the virtues together . . ."

32. Contra Käseman, *Romans*, 171-85.

33. Against Wasserman, however, I think that the death spoken of here is not just the death of the soul defined as its domination by the passions and the failure of reason to gain control. The death that Paul has in mind has to be "condemnation" at the final judgment (Rom 8:1, 3, 12). This, I think, is clear from other passages in Paul. But

is not, however, a price named for eternal life, which is the gift of God (χάρισμα τοῦ θεοῦ). At first this would seem to support the usual (ultimately incoherent) soteriological readings of Paul in which unrepentant sinners are justly condemned for what are genuinely their own misdeeds, but repentant sinners are given eternal life completely free of any responsibility on their own part. The first part of this seems to be on the mark, but the latter is more complicated.

Specifically, Paul has outlined a big task for the Christian by exhorting her to allow the passions to dominate no longer. This means that while God will exact payment for shameful deeds in the form of death, it is not the case that there is nothing that can be done to receive eternal life. The entire imperative force of this section speaks against this. Rather, Paul says, God gives the holy and just members of the church eternal life. Thus, χάρισμα, as we noted above, simply means "gifted thing," and so we can render v. 23b "but what God gives is eternal life." There *is* therefore a contrast to be noted between "wages" and "gift": the former costs and the latter is free. But this does not name two ways to salvation, one of which involves an account of "works" and one which does not. *It simply names the respective ends of the sinful life and the holy life*. One ends in death and one ends in eternal life. Again we must leave both our Anselmian calculus and our Lutheran revision thereof behind in order to understand Paul.

I have been arguing that 6:12–23 is not engaged in a discussion of sin as a power. The Apostle is talking rather about the way that people in the church behave. Fundamentally, Paul is concerned that the Romans continue in obedience to God and not let their passions rule over them. The latter he names "sin." What this reveals, as we have mentioned, is that Paul has a theological reading of the passions—the practices that embody their indulgence are grounds for condemnation on the day of judgment.

Wasserman is not wrong that the "death of the soul" also fits the discourse. So Philo *Fug.* 58: "Goodness and virtue is life, evil and wickedness is death. This is a most noble definition of deathless life, to be possessed by a love of God and a friendship for God with which flesh and body have no concern." *Leg.* 1.105–7: "The death of man is the separation of the soul from the body, but the death of the soul is the decay of virtue and the bringing in of wickedness." See also her references to Philo (Wasserman, "Paul Among the Philosophers" 400): *Leg.* 78; *Post* 73; *Mos.* 1.279; *Gig* 14; *Leg.* 1.32, 35; 2.93; 3.52; *Post.* 12, 45; *Migr.* 21, *Her.* 201; *Contr.* 87; *Mut.* 213. Cf. Zeller, "Life and Death of the Soul," 19–55. So also Origen, *Comm. Rom.* 6.6.7, thinks the death that is the wages of sin is not death from separation of body and soul, but the soul's separation from God by means of sin. Cf. also James 1:14 "Each is tempted by his own desire (ἐπιθυμίας), being lured and enticed by it; then, when ἐπιθυμία has conceived, it gives birth to sin, and sin, when fully grown, gives birth to death."

Because of this it is vitally important that this most basic change in the life of the Romans be maintained. *Paul has not yet told us how it is that this change comes about.* That is to come in Romans 8:1–30, treated below.

I have, moreover, argued for a particular resolution of the problem of the "imperative versus the indicative."[34] I suggest that the indicatives point to the visible, stable, and yet contingent change in behavior undergone by Christians in the process of conversion. It is simply a fact that they do live differently than they used to: their passions no longer rule them and they are now just and holy. Because this change is contingent, however, and involves much striving and training, Paul must at the same time exhort the church to stay on this path that they have taken. They are genuinely holy and just, but this is not immutable. The indicative statements do not refer to a once-and-for-all permanent state, either in the nature of the cosmos, the spiritual realm, or in the church member herself. What it does indicate is a type of behavior that is true of the church at this time. They have been freed from sin and are now slaves to righteousness; this names the fact that their passions used to control them and now do not. They live in a visibly different way than they used to, now in a way that is obedient to God.

Rom 6:1–11 as Description of Virtuous Practice

With this position in place we can grasp better what is going on in vv. 1–11. Paul answers the interlocutor's question by asking how those who have died to sin can live in it any more (6:2). In a section of Romans that is usually held up as the paradigm for the indicative side of the usual dichotomy, it is to be noted just how hortatory Paul's language is: "How shall we live in sin anymore since we have died to it?"

Noting this, and leaning on the interpretation I have offered for vv. 12–23, I suggest that what Paul means is that the church has "died" to its passions, so it is no longer a slave of them.[35] He goes on and estab-

---

34. So see the typical position, to which it is possible to reduce most other versions: Parson, "Being Precedes Act," 99–127; Reed, "Indicative and Imperative," 224–57; also Vlainic "Be What You Are," 55–76. On Paul and sinlessness Windisch, "Das Problem," 265–81. Of course, any major topical work on Paul that contains a section on "eschatology" will treat this question, e.g., Beker, *Paul*, 275–78, Furnish, *Theology and Ethics*, 208–26.

35. Death is a normal term in classical accounts of human action. Cf. Philo, *Leg.* 3.74: "When, O soul, will you realize that you are a corpse-bearer? At that time you will be no lover of the body, but a lover of God." Cited in Wasserman, *Death of the Soul*, 133.

lishes that this "death" is part and parcel of baptism: "those of us who were baptized into Christ Jesus, into his death we were baptized. Through baptism, therefore, we have been buried with him into death" (6:3). Importantly, no longer obeying the passions is being aligned with the act of baptism into Christ. Of course, as we have seen, many theories about the nature of this "participation with Christ" have been advanced. But our previous exegetical work allows us to see that an obvious way that the baptizand participates with Christ's death is through her practices. Since the Christians in Rome no longer obey their passions they are said to have "died to sin" and it is *this* dying that Paul takes up and unifies with Christ's death. The church therefore participates in this death, to use the language of Rom 6:11, by not letting the body's desires rule. This is the Christian's death to sin (6:1).

In the same way that Christ was raised so also the church walks in newness of life (6:5). Christ died and the church is baptized into his death and so dies its own death to the passions, with him. Paul therefore names baptism as the time when Christians leave the old pagan life and started living a new one. He says that they *were* baptized (ἐβαπτίσθημεν), and this is the basis of the fact that they are *currently* holy. Nowhere in this passage is evinced any notion of the possible separation between baptism and holiness. Baptism is a death with Christ *because* in it the church dies to sin. Paul does not say that the church is mystically joined to Christ in it. The participation with Christ is by means of new practices.[36]

Until now the focus has been on the negative aspect of *not* living a sinful life. This is the life the church dies to in baptism. But then (6:4) Paul turns his eye to the participation in the resurrection: just as Christ was raised, so also the church ought to "live a new life" (ἐν καινότητι ζωῆς περιπατήσωμεν). Church members died, in other words, in order that they might live a different life. It is not just that the church has died to sin, but that it now lives to holiness. The Apostle elaborates: "We became partakers in *a figure* of his death" (σύμφυτοι γεγόναμεν τῷ ὁμοιώματι τοῦ θανάτου αὐτοῦ).[37] And the thesis that we are advancing gives good reason for this:

---

36. See below for how the Spirit integrates with this claim, but this fits nicely with Aquinas, *in Rom* 6.1: Paul claims here that *per bona opera vitae procedamus. Vita enim peccati vetustatem habet, quia in corruptionem nos ducit. Unde et novitas vitae dicitur per quam aliquis redit ad integritatem, ut scilicet sit sine peccato.*

37. On ὁμοιώματι cf. Schneider, "ὅμοιος, ὁμοιότης, κτλ," in *TDNT* 5:191–98: "The likeness of the death of Jesus is that by baptism the believer is set in a position which is *like* the death of Jesus . . . Not the act of baptism, but the ἀποθανεῖν τῇ ἁμαρτίᾳ (v. 10) effected by baptism, is the likeness of the death of Christ" (my italics).

The Practice of the Body of Christ

we did not *exactly* become partakers of his death, since we are still alive in our mortal bodies. Rather, our death to sin is a figure of that death because our body is the site of the passions and so we have to, in a way, "kill it" (more on this below).

This means that the church is now in a fit condition to receive new bodies at the final resurrection (6:23; cf. 1 Cor 15:42–58; see below). The present "likeness" of Christ's death and newness of life presently are necessary for the future resurrection when church bodies will inherit eternal life. Hence Paul says (6:5) that the current death to the passions is necessary for the future resurrection, for only if (εἰ) they are partakers of the figure of his death will they also be partakers of his resurrection (ἀλλὰ καὶ τῆς ἀναστάσεως ἐσόμεθα). We see therefore a threefold division of participation by practice: (1) participation in Christ's death by killing the body's passions, (2) participation in Christ's resurrection by subsequently living in newness of life, and (3) participation in Christ's resurrection by receiving new bodies at the eschaton. We participate in Christ by what we do.

In vv. 6–11 the relationship between Christ's death and Christian holiness begins to emerge. Paul spells out further (v. 6) the appearance of the church's new way of life, again with reference to Christ's death, by saying that the old human has been crucified along with Christ (ὁ παλαιὸς ἡμῶν ἄνθρωπος συνεσταυρώθη) in order to condemn the sinful body (ἵνα καταργηθῇ τὸ σῶμα τῆς ἁμαρτίας). What this means is that, introducing for the first time the topic of slavery, "we no longer serve sin" (τοῦ μηκέτι δουλεύειν ἡμᾶς τῇ ἁμαρτίᾳ). He then concludes this section (vv. 10–11) by recapping again the topic of dying with Christ as a change of life, this time more explicitly.

> If we died with Christ we trust that also we shall live along with him, knowing that Christ, being raised from the dead no longer dies. Death no longer rules over him. For he died to sin once, and now that he lives, he lives with God. It is the same with you! Consider yourselves dead to sin but alive to God in Christ Jesus.

Here we get the comparison set out more carefully. Just as Christ died one time and doesn't die anymore, so also there can be no more "death" for the member of the church, since the church has "died" to the passions themselves (v. 11).

But again we have to be clear about what Paul is saying, so that we do not end up neglecting the hortatory aspect of this passage. Paul does not, on my reading, mean to say that it is literally impossible for their souls again to die in the same way that that it is impossible for Christ to be crucified and die. That is not the aspect of the analogy he is pressing. Rather, he is imploring them to make their rejection of the passions so final as to be like Christ who can never again suffer his passion. Their rejection of the passions *should* be permanent, but because it is their practices, and not any sort of mystical superglue, that attach them to Christ, it can never be finally secured short of the eschaton or the death of the body in the usual sense.[38]

Finally, Rom 6 is, moreover, clearly a development on the theology of Rom 5, and this in multiple ways, so that it is always a problem when the two chapters are read independently of each other. Virtually all of the vocabulary overlaps, as a glance at the chapters side by side bears out. First, and most obviously, both chapters treat the themes of sin and justice. I have found in Rom 6 a confirmation of the nature of sin as disobedience that I argued for in Rom 5. Sin entered the world by means of everyone performing sinful acts (5:12, 18), and these are the very acts to which the church was once enslaved (6:17-20). Sin is not a cosmic power that had to be combated by another cosmic power called "grace" or "righteousness," but particular acts in obedience to the passions (6:12) and disobedience to God (5:14, 18). The obedience of Christ (5:19) set the church free from the pattern of Adam's disobedience (5:18) so that it no longer obeys the passions (6:12) but now is obedient to God. The "old human" (6:6), then, comes into focus as the Adamic human (5:14–15), who was crucified with Christ (6:8). The crucifixion (6:6) of the Adamic human is death to Adam's disobedient trespass (5:16, 19a), and so through Christ's act of obedience (5:19b) a new life of obedience (6:16) has been opened up that is no longer obedience to the passions but to God. This is the just and holy life (5:21; 6:19, 22), but it is equally one that God has *given* (5:15; 6:23) through the just act of Christ's obedience unto death. By participation in that death through "dying" to sin and so being holy and just the church makes itself fit for the fullest installment of participation—eternal life in new bodies (5:21; 6:23). These new bodies will be God's gift (6:23), and yet they can and must be prepared for, since this gift will follow upon God's prior gift of a just way of life (5:19, 6:18, et cetera).

---

38. Cf. Cicero, *Resp.* 1.1.2: "It is not enough to possess (*habere*) virtue as some sort of art (*artem*), unless you make use (*utere*) of it. For an art, even though never used, can still remain in your possession by the very fact of your knowledge of it, but virtue depends entirely upon its use (*virtus in usu sui tota posita est*)."

Rom 7: No Virtues Without the Spirit

Romans 7 is outside the scope of my study and I do not need to treat it to establish my thesis. Wasserman's work is determinative on this topic, and the general thrust of her reading seems right. I should comment on this text briefly, however, since something like Wasserman's reading sets up nicely what I will be saying below about Rom 8. I have differences with her thesis in detail, but this is neither the place to air those nor to set out her reading fully.

Rom 7:1-6 discusses the way that the church has died to the law so that, just as in Rom 5-6, it is in a changed situation. In 7:7 an interlocutor appears who opens a discussion of the law and the doing of its commands. Whoever the hypothetical speaker is in vv. 7-25, it is not Paul qua Christian and it is not one of the Christians about whom Paul has been speaking in Rom 5:1—7:6. Whether the speaker is "Reason" personified, the pre-Christian gentile, the immature Christian, or the gentile Christian now trying to follow the law, the character of this person breaks sharply with that which has come before. She is unable to please God and is involved in a losing struggle with sin and the passions, in contrast to the previous conversation up to 7:6 in which Paul was very clear that the Christian is living a more or less sinless life where her passions no longer rule.[39] Rom 5:12—7:6 depicts, that is, the church as it should be—holy and just—while in Rom 7:7-25 something is wrong.

The terms that Paul puts in this speaker's mouth further substantiate my theory about the nature of the discussion in chapters 5-6 and those to come in chapter 8. In this section the good (τὸ καλόν, τὸ ἀγαθὸν: vv. 13, 21) and the evil (τὸ κακὸν: v. 21) are defined patently in terms of acts and not in terms of powers. "Sin" is spelled out in terms of ἐπιθυμία (vv. 7, 8), breaking the commandment (vv. 8, 9, 10, 11), and the speaker is enslaved to the παθήματα (cf. v. 5). Both the good and the evil are put in terms of what is "done" (κατεργάζομαι, ποιῶ, πράσσω: vv. 8, 15, 16, 17, 18). The usual Lutheran-influenced reading of this passage would say that it is exactly the attempting to *do* good that constitutes the speaker's futility. But

---

39. Reason personified: Wasserman, "Paul Among the Philosophers," 405. The immature Christian: Origen, *Comm. Rom.* 6.8.9 (34). He goes on in 6.9.2 (36-37), to note: "Not only are there a diversity of law here but a diversity of *personae*. For Paul has said elsewhere . . . but now he claims . . . We should conclude from these things that it is the custom of holy scripture to imperceptibly change the *personae* and the subject matter and the reasons that it seems to discuss and the designations. . . . He has now taken on himself the *persona* of the weak." The pre-Christian Gentile: Chrysostom, *Hom. Rom.* 12-13. Gentile Christian observing the law: Stowers, *Rereading*, 258-84.

Practicing Participation

this is unlikely, since there is such a high level of overlap between the terminology of Rom 5–6 and 7. Paul is concerned in *all* these chapters with sin as the performance of certain acts in obedience to the passions and in disobedience to God's law. That is the topic throughout. The difference lies in the fact that in 7:7–25 the speaker is in the midst of a losing struggle with the passions she is free from in 5:12—7:6.

Rom 8:1–18: Killing the Sinful Body By Practicing the Spirit

Rom 8:1–18 follows precisely as an answer to the basic problem (whatever it is exactly) of Rom 7:7–25. The thematic unity of the notion of sin across Rom 5–7 means that whatever the specific history of the *persona* in Rom 7:7–25, her fundamental ailment is the same as that which Paul's gospel in Rom 5:1—7:6 treats: an inability to control her passions and submit to God's law. In Rom 8 we see in a more focused way just *how* Paul imagines such an ailment is relieved. Rom 5 therefore presents the *what* of Christian life in terms of holiness and justice, in contrast to the body of sin of Rom 7:7–25 which is the *what* and a bit of the *how* of the life enslaved to the passions. In Rom 6 Paul sets out the beginning of *how* this comes about: participation in Christ. Rom 8 is going to tell us more exactly what this entails.

Rom 8:1 opens as a response to the sorry state of Rom 7, and specifically the worry about death, saying that there is no condemnation for those in Christ. My reading argues that Paul does not name a cosmic state of the universe, much less a forensic status we hold before God, but rather the state of holiness that the church comes to stand in by no longer being slaves it its passions.[40] The rest of the chapter goes on to sort out how this is possible.

Verse 2 picks up the theme of the Spirit, which will dominate the discussion presently, for nearly the first time in the letter. There are glimpses of the Spirit in 5:5 and most recently in 7:6, when the church is said to be slaves to it and not to the oldness of the letter (ὥστε δουλεύειν ἡμᾶς ἐν καινότητι πνεύματος καὶ οὐ παλαιότητι γράμματος). Here Paul says something similar, except this time the Spirit itself appears as a νόμος: the law of the Spirit of life (8:2). The latter has liberated the church from another law, the law of sin and of death, the contextual significance being that this is the solution to the struggle of Rom 7. Here a new law appears

---

40. For exactly this reading see Origen, *Comm. Rom.*, 6.11.2 on Rom 8:1.

that has done away with that losing battle and, instead of ending in death, it will bring life.[41] The past tense of the verb (ἠλευθέρωσέν) means, as we have seen, that Paul does not assume his hearers *are* currently in a losing battle. On the contrary, they are freed from sin as set out in 5:1—7:6, so that the Spirit's law has *already* set them free from slavery to the passions.[42] How?

"God condemned sin" (8:3). That is Paul's answer, and the basic grammar of the next sentence. The struggler of Rom 7:7–25 was himself enslaved to a body of death because of sin. *He* was fit to be condemned; but instead God condemned *sin* by sending his Son. He did this "in his flesh" (ἐν τῇ σαρκί), so that we are left to conclude that somehow the death of Christ's flesh, which was "like the flesh of sin" (ἐν ὁμοιώματι σαρκὸς ἁμαρτίας), was the condemnation of sin to death.

Notice that Paul does *not* say that Christ's death *is* sin's death nor that the cross was what killed sin in the church. Rather, victory over sin requires the effort of the sinner as well (see below). But the work of the Son *has* pronounced the sentence of death (κατέκρινεν) so that sin is set to be killed (8:3). We are not yet told how it is to be killed; that will wait for 8:13 and have to be filled out in chapters 12–15; but Paul is getting there.

He pauses, however, to say something about the significance of this (8:4). For if sin is set to be killed, it means that the just acts of the law can finally be fulfilled (τὸ δικαίωμα τοῦ νόμου πληρωθῇ). The key to this, however, will be a certain way of life (περιπατοῦσιν) which he names "not according to the flesh but according to the spirit." The just practice that was the goal of the struggle in Rom 7:7–25 can now be fulfilled by means of a different way of life that involves the spirit (on the lower-case see below). But what does it mean to walk in the spirit?

The spirit's φρόνημα (8:6–7) appears significant. The Vulgate translates φρόνημα variously as *prudentia* or *sapientia*. Such renderings suggest that Paul is after something rather different from the usual English translation of "think" or "be minded." What is the difference? First, I don't think Paul is concerned with the instrumental reason of post-classical rationality as Taylor expounds it (and we saw in chapter 1). Rather, the

---

41. It will be left to the next chapter to expound exactly what this new law is, but I do think that it is genuinely a law. See also Rom 6:7: διότι τὸ φρόνημα τῆς σαρκὸς ἔχθρα εἰς θεόν, τῷ γὰρ νόμῳ τοῦ θεοῦ οὐχ ὑποτάσσεται, οὐδὲ γὰρ δύναται· This is to oppose again Lutheran readings that would see any notion of law as legalistic. On the contrary, Paul has a very full account of what it looks like to be slaves to righteousness. The new law is not "freedom" per se. It is being bound to another way of life.

42. On freedom as freedom from the passions see Philo, *Prob.*, 42; Epictetus, *Ench.* 41.

Practicing Participation

φρόνημα/φρονέω family of words is most often used of virtues that are directed towards certain ends.[43] In similar discussions of human agency, it concerns precisely that part of the subject that is in charge of acting, and this always for some end.[44] The φρόνημα is the part of the body that is in charge of φρόνησις or practical deliberation, and this places it right in the heart of classical discussions of human action. Thus Paul is concerned not so much with what we would call "thinking" but "doing."[45] This grammar is essential for making sense of what follows.

Paul says that those who live according to the flesh (οἱ κατὰ σάρκα ὄντες) are prudent toward (φρονοῦσιν) matters of the flesh and those who live according to the spirit are prudent toward the things of the spirit (8:5). Paul speaks in a long tradition of philosophical discussion about the way that one lives, as usual designating different ways of life with various prepositions (κατά, παρά, etc.). Most famous is the tradition, popular in Paul's time especially among the Stoics, but reaching back all the way to Plato and Aristotle, of life according to nature or against nature.[46] These were the ends to which one's life was ordered—one's virtues and vices, particular habits, demonstrated in particular actions, tended in one direction or another. Paul simply states the rather mundane axiom that one who is practiced in certain actions, one who lives in certain ways, is skilled in pursuing matters that pertain to those ends. And so, regarding the flesh and the spirit, each is well-trained regarding its own way of life.

That the φρόνημα-family of words contains in Paul's grammar a significant notion of the telos of human action is confirmed in in v.7. He says literally that "the fleshly prudence is death, but the pneumatic prudence is life and peace." There can be little doubt from the foregoing context that these are the *ends* of a particular way of life, (6:21–22: τὸ γὰρ τέλος ἐκείνων θάνατος . . . τὸ δὲ τέλος ζωὴν αἰώνιον; cf. also 5:21; 6:23; 7:24, etc.) and that here death and life are called φρονήματα under the latter's teleological aspect. If this is the case, it appears that Paul has a teleological

---

43. Aristotle, *N.E.*, 6.5.1-2: "We speak of people as φρονίμους when they reason well towards some τέλος."

44. See *Let. Aris.*, 124; Philo, *Leg. All.* 1.66; 3.193.

45. Thus Philo (*Leg.* 1.74) says that fro,nhma consists in both words and deeds. Hence it comes close to "habit" or "disposition" in *Mos.* 1.309, 325. Cf. also Chrysostom, *Hom. Rom.* 13: "It is vice then he means by carnal mindedness, and by spiritual mindedness the grace given, and the working of it discernible in the right determination."

46. There are many works on this topic, but for primary sources see the works of Koester, "NOMOS FUSEWS," 521–41. Note also the list of citations from *Stoicorum Veterum Fragmenta* in Koester's, "φύσις, φυσικός; κτλ," 264–65.

analysis of human action. Each person's prudence directs his action toward a certain end—either death or life. Thus, even though one does not know she intends such ends, each action will tend in one direction or another depending on each one's prudence. We should note, moreover, that each one of these ends is a condition of the body: either dead or alive.

These are the ends to which each action moves—either to eschatological (which is also to say teleological) death in the destruction of the body, or eschatological life in a new body. Thus φρόνημα actually names for Paul a certain disposition of the body, such that the eschatological nature of the body appears as a completion of an already partly-established habit.[47]

Verses 7–8 confirm two of our hypotheses. First, Paul does think that there is still a law of God that must be fulfilled, since fleshly prudence does not and cannot "submit to God's law" (τὸ φρόνημα τῆς σαρκὸς τῷ νόμῳ τοῦ θεοῦ οὐχ ὑποτάσσεται). The question is not for Paul whether there still is a law, but how it might be possible to submit to it. Second, these same verses confirm that we are on the right track in thinking that Paul is concerned primarily with certain dispositions, since fleshly prudence does not and cannot *submit to* and *please* God, a fleshly habit does not allow certain types of behavior.

Paul has already been talking a lot about the spirit. But I submit that in 8:1–8 he has not been talking about God's Spirit.[48] That there are two different πνεύματα in play at this point is shown clearly by v. 16: "the Spirit testifies along with our spirit."[49] What is Paul up to? In vv. 1–8 he poses the common classical contrast between the life that focuses on the needs of the body and the life of the mind or of the soul.[50] Life "according to the spirit" is a synonymous expression.[51] Paul is saying, almost prosaically,

---

47. That these terms have this bodily component in a classical account appears when Chrysostom, *Hom. Rom.*13, says that the Spirit's job is to "persuade our flesh to get acquainted with its proper position."

48. So see Stowers, "Pauline Participation," 362–63.

49. This same division can be seen in 1 Cor 2:11–15.

50. Cf. Heb 12:22–23, where pneu/ma is used basically for "soul": "You have come to Mount Zion ... to the pneu,masi of the righteous made perfect."

51. So πνεῦμα is always in roughly the same grammatical family as ψυχή λογικόν νοῦς φρόνημά or ἡγεμονικόν, even if it plays various different roles depending on the anthropology. See Cicero, *Tusc.* I.IX.19. Galen at least twice says that the yuch, is made out of pneu/ma (*On Hippocrates' and Plato's Doctrines* 5.3.8; *On Hippocrates' Epidemics* 6.270, 26–28). Sextus Empiricus sees the yuch, as the same as the ἡγεμονικόν (*Against the Professors* 7.234), while at one point identifies ψυχή πνεῦμά ανδ ἡγεμονικόν (Calcidius 220); Aetius, in another threefold identification, sees little difference between

that the life of the body and the flesh is the life of sin, and that instead the members of the church should live by reason, by their own mind or spirit, the best part of their soul that, in a good person, should govern and control the lower, irrational parts of the soul. That Paul would exhort them to rule their sinful passions by the leading part of their soul was simply to be expected. After all, he has just spent a lot of time, especially in Rom 6, saying that their passions do not rule, and telling them to be sure to keep things that way. This was everybody's goal, but the problem of the passions persisted. So at first he seems to give the standard answer: let the right part of your soul rule and you will not be subject to sin and condemned.[52] This was common advice, but he has not yet set out his own Christocentric, pneumatological version.

So, in v.9, Paul introduces another kind of Spirit. "For you are not in the flesh if the Spirit *of God* dwells in you." Paul reveals what he has not yet said—that the way one has to order one's own πνεῦμα is with God's πνεῦμα. But so what? If everything is a matter of having this Spirit or not, why does Paul speak as though there is something church members can do about it?

I suggest the answer lies in two places. First, it is likely that Paul is pointing to baptism. The Spirit is involved in texts that mention baptism (1 Cor 12:13; Eph 4:1-16), and this in part because the Spirit is received for the first time in that event.[53] Moreover, Paul opened the present discussion by relating the intimate connection between baptism and death to sin (Rom 6:3). It is to be expected that the Spirit would figure in this discussion. There is therefore a threefold mutual inclusion in Paul's theology between baptism, holiness and the Spirit. If this is true, v.9 has a shade of warning to it: "if indeed you still have the Spirit of God you received in baptism—if you've not done anything to lose it . . ."

Second, and therefore, v.9 points back to the previous verses. The Spirit is indeed something that is given at baptism, but as the hortatory nature of vv. 4-9a makes clear, it is also something that must be continually

---

πνεῦμά ψυχή, and λογικόν (Aetius 4.21.1-4). Iamblichus, *On the Soul* identifies the πνεῦμα almost completely with the ἡγεμονικόν (Stobaeus 1.368.12-20). These citations could be expanded. I am indebted to Long and Sedley, *Hellenistic Philosophers*, 320-41, for most of these, and for the Hellenistic texts cited in the notes below with English titles.

52. This is what Chrysostom (*Hom. Rom.* 13) heard: "Thus the soul and the flesh belong to things indifferent, since each may become either the one or the other. But the spirit belongs to things good, and at no time becometh any other thing. Again, the mind of the flesh, that is, ill-doing, belongs to things always bad."

53. See chapter 4 below.

practiced. "If you practice the Spirit of God," says Paul, "then you will not be in the flesh, and in this way you will avoid condemnation." V. 9b helps establish this, where we learn that this is not just the Spirit of God, but now it is *of Christ*, which "someone" (τις) needs to have in order to be "Christ's." The last mention we have had of Christ is in 8:1, and it is significant that there those who are "in him" are said to have no condemnation. For "having the Spirit of Christ" appears to be equivalent to being "in Christ." Both involve elements of the indwelling of Christ or his Spirit *and inseparably* a particular way of life (since this is what 8:1 addresses). This is evinced by the secondary, but early textual tradition that places "to those who walk not according to the flesh but according to the Spirit" at the end of 8:1. It does not seem to have occurred to Paul that someone might be baptized and go on living the same way as before. Baptism imparts the Spirit and at the same time a changed way of life that is typical of the Spirit and so can be phrased "living in the Spirit." This practice is the only way that one will be able to please God and avoid condemnation.

This is, on other words, Paul's more detailed solution to the problem of the passions we said was forthcoming. As part of this, the Apostle is unpacking a significant amount of pneumatology. He is engaged in a discussion of what it is that allows the control of the passions, having begun by appeal to the spirit as the ruling part of the soul. He then reveals, in v.9a, that what is necessary for this task is God's πνεῦμα, and, giving further definition, he says that this is actually Christ's own. The force, therefore, of the statement that if someone does not have Christ's Spirit he is not of him, must be to point back to 8:1 and the claim that condemnation is avoided by those in Christ. Again the hortatory dimension of the passage comes to the fore: having Christ's Spirit is not just something that happens or not, as it were from the top down. Rather, the Spirit's agency comes alongside human agency (see below). This cooperation is manifested in a particular way of life that he names "according to the Spirit." The final definition of the Spirit then comes in v. 11: "the Spirit *of the one raising Jesus from the dead."* The broadly conceived leading principle of the soul has come by the end of the section to be named *very* specifically in relation to Christ and his resurrection.

Paul is conveying the nature of this Spirit as it relates to the saving work of sanctification. Its mode is outlined in vv. 10 and 13. In the latter Paul says to "put to death the deeds of the body by the Spirit" (πνεύματι τὰς πράξεις τοῦ σώματος θανατοῦτε). The grammar of this sentence is very important: it is an *exhortation* (θανατοῦτε) to behave in a particular way - to kill the passions *by means of the Spirit* that has been defined as Christ's.

This fits with what we have seen so far in terms of the Spirit both being an abiding presence and a way of life. The Spirit is apparently something that can be practiced, and so, exhorted. This will be confirmed presently.

But this is not the first time in the letter that we have seen something like this. In Rom 6:6 Paul said that the sinful body was annulled so that we are no longer slaves to sin (καταργηθῇ τὸ σῶμα τῆς ἁμαρτίας τοῦ μηκέτι δουλεύειν ἡμᾶς τῇ ἁμαρτίᾳ). What is potentially surprising about these verses is the relatively pessimistic way that Paul talks about the body. It is more or less the locus of the passions and nothing else. Later commentators like Chrysostom point this out by spending lots of time talking about how for Paul the body *itself* is not sinful but indifferent.[54] I think this is a good reading of Paul, for nowhere is the body, in and of itself, denoted as sinful or for death. It remains the case, however, that the body and its acts are not to be *treated* indifferently, but to be fought *against*. The practices of the *body*—Paul does not even say the *evil* practices!—are to be killed. This means that in order to avoid the reading that has Paul condemning everything that the body does (i.e., all its acts—which would be to commend suicide), the grammar of the "body" to which the practices belong must be at least that it *tends* towards sin, or at most that it is inherently sinful. The latter is ruled out since we have seen plenty of evidence that shows that in the Spirit holy bodily acts body are not only possible but normative.

So for Paul the body itself tends towards sin, and we've seen good reasons above to think that this is because it is the seat of the passions: Rom 6–8 confirms that desires, passions, wickedness, and sin are of the body, the flesh, or the body-parts. Paul really does mean that if one lives "according to the *flesh*" (v. 13a) she is about to die. But in order to view this correctly we have to remember that Paul has given ample evidence that he views his converts as being in a stable, yet contingent moral position. Their bodies are still susceptible to sin, but it has a much weaker pull on them than on those not in Christ. But this just means that Paul has a view of the body similar to that of someone steeped in classical human action like Augustine or Aquinas. The body is indeed created by God, but it has been corrupted by sin to tend toward the fulfillment of the passions.[55] This

---

54. *Hom. Rom.* 13.

55. This is exactly what Aquinas said *in Rom* 6.3: *Dicit ergo primo: dictum est quod vetus homo noster simul crucifixus est, ut destruatur corpus peccati, per quod datur intelligi, quod virtus peccati in tantum diminuta est, ut nobis dominari non possit. Ergo peccatum, de caetero, non regnet in vestro mortali corpore. Non autem dicit: non sit peccatum in vestro mortali corpore, quia quamdiu corpus nostrum est mortale, id est necessitati mortis addictum, non potest esse quin in corpore nostro sit peccatum, id est fomes peccati. Sed ex quo a Deo liberati sumus a regno peccati debemus conari, quod*

appears to be a real feature of the present nature of human flesh itself. This is the body of sin, the body whose practices are evil. By baptism and the Spirit, however, that can be changed, for that body is capable of tending in a new direction. And if this is so, and we deal here literally with the habits of the physical body, it is not merely metaphorical for Paul to say that the old, sinful person has died. The flesh and bones of the new body are physically and so literally different through putting its deeds to death. Habits are inclinations of the body, and so to change a habit is to change one's body.

Performing different acts thus literally creates a different body—one in continuity with the first, but a different body nonetheless. However new and different, and however stable, the maintenance of this body is contingent upon continuing in its practices.[56] For this reason, therefore, just as he has before, Paul exhorts even those in such a stable condition to continue to be vigilant, for the contingency of salvation, and the simple fact that they continue in a body that will not be corruption-free until the eschaton's new bodies, means that they still have to put to death the practices of the sinful body.[57]

This raises the question of whether the future verb ζῳοποιήσει in v. 11 is an eschatological future or a logical future. Most have not considered the latter. Yet, the former is unlikely, since the rest of the sentence suggests that this is something already happening among his churches. Paul has just said (v. 10) that the body is *currently* dead (τὸ σῶμα νέκρον) but "Spirit is life (ζωή τὸ πνεῦμα) because of righteousness." The translation of ζωή as "alive" is highly favored in current translations, but this is simply not what Paul says: ζωή is not an adjective! Again Paul is working in contrasts which are not meant to be exact opposites. What exactly is he saying?

---

peccatum in corpore nostro dominium iam amissum in nobis non recuperet. Et hoc est quod dicit non regnet peccatum in vestro mortali corpore. Et hoc quidem necessarium est cavere, dum corpus mortale gerimus, quia dicitur Sap. IX, 15: corpus quod corrumpitur aggravat animam, et cetera.

56. Hence Aquinas, *in Rom* 6:2, says that one who has died to sin lives with the risen Christ in such a way that he has the *capacity* of never returning to sin.

57. The apparent tension here between the habit of the good and still needing to strive against the bad is a common one in ancient virtue ethics. How can it be that we still have to strive for the good if our bodies are habituated for it? The answer has to be that the sinful tendency of the body, though able to be severely contained, is never quite done away with. And Paul knows this, and has a solution for it: the gift of an entirely new body made of different, pneumatic material (1 Cor 15). See Wasserman, *Death of the Soul*, 134–35.

I suggest that both statements in v.10b have an elided middle. Sin does not kill the body (Wasserman has shown that it would be more likely to say it kills the soul[58]), but rather *because* the body is a sort of petri dish for sin, it is necessary that the Christian kill that body to prevent the sin from growing, and this is only possible with the Spirit. Moreover, righteousness itself does not make the Spirit life (what would that mean?). Rather, the Spirit that comes inseparably with just practice (righteousness) *progressively vivifies the body as it dies to sin*, "replacing" that old corrupt flesh slowly as it is transformed more and more toward the perfection it can only receive in the eschatological body. Thus Stowers says rightly that Christians are literally "materially improved people."[59] I suspect that this is the rationale for the statement that "if Christ is in you the body is dead because of sin but the Spirit is life because of righteousness."

Thus, "the Spirit is life" (not "the Spirit is alive") makes more sense than the usual translation. It obviates the conceptual problem with affirming that the Spirit is "alive." Was there a question about it being dead? What would it be like for a spirit to be dead? But more importantly, this translation allows Paul to say that the Spirit supplies to the dead body exactly what it is wanting—life. How is it that the church continues to live if its bodies are dead? The answer, says v. 10, is that the Spirit gives it life—and an entirely different quality of life, as we have seen.

This brings us back to ζῳοποιήσει. At this point we can further note the significance of the fact that God shall make alive *mortal* bodies. The dead bodies we have been talking about are precisely those bodies that have been killed because they tend toward sin. Life replaces that dead flesh by the Spirit presently (v.10)—prior to the eschaton. That God will make "mortal bodies" live must refer to the present bodies that are being invested with life. For the only other kind of body that Paul knows is an immortal body—the body of the resurrection—and it is not that body that is made alive.[60] That body is *made of* Spirit (σῶμα πνευματικόν, 1 Cor 15:44; see Chapter 4 below); this body is made alive through the Holy Spirit dwelling in it (διὰ τοῦ ἐνοικοῦντος αὐτοῦ πνεύματος ἐν ὑμῖν).[61] Thus ζῳοποιήσει conveys the present pneumatic vivification (ζωή τὸ πνεῦμα) of the body.

---

58. Wasserman, *Death of the Soul*, 60–67.

59. Stowers, "Pauline Participation," 365.

60. Paul of course does use ζῳοποιέω for the future resurrection in 1 Cor 15:22, 45. But as we have seen, the present change in the body is intimately connected to the future, and so there is no good reason not to use the verb in both cases.

61. Martin, *Corinthian Body*, 123–36. See chapter 4 below.

The Practice of the Body of Christ

Hence realized eschatology is at the heart of the process of making the church holy. The Spirit that raised Jesus from the dead already breaks in, before the general resurrection, and starts to vivify bodies precisely as they die. This close connection between Spirit as sanctifier of the present body and as the very constituent of the resurrected body is unsurprising if our thesis about salvation as the repositioning of bodies is on the mark.

Verse 14a is usually rendered "as many as are led by the Spirit of God." The grammar of "leading" has become a dominant analogy on which to understand the relationship between the Spirit and the church. But our discussion opens up the possibility of translating ἄγονται as a middle. This is a common use of ἄγω in the sorts of ethical discussions like I am arguing Paul is in the midst of.[62] "As many as *conduct themselves* by the Spirit of God" would parallel the dual agency involved in the command to "put to death the deeds of the body by the Spirit" (v. 13), and the dual agency made explicit in esp. vv. 26–30 (see below). Again, the Spirit is viewed in terms of something that can be practiced, something with which the church can cooperate. Such cooperation is evident again in the claim that this same Spirit "co-testifies" with our spirit (συμμαρτυρεῖ τῷ πνεύματι ἡμῶν) that we are sons of God (v. 16b). Bondage and fear (v. 14)—those things *away from* which the church conducts itself, but to which it is possible to return—are likewise a normal way of describing the passions.[63]

We have already dealt with putting to death the deeds of the body (v. 13). We can now add that Paul sees this process as one of suffering with Christ (and so we are tied in closely at this point to Rom 6:1–3). Christ's body suffered when it died, and ecclesial bodies suffer too (συμπάσχομεν) when they die to sin. There are of course times in Paul's letters when such suffering involves enduring persecution (e.g., 2 Cor 1:4-7), but πάσχω is also common in discussions of the passions.[64] The parallel is as it was before: the church participates in Christ's death when the faithful put to death their own bodies' bondage to the passions. This is what is it is to "co-suffer"

---

62. BDAG, ἄγω, 16. Thus, "conduct oneself" as a true middle is much more elegant than making up a category such as the "permissive passive."

63. See Stobaeus 2.88–91; Andronicus, *On Passions* I; Diogenes Laertius 7.115; Galen, *On Hippocrates' and Plato's Doctrines* 3.1.25. Chrysostom says in *Sac.* 6:12 that "[as with] conflict and battle: so it is with the passions of the soul. He who makes them weak, placed them in subjection to right reason; but he who nourishes them carefully makes his battle with them harder and renders them so formidable that he passes all his time in bondage and fear."

64. *TDNT*, "πάσχω κτλ", 905–7.

(συμπάσχομεν) with Christ, and it is clearly mandatory for salvation: only *if* (εἴπερ) the church suffers will it be glorified with new bodies.

Rom 8:18–30: The God Who Cooperates

Unworthy Passions and New Bodies

We saw that the reason that we have to put to death the evil passions has to do with the reception of new bodies. Paul now moves on (v. 18) to spell out that this is because "the passions of this age are not worthy of the glory about to be revealed in us" (οὐκ ἄξια τὰ παθήματα τοῦ νῦν καιροῦ πρὸς τὴν μέλλουσαν δόξαν ἀποκαλυφθῆναι εἰς ἡμᾶς). I argue, that is, that τὰ παθήματα names the passions of classical action theory and not just of "suffering" in general. There are very good reasons to do so.

First, the most recent use of παθήματα before 8:18 undoubtedly refers to these same passions: "When you were in the flesh the sinful passions (παθήματα τῶν ἁμαρτιῶν) worked in our bodies to make us bear fruit to death" (7:5). Second, the usual translation simply makes the verse say something that the Greek does not. Paul is not *comparing* present suffering to future bliss and thereby exhorting the church to stick things out for the sake of something much better to come. This poor reading (1) would supply the word "compare" which is simply not present in the sentence and (2) is quite out of keeping with Paul's discourse. The Apostle has been concerned with how it is that Christians can live in such a way that they may control their passions. As he moves, therefore, to consider the glory that is given to those who do so (v. 17), he states another reason why present renovation of life is necessary for future blessedness: the passions of this body are not worthy *of* the glory of the resurrected body. Indeed, as we have seen, that resurrected body can be viewed as the completion of the body that has been taught to act correctly in obedience to God. Thus, v. 18 in one way introduces the following verses, but it also stands as an important preliminary conclusion to, and rationale for, the whole discussion of human action begun in 6:1.

The background and referent of the next few verses (19–24) are matters of intense speculation, but they fit the reading that I am giving well.[65] The creation is eagerly awaiting (ἀποκαραδοκία is a hapax legomenon particular to Paul, only appearing elsewhere in Phil 1:20) the revelation of the

---

65. Vögtle, *Röm 8:* 18–22. See in addition the more recent bibliography in Jewett, *Romans*, 511–20.

sons of God because it was subjected to futility (ματαιότητι; vv. 19-20). The grammar of ματαιότητι takes its place firmly in discussions of pagan idolatry and slavery to the passions.[66] It normally describes the nature of something—almost always a human being—when involved in typically pagan activities, but especially when in bondage to unruly desires. Paul himself uses the word this way (Rom 1:21; 1 Cor 3:20; Eph 4:17). Here not only humans, but the entire creation (v. 21), suffers from one and the same malady of bondage (δουλείας) to vice. It is important to note that *at this point*, and not before, Paul broadens the scope of the discussion from human action to a view of the whole cosmos. But even then it is the creation as a whole that is described by analogy to a condition of human action ("futility") and not visa-versa.

Paul then once again (v. 21) applies to the church the language of "slavery" that was first applied to human action in Rom 6 and 8:1. This time, however, the accent is slightly different. The freedom (ἐλευθήσεται, ἐλευθερίαν) of the sons of God is no longer considered as a present freedom that they have from domination by the passions, but as a future, complete freedom from the old body of sin by its replacement with a new body. This is the "freedom of the glory of the sons of God" (v. 21b)—the new body that is the replacement of that old one that is marked by some degree of slavery (even in those who are slaves of righteousness) and of corruption (φθορᾶς; cf. 1 Cor 15:42) that it shares with the creation itself.

Thus, quite importantly, we should underline that *this* is the proper place to talk about the "now and not yet" in Pauline soteriology. "Partially realized eschatology" is not a tension that exists because of two different cosmic states, one of which has only been realized "in principle." Paul's "now and not yet" names what must be the case if both what Paul says in Rom 6:1-11 about present freedom from the passions *and* what he says here are to be taken together: the body is partly redeemed *now* but *not yet* to the extent that it will be.

Thus until the church has those new bodies (ἀπολύτρωσιν τοῦ σώματος ἡμῶν, v. 23) it still labors under the weight of a sinful body that cannot entirely be snuffed out. As we have seen, the passions *have* been put down (Rom 6:1-11), but the church must be in constant vigilance so as not to let them get another foothold (Rom 6:12-23). This requires constant effort, and so the church "groans" (στενάζομεν) as it works (v. 23). "Groaning" is once again a common classical way that the effort of striving

---

66. So, Wisdom 13:1; and see the parallels in Philo *Contempl.* 3-8; *Decal.* 52-81; Isa 44:9; Jer 10:3, 14; 1 *Cl.* 7:2. See also Ricken, "Hellenistische Vorlage?," 54-86.

for virtue is described.⁶⁷ What is not so usual is Paul's contention that this state is common to the entire creation: "all creation groans and travails together until the present time" (v. 22). The *focus* however, is not on the non-human creation but on the church, for Paul immediately returns to it (v. 23); only vv. 19-22 depart from the discussion of human action, applying its description to the creation as a whole. V. 23 returns the discussion to the church. Hence the futile condition of the "entire creation" appears not as a cosmic *qualifier* or limitation of the church's nature (the church being caught in cosmic forces), but as her *consolation*, since it groans with her in sympathy.

Verses 19-24 continue Paul's concern with the incremental perfection of the human body—this time articulating the need for it finally to be freed from its tendency toward sin by being replaced with another body (v. 23b). This confirms our earlier argument that the Spirit's role in working holiness before the final resurrection is intimately connected with the body itself. For even though the church has the first fruits of the Spirit (v. 23a), Paul appears to be saying that the faithful groan while still awaiting new bodies. This presumes that the Spirit has done something vital to our present bodies but that this is not yet quite enough to stop groaning under the possible attacks of the passions. The latter is hard work that requires perseverance (δι' ὑπομονῆς ἀπεκδεχόμεθα; v. 25).

Cooperation Towards the Good

Rom 8:26-30 forms something of a paragraph of its own and is vital evidence for the question of agency. In fact, we find here one of the only texts that speaks directly to the relationship between the Spirit's action and the church's: "the Spirit cooperates with our weakness" (τὸ πνεῦμα συναντιλαμβάνεται τῇ ἀσθενείᾳ ἡμῶν, v. 26). On our reading, the body is weak because it is a body of corruption tending toward sin and not yet one

67. This is ubiquitous, for example, in Philo, e.g., *Leg.* 3.211: "Therefore it is not sufficient for the unfortunate external sense to be abundantly occupied with pains, but it must also be full of groaning (τῷ στεναγμῷ). Now groaning is a violent and intense pain. For we are very often in pain without groaning. But, when we groan, we are under the influence of most grievous and thickly pressing pain. Now, groaning is of a twofold nature. One kind is that which arises in those who desire and are very eager for august objects and who do not succeed in them, which is wicked; the other kind is that which proceeds from persons who repent and are distressed for previous sins, and who say, 'Miserable are we, how long a time have we passed infected with the disease of foolishness, and in the practice of all kinds of folly and iniquity.'" The same sort of discourse appears in *Leg* 3:212; *Det.* 1:93; *Deus.* 1:115, 138; *Mig.*15, 155.

of incorruption. This is "our weakness." The fundamental way that Paul characterizes the relation of the Spirit to our agency is that of "helping." Συναντιλαμβάνω is another Pauline hapax because of the unusual συν- prefix. But we here get a glimpse of the fact that this prefix indicates exactly the nature of our relationship to the Spirit—that of doing something "with" it. Ἀντιλαμβάνω is itself common enough and means "help."[68] But Paul emphasizes the "with-ness" of this helping by adding what amounts to the intensifying prefix συν-. The Spirit *helps* the church's weak bodies. Toward what?

Toward, says Paul, the good: "God cooperates in all things toward the good" (v. 28). The Greek printed in NA27 (τοῖς ἀγαπῶσιν τὸν θεὸν πάντα συνεργεῖ εἰς ἀγαθόν) is usually rendered into English as "all things work together for good for those who love him," or some variation thereof.[69] But this is textually and lexically problematic.

The textual issue admits a fairly easy solution. First, Jewett's claim that the subject of συνεργεῖ in v. 28 is the same as it was at the end of v. 27—the Spirit—cannot stand, since this would entail that the Spirit is the subject of all the rest of the verbs in the paragraph (through v. 30).[70] This leads, among other improbabilities, to making Paul speak of the Spirit's Son (τοῦ υἱοῦ αὐτοῦ; v. 29)! So the subject of συνεργεῖ must be ὁ θεός , contra NA27, but with all the best manuscript evidence (P46, A, B, etc.) except ℵ. That this makes the sentence slightly redundant cannot overcome the arguments in its favor. The only problem with the rest of Jewett's argument at this point is that it is overly complex. He imagines that πάντα is *not* the direct object and that Paul elides a κατά, so that what he really meant to say was that the Spirit κατὰ πάντα συνεργεῖ εἰς ἀγαθόν.[71] But this is an unnecessary move since in either case the phrase refers to the same thing, namely, that at each moment the Spirit (or God in our reading) cooperates. It is better to simply take πάντα as the direct object of συνεργεῖ.

Second, συνεργεῖ is close to a synonym of συναντιλαμβάνεται and should be rendered "works with" or "cooperates." Moreover, since there is a dative candidate for the indirect object of συνεργεῖ, we should make use of it. Thus τοῖς ἀγαπῶσιν names the party cooperating with God. Paul emphasizes, then, the duality of agency involved in getting to the good:

68. Liddell, Scott, and Jones, " ἀντιλαμβάνω," in *A Greek-English Lexicon*, 157.
69. Hence, NRSV, NIV, NAB, NKJV.
70. Jewett, *Romans*, 15.
71. Ibid.

both God and the human actor are involved. What Paul says here is that "God cooperates with those who love God in all things toward the good" (ὁ θεὸς τοῖς ἀγαπῶσιν τὸν θεὸν πάντα συνεργεῖ εἰς ἀγαθόν).

This is Paul's basic claim in this paragraph, but he has more to say concerning it. First, he says that one way God helps is the Spirit's assistance in prayer (v. 27). One component of this is that each church member is able to search her heart (ὁ δὲ ἐραυνῶν τὰς καρδίας) and understand something of the wisdom (φρόνημα) of the Spirit itself. And the use of φρόνημα here makes good sense. We saw earlier that implicit in the grammar of "wisdom" is movement toward some *telos*, and Paul is just about to name τὸ ἀγαθόν as such (v. 28). Thus one way that the Spirit cooperates is by being searched out in the hearts of those who pray and imparting wisdom about how to get to the good.

Second, this process of cooperation toward the good involves a transformation into the image of Christ. God ordained that all those whom he calls become conformed to the image of his Son (συμμόρφους τῆς εἰκόνος τοῦ υἱοῦ αὐτοῦ, v.29). Once again a συν- compound shows up, this time not indicating a duality of *agency* but of *form*. One form, that of the Christian, is changed into the form of another, that of Christ, so that they become co-forms (συμμόρφους). Thus the good for Paul, as we have seen and will see more extensively in the next chapter, has everything to do with being conformed to actions similar to those of Christ.

The rest of v. 29 confirms that the focus is on transformation into Christ's image, consonant with what has gone before in this chapter. Thus, though v. 29b is sometimes read with an emphasis on the Christological claim that *Christ* is the firstborn, in a proper reading things should be the other way around. Paul has just argued that church members are sons of God and co-heirs with Christ. He now claims that, however glorious Christ is, he is merely the *first*born among *many* siblings (πρωτότοκον ἐν πολλοῖς ἀδελφοῖς), and these are siblings precisely because they are all God's children (cf. 8:17: τέκνα). Thus, this transformation into the image of the Son by working with the Spirit toward the good is a soteriological necessity because the gift of a new glorious resurrected body depends upon it (as implied in v.30).

Conclusion: Human Agency in Rom 6-8

Several considerations drawn from this exegesis are in order.

First, I said above that in some ways this reading flips the "cosmic powers" reading on its head. We can now see that what this hermeneutic opens space for—and in the end what it demands—is a virtue ethic. For it posits a church with a stable yet contingent way of life that can intelligibly be *both* exhorted and described. This is simply to say that Paul is speaking the language of classical action theory. To put things in those terms: Rom 6:1–11 describes a "habit" of the body that has a particular relationship to baptism and Christ's death. A habit does not describe a human possibility, but the contingent anthropological state of persisting in particular bodily acts. Rom 6:1–11 is Paul's way of saying "you now have virtuous habits," and this itself functions as both (1) praise and (2) an implied exhortation to preserve that habit of justice. Rom 6:12–23 provide an more explicit exhortation, which is possible and necessary because it is always possible to lose good habits and return to obey the passions through inattentiveness. Rom 8:1–30 then give the specifics of how it is that such a transformation of habits has come about in terms of the Spirit's synergistic involvement in putting to death the habits and passions of the body and progressing toward the good.

Second, I have argued that the church is "attached" to Christ by means of its cooperative practice of the Spirit. The content of those practices is only specified here to the extent that it is the rejection of the passions, of sin. Paul leaves exposition of the positive content to Rom 12–15. What we must hold together is that participation in the death of Christ is "real" and that this participation is a visible one borne out in the church's acts. The former is necessary to avoid flattening out Paul's συν- compounds into simple heuristic metaphors about the moral life. Rather, I have argued that Paul has a full notion of the church's union with Christ through present pneumatic vivification. The latter is necessary in order to prevent those same compounds from losing their proper grammar as part of what the church does—the compounds name real practices that involve genuine human agency.

Third, this involves a very different place for the πνεῦμα than usual discussions allow, although one I have contended is thoroughly evident in the text. At bottom, it is the Spirit that "qualifies" the church with Christ's characteristics (habits) in the process of vivification. One basic point of the grammar of πνεῦμα for Paul and the ancient world more generally is that one who has a particular kind of πνεῦμα has her behavior shaped by

Practicing Participation

it. This is true whether we are talking about something like demon possession with "evil spirits" or about philosophically sophisticated discussions of anthropology where the type of πνεῦμα someone has determines what sort of physical and moral qualities she possesses.[72] My reading presses against the notion that Paul speaks of πνεῦμα in terms of possession, but the simple point that the the spirit acts as *qualifier* is the same regardless. This provides one reason why Paul thinks that those who have the Spirit of Christ will act like Christ in suffering (Rom 8:9, 17). Thus the Spirit plays a non-negotiable role in the church's participation in both Christ's death and resurrection, since when it receives this Spirit it will act like Christ. This is, however, a joint ecclesial-pnuematic agency. Everything Paul says presumes both the church's responsibility to act and that such action is genuinely human. This is a key difference between Paul's grammar of the πνεῦμα and, again, something like demon possession (or a heavy-handed notion of *possession* by God's Spirit for that matter). The pneumatic nature is qualifying in either case. But for Paul (as for someone like Chrysostom or Aquinas as the notes show) it appears that the more hard, human work is done, the more the Spirit participates in that work and makes it ever more fruitful—precisely because part of having the Spirit is a disposition to act in a certain way. In this way Paul's grammar of the Spirit also comes close to the classical language of virtue: a virtue is a state of the soul that tends to make its body act in certain ways.

---

72. This is true across various traditions. One's πνεῦμα determines *who* and *how* one is. So, Reesor, *Early Stoic Philosophy*, 4: "The pneuma is responsible for the qualifications (ποια) in the corporeal body (σομα), whether the qualification is hard or white, a disposition, such as 'being a scholar', or a condition, such as 'being posted in an advanced position'. The pneuma is responsible for the conditions of the soul, and the status of the individual, as well as for the physical conditions of the body." The Stoics called this quality produced by the movement of the πνεῦμα α ἕξις—a "state" or "tenor" (cf. e.g., Stobaeus 1.777–79.17). But the qualifying nature of the pneu/ma extended beyond the qualification of substances like rock and iron to the qualification of people's bodies, natures, and moral behavior. Thus Simplicius (*On Aristotle's Categories* 237.25) places virtue under things qualified by pneu/ma. Cf. Seneca, *On Mercy* 1.5.5. Thus Luckman writes that "[n]ot only is every soul a fragment of the world soul, but each soul is a bit of unified πνεῦμα and all psychic phenomena—including passions and emotions—are states of this πνεῦμα, or simply are this pneu/ma in some degree of tension." In other words, the kind of πνεῦμα one has determines who and how one is. See also Galen, *On Sustaining* Causes 1.1–2.4, and the clear discussion in Long and Sedley, *Hellenistic Philosophers*, 1.288–89 and Luckmann, "Pneumatology and Asceticism" 106–43. Also Isaacs, *Pneuma in Hellenistic Judaism*, 70–82. Levinson, *The Spirit*, 71, 92–95, 223–26.

The Practice of the Body of Christ

Fourth, it follows that Paul's soteriology is fundamentally about what the church does with its bodies. This is what agency treats. He is clear that bodies will be bound to one master or another and that they have to do and be disposed to do certain things to be pleasing to God. He says that they have to walk in newness of life, and so implies a soteriologically vital praxis. He says that they are slaves to serve whomever they obey and that this determines the end—death or eternal life. The most important thing about eternal life is that in it the church receives new bodies (1 Cor 15, 2 Cor 5, etc.). This is why the Apostle is so concerned that bodies tend toward sin. The church is involved by participation in Christ in a movement that will climax in bodies that are fully clean of sin. Since the ultimate telos is these bodies, the motion toward those bodies must be one in which the various parts of the present body are rendered in service to God. Doing the latter is the means to the former. In other words, taking the things Paul says about the body—both present and eschatological—as a single piece of teleological reasoning proves to be enlightening of texts about both future bodies (i.e., 1 Cor 15, etc.) and present ones (Rom 6-8). That Paul sees Christianity as a matter of the condition of the body is simply to say that in order to faithfully understand him we have to recognize that he is speaking within a classical account of agency. Rom 6-8 finds its place right in the middle of such discourse, so that what Paul is presenting is actually the first Christian theological ethics.

Fifth, that Paul treats the body as part of what it is to be virtuous offers a deeper theological reason than is generally offered for the well-recognized fact that Paul was an ascetic.[73] Though unfortunately this discussion is still usually limited to his views on sex, there is some indication that this tide may be turning.[74] In contrast to the tendency of current scholarship, I am suggesting a Pauline ascesis much more broadly conceived, and much more integral to his theology as a whole. For—anticipating our next chapter—what will emerge is that Paul advocated a regimen of corporal discipline that would mean the triumph over sin by fighting against its foothold in the body. We see this discipline—this "Rule of St. Paul"—primarily in the form of the church practices of Rom 12-15. Below I will argue that this daily solution to the passions involves the constant presence, demand, and practice of the church.

---

73. E.g., Moxnes, "Asceticism," 3–29; Hunter, "1 Cor 7," 163–91. See the bibliography and overview by Brown, *Body and Society*, 5–64. That the earliest readers of Paul read him this way is demonstrated by Clark, *Reading Renunciation*, 259–370.

74. So, see the essays collected by Vaage et. al, eds., *Asceticism*, 159–330.

Practicing Participation

Sixth, I can further focus these arguments and a few others by making clear the ways in which this reading differs from Wasserman's. First, it is difficult to see in her reading how Paul differs from a common popular Hellenistic philosopher—except that Christ and the Spirit are appended at the end as additional helping agents. She thus flattens out Paul and in fact demythologizes him by suggesting that all this language is really about moral-psychological transformation *and nothing more*. One way that she does this and therein distorts Paul is in her insistence that his primary concern is with *control*. Indeed, she classes huge chunks of Pauline text as so concerned:

> In spite of the many proposals for holding the indicative together with the imperative in Paul's thought, the discourse of soul-death obviates these tensions and provides a contextual explanation for the metaphors that can be anchored historically . . . Understood in this way, Paul's already statements explain a new form of self-mastery, whereas his not yet statements warn that the lower faculties still threaten.[75]

I am so close to agreeing with this that it is important to point out where I differ from it. It may seem a quibble, but in fact it is of the greatest significance. First, neither the term, nor the concept of "control" or "self-mastery" appears in Rom 6–8. For Paul the goal of not letting the passions rule is not that the church might control itself but that it might be transformed into Christ, and the difference is not one of pious semantics. Far from control of the self, Paul, as we have seen, indicates what is much more like a *loss* of control brought about through the transformation of the very nature of the body. Wasserman, on the other hand, flattens Paul's full and complex notion of participation into *simply* a new mode of behavior. New behavior it entails indeed, but such action only gains its intelligibility from a theological ascesis that Wasserman lacks. Paul's asceticism appears to be one that does not seek control but rather strives to give up control in order to be obedient to God. Wasserman does not seem open to conceiving of salvation in terms of union with Christ by the practice of such obedience.

Next, I have sketched the bare outlines of the "process" that brings about the transformation Paul describes: the church participates in Christ's death by submitting its sinful passions to his death and by being vivified in his resurrection by the Spirit's replacement of that dying body slowly by life. Wasserman, however, says only that this transformation was "brought

---

75. Wasserman, *Death of the Soul*, 134.

about by God's work in Christ" but that "sin's rule still threatens."[76] By this language, however, she ironically risks reinstating a view of these chapters in which "God's work in Christ" has changed an ontological, cosmic condition. Specifically, though she interprets Paul's analysis of the *problem* in terms of Hellenistic moral philosophy, at crucial points in her description of Paul's *solution* to the problem she leans back on the consensus in a way that comes dangerously close to obviating human agency. (And of course in this she is at odds with the very tradition of Hellenistic ethics itself.) So she thinks that Paul

> does not propose that the Gentiles learn to behave better by spending their lives with a moral teacher in an arduous battle toward virtue. Rather he seems to assume that baptism in chapter 6 and πνεῦμα in chapter 8 serve to restore the lost capacity for self control that is a condition of obedience to God . . . His solution, an infusion of divine πνεῦμα, is distinctive but also makes sense of his apocalyptic conviction that God is about to judge the world for its sins. That is, this understanding of God's coming judgment requires a nearly immediate solution to the problem of sin.[77]

These lines stand in marked and puzzling contrast with many of the best points of Wasserman's thesis, and especially with her emphasis that Paul is often *exhorting* the Romans. This is itself good reason to doubt that Paul sees the solution to sin as an infusion of spirit that automatically fixes the problem. Never does Paul assume that becoming holy is magic.

Seventh, what are the implications of my account for Paul's view of Christ's death? This is too big a question to be addressed comprehensively here, but a couple of important parameters can be laid down.

On the one hand, that Paul moves *from* the basis of union with Christ by baptism *to* a dying with Christ *to* death to sin (Rom 6:1–3) means that participation in Christ's death is not just a metaphor for controlling the passions. This in turn means that Christ's death does more work for Paul than illustrating moral transformation. Christ's death is not a mere "symbol" for making sense out of the church, and the transformation of the church is not all that can be said of Christ's death. I indicated in the last chapter that sketching Paul's account of Christ's death would have to include passages like Rom 3:21–6 and include notions such as sacrifice, forgiveness, and previous sins.

76. Ibid., 136.
77. Ibid., 135.

On the other hand, we must recon seriously with the fact that most of the time that Paul talks about Christ's death he does so in relation to the holiness of the church. This ought not to be surprising if God was in Christ reconciling the world to himself by forgiving sins and making the church holy. Still, the deep way that the church appears at times to be *already* present *in* Christ's death and resurrection for Paul (Rom 6:1–3; 1 Cor 6:20; 2 Cor 4:10; 5:14–17; Gal 2:20; Col 1:24) is too often unrecognized. The fact that Paul almost always talks about Christ's death in terms of how the church participates in it means that exploring that connection might tell us more about Paul's view of what happened on the cross. This topic is ripe for further exploration.

In the last chapter I argued that for Paul the church is a community that God has given the just practice of obedience. This chapter has specified how Paul thinks that just practice is possible, by suggesting that Paul has a classical account of human agency that is pneumatologically and Christologically qualified. Of course, compared with the work of later thinkers, Paul has given us just the bare bones of the matter. Many questions remain unanswered. Theoretical questions concern the nature human action in general and of virtues, desires, passions, and intentions in particular. Practical questions (which are ultimately inseparable from the theoretical) surround just what this holy life Paul is commending looks like. Paul simply does not give us an account of the former, if he had one at all. The latter, however, he developed at length, and it is impossible to understand what he says in Rom 5–8 apart from the detailed practices that make up the community those chapters address. We turn therefore to an exploration of Rom 12–15.

4

Romans 12–15 as the Practice of the Body of Christ

Introduction: A Body of God in the City of Caesar

IN THIS CHAPTER I ARGUE THAT IN ROM 12–15 PAUL DETAILS WHAT THE way of life he has set out so far looks like "on the ground," in the day to day life of the church. This is another view of the same holistic and communal salvation he has been talking about throughout, and which in Romans he presents at several different levels. In what follows I will argue that Rom 12–15 is not a special "subsection" of salvation, as if salvation began at the individual level and now we have to know how to act with each other. This is *not* the "result," the "outworking," the "application," or the "implication," of salvation, but its very content.[1] This is because, as I have already suggested, imperatives and hortatory sections have been present throughout the preceding chapters just as they are in Rom 12–15, and so the latter can only be viewed as another look at the distinct practices of the church.

I suggest that Romans 12–15 in some ways parallels parts of Plato's or Cicero's *Republics*, or Aristotle's *Politics*. It prescribes roles, chastises certain vices, and commends certain virtues. This section of the letter, therefore, provides the final complement of a classical theory of human action: a description of the specific virtues, vices, actions, and rules that make up a "practice" in the MacIntyrian sense. These are the actions the habitual practice of which constitutes what Paul means by a just practice (Rom 5) and a life free from the sinful passions of the body and serving God obediently (Rom 6–8).

---

1. I take it that this is what Troels Engberg-Pedersen, *Paul*, 262, means when he says that Paul "wishes these so called ethical matters to be understood as actually constituting the very content of the movement I*X."

Romans 12-15 as the Practice of the Body of Christ

Specifically, I argue that Paul claims that this is the body of the true φρόνιμοι, so that she who is part of it is the true Sage. In it the central virtue of ἀγάπη is advocated over and against other well-known antique virtues as the means to τὸ ἀγαθός. Throughout we find the exhortation to humility and abandonment of honor in favor of submission to persecution and even death that is typical of Christ. As Christ's body, the church could act in no other way. At the heart of this virtue of ἀγάπη, I suggest, stands the practice of ἡ ἀγάπη, the "love feast" or Eucharistic meal.[2] Indeed, I argue, it is from this instantiation of Christ's body that the church's practice of Christ takes its particular Christic forms of life.

In these chapters, I suggest, everything is, in one way or another, literally the practice of Christ's body. This is Paul's explication of what it means to do everything like, or rather, as, Christ. The structure and topics of Rom 12:1—15:6 unfold as one progression, which begins with the logic of the Agape as the embodiment of the community as the body of Christ. This section of the letter can be separated into three main divisions, the third of which takes up the majority of space:

a. 12:1-2   Transition and introduction
b. 12:3-8   Prologue: The Gifted Virtues of Christ's Body
c. 12:9—15:6   Partaking of the Agape Unhypocritcally
   i. 12:9-21   A Critique of the Philosophy of Honor
   ii. 13:1-7   Loving the Romans
   iii. 13:8-14   Agape and Christ
   iv. 14:1—5:6   Food at the Agape

After a dense transitional opening (12:1-2), the second section (12:3-8) is Paul's description of the church as the Body of Christ and its division into what are usually called different "ministries." But what Paul says here is that this is the practice (πρᾶξις) of the body, and I shall suggest below that Paul here enumerates the different virtues of Christ's body. The third section (12:9—15:13) I read as an extended instruction on the proper

---

2. I use Love Feast, Agape, Lord's Supper, and Eucharist in what follows all to refer to the same meal with bread and the cup around which the worshipping church gathered. I do not shy away from using "Eucharist" since, as I will show, I think Paul also used this term along with the other synonyms. Nothing in the argument that follows depends on an overly detailed reconstruction of the specific nature of this worship-meal. I have in mind only a regular gathering of the community around shared food, in which (ideally) everyone was able to participate, regardless of ability to contribute. At some point in this meal there was shared a "cup of blessing" and "broken bread" which were respectively the blood and body of Christ. See below for the literature.

The Practice of the Body of Christ

conduct for ἡ ἀγάπη (12:9),—the Love Feast or Eucharist. This section is of one piece with 12:3-8, since for Paul the Eucharist is exactly a "participation with the body and blood of Christ" (κοινωνία τοῦ αἵματος καὶ τοῦ σώματος τοῦ Χριστοῦ; 1 Cor 10:16). Thus Paul's discussion of the virtues of Christ's body flows directly and logically into his discussion of the practice in which they have communion with Christ's body.

Within this third section stand four interrelated sections, all of which set forth the practices in which the community partakes of the Agape unhypocritically (12:9). In the first section (12:9-21) Paul introduces two themes that he will then develop in the following: practices internal to the church and practices external to it (i.e., domestic and foreign policy). The latter Paul takes up in the second subsection (13:1-7) by advocating peaceful relations with the superpower, and the former he takes up in the long section on food preferences at the Agape (14:1—15:6).[3]

All these sections are connected to the Agape and the prologue on Christ's body because if the church is Christ's body, functions as his body-parts, and is nourished as such by his body and blood, then this requires a certain way of life, a certain discipline. The church must practice Christ since to fail to practice Christ means to fail to be Christ, the very participation and identification in which their salvation consists. All of these imperatives then, are a command to continue to be Christians, to be Christ by their virtues (12:3-8, cf. 13:11-14), by their liturgy (12:9, cf. 12:6-8, 14:6), by their relations with each other (14:1—15:7), with those who persecute them (12:14-21), with the Roman authorities (13:1-7), and with their neighbors (13:8-10).

The argument proceeds as follows. First, before coming directly to exegesis of 12:3-8, I make several extended arguments regarding its context and theology, and it is here that I deal with Rom 14—15:6. In light of this foundational piece I then come back to the transition in 12:1-2. I then move on and show that the remainder of the passage Rom 12:9—13:14 is best read in light of 12:3-8 specifically and Rom 5-8 more generally. I then tie all of this together and point us towards the final chapter.

---

3. I treat Rom 14—15:6 in the argument of this chapter, but only in arguing that its context is Eucharistic. I do not come back again and give a full exegesis, for this is not my concern here. Happily, this means that I do not get bogged down in all the difficult issues surrounding who exactly the strong and the weak are, what the problems entail, etc. My argument is rather that this section simply fits my hypothesis that Rom 12-15 largely treats liturgical concerns, since the section regards what sort of food is appropriate to eat, and the main context in which we know of Christians eating together is the Lord's Supper.

Rom 12:3-8: The Charismatic Virtues of Christ's Body

Introduction

In Rom 12:3 Paul moves from his transition in 12:1-2 (treated below) to an explication of the how the church is to live as Christ's body. Rom 12:3-8 constitutes the center of the praxeological content of salvation in Christ. These verses depend upon the discussion of Rom 5-8 and 12:1-2 and point the way forward to an explication of the minutiae of community life. In other words, these verses are something of a hinge between the macro-level of salvation previously set out in Rom 5-8, and the microcosm of salvation as it is practiced at the level of the local church.

But before I come to give my reading of this section, I have to set out some broader intricacies of Pauline theology and of the topic of Rom 12—15:1 Cor 10-14, and especially 1 Cor 12 are important here, since these texts allow us to appreciate salient traits about Paul's doctrine of the body of Christ that do not show up in the more condensed account of Romans 12:3-8.[4] I come back to treat this entire section below, but several smaller studies are prerequisite.

Body, City and Virtue

The center of Rom 12:3-8 is Paul's statement that καθάπερ γὰρ ἐν ἑνὶ σώματι πολλὰ μέλη ἔχομεν, τὰ δὲ μέλη πάντα οὐ τὴν αὐτὴν ἔχει πρᾶξιν, οὕτως οἱ πολλοὶ ἓν σῶμά ἐσμεν ἐν Χριστῷ, τὸ δὲ καθ' εἷς ἀλλήλων μέλη. It is well known that Paul was not the first to name a group of people a "body." The best collection of this literature into one place is the study by Lee.[5] There is no reason to re-present the evidence at length.[6] However,

---

4. Thus Horrell, *Solidarity*, 121, thinks that Rom 12:3-8 is a "summary" of 1 Cor 12. On the relationship of the two pericopes see principally Fee, *Presence*, 146-203, 605-11, 886-89.

5. Lee, *Body of Christ*, 29-45; the whole work is relevant. Puzzling is the use of Cicero throughout the work indiscriminately as a Stoic per se. Of course, Cicero explicitly says at various places that he is not an adherent to any particular school, but that on each issue he weighs the arguments of each and comes to the appropriate conclusion. This, however, if anything, would only *strengthen* her argument by broadening her base.

6. See esp. Seneca, *Ira.* 2.31.6-8; Cicero, *Top.* 6.30, *Off.* 1.7.22, *Fin.* 3.19.645; Dio Chrysostom, *Apam.* 41.9, 2 *Tars.* 34.20, *Nicaeen* 39.5, 3*Reg* 3.108; Dionysus of Halicarnassus *Ant. Rom.* 6.86; Livy, *History of Rome* 2.32.8-12. Parts of society were also variously identified as different parts of the body: belly (Plutarch *Cor.* 6.2-3;); head (Philo *QG* 2.9, *Praem.* 125, 114, *Abr.* 74.). On disease: Philo, *Decal* 150; Dio Chyrsostom 2

one connection that neither Lee nor others make is that action discourse in classical terms is fundamentally a discourse about the *body* in an even stronger way than we have seen so far. MacIntyre does not highlight this, but for many of the classical authors he treats, the body is utilized to describe human action, human society and human relationships, in a mutually parasitic way, so that to talk about human action is to talk about the body and vise versa. This is vitally important for understanding the dynamics of Rom 12–15.

Aristotle speaks of the body at the beginning of both his *Nicomachean Ethics* and his *Politics*. In the former, he discusses happiness as the ultimate end of human action, since it is the reason that all other things are pursued, and it is pursued to no further end. He then asks what constitutes this happiness by inquiring into the function/work (ἔργον) of man[7]: "Must we not assume that, just as the eye, the hand, the foot, and each of the various members manifestly has a certain function (ἔργον) of its own, so a human being also has a certain function over and above all the functions of his particular members?"[8] The equation is familiar enough, but the context is important. Aristotle goes on to say that the function/work of the human being is the exercise of virtue.

> Now if the function (ἔργον) of man is an activity of soul which follows or at any rate is not without rational principle, and if we say "so-and-so" and "a good so-and-so" have a function which is the same in kind, e.g., a lyre, and a good lyre-player, and so without qualification in all cases, supremacy of virtue (ἀρετήν) in respect of goodness being added to the function (for the function of a lyre-player is to play the lyre, and that of a good lyre-player is to do so well): if this is the case, and we state the function of man to be a certain kind of life, and this to be an activity or actions (ἐνέργειαν καὶ πράξεις) of the soul implying a rational principle, and the function of a good man to be the good and noble performance of these, and if any action is well-performed when it is performed in accordance with the appropriate virtue (τὴν ἀρετήν): if this is the case, human good turns out to be activity of soul in accordance with virtue (κατ' ἀρετήν), and if

---

Tars. 34.20; Josephus, *B.J.* 4.406–7; Dio Chrysostom, *Isthmus.* 9.1–2; Marcus Aurelius *Med* 2.1; Epictetus, *Diatr.* 2.10.2–4, 2.5.24–8. Some of this material is also covered, but quite thinly, in Kim, *Christ's Body in Corinth*, 39–64.

7. I use "man" here and in what follows advisedly, since for Aristotle women are not really capable of the good life in the same way that men are. Nevertheless, as with the English "man," his ἄνθρωπος at least grammatically includes them.

8. Aristotle, *N.E.* 1.7.12. Translations are from the Loeb with modifications.

there are many virtues (αἱ ἀρεταί), in accordance with the best and most complete.[9]

The reference to the body is not, in this instance, primarily focused on pointing out the ways that it is a microcosm of a *society* (Aristotle will do that too, see below), but to show that it is a microcosm of *human action*. The members of the body perform certain actions and functions (the preferred word is πράξεις) in better or worse ways depending upon what the good for that certain part of the body is which contributes more or less to the good of the whole body. In the same way a man performs πράξεις better or worse in reference to the good for man. To perform this function well is to practice it according to virtue. As we have learned from MacIntyre, a virtue is a tendency to practice that leads to the attainment of the good for man and to be virtuous is to tend to act in pursuit of the good.

Directly after this theorizing about the nature of the good and the function of man, he says: "Let this serve as an outline of the good; for we must presumably first sketch it roughly, and then later fill in the details. But it would seem that any one is capable of carrying on and articulating what has once been well outlined."[10] These details, it must be remembered, however, are not merely the "expression" or the "outworking" of some good that has been ascertained theoretically. Rather, the good itself can only be attained for Aristotle in *action*: the good cannot be other than the-good-that-is-practiced. He says that "we identify the telos with certain actions and activities; for thus it falls among goods of the soul and not among external goods . . . We have defined happiness practically as a sort of good life and good action."[11]

As in the *Ethics*, body-discourse is fundamental to the work he sets himself to do in the *Politics*. He writes:

> The polis is by nature clearly prior to the family and to each of us (ἕκαστος ἡμῶν), since the whole is of necessity prior to the part; for example, if the whole body be destroyed, there will be no foot or hand, except in an equivocal sense, as we might speak of a stone hand; for when destroyed the hand will be no better than that. But things are defined by their function and power (τῷ ἔργῳ καὶ τῇ δυνάμει); and we ought not to say that they are the same, but only that they have the same name.[12]

---

9. *N.E.* 1.7.14–15.
10. *N.E.* 1.7.16.
11. *N.E.* 1.8.1.
12. *Pol.* 1253a19–25.

The word σῶμα is not used in this passage, but the reference of the body is obvious. Feet and hands are secondary to the whole in the same way that the person and the family are secondary to the primary unit of social relations, the polis. Each person (Aristotle does not know the word or concept "individual") thus is who he is by his place in the whole polis, and this place is marked out by its "function and power."

That Aristotle uses the same words here to define the place of each in the polis as he did defining the nature of human action in the *Ethics* is anything but incidental. For the proper function of the human turns out to be just that action which fits his place in the polis and leads to its flourishing. The two uses of the body-discourse are really of the same grammatical piece. Here, however, Aristotle's point is that each part is dependent upon the whole in such a way that without the whole it will be nothing and that without its proper relation to the whole in terms of its *function* therein, it has ceased to be what it is called.

Thus life-together-for-a-common-goal, or what Aristotle called κοινωνία, is part of what it means to be truly human:

> The proof that the polis is a creation of nature and prior to each of us is that each of us, when isolated, is not self-sufficing; and therefore he is like the various body parts in relation to the whole. But he who is unable to live in society (κοινωνεῖν), or who has no need because he is sufficient for himself, must be either a beast or a god: he is no part of a polis. An instinct towards life-together (ὁρμὴ ἐπὶ κοινωνίαν) is in all men by nature.

Beasts and gods are mentioned not because of their respective moral qualities, but precisely because they are not *human*: they are two *other types of beings* in the world. A human, however, is by definition part of κοινωνία, and so if something is *not* part of it, that thing must be some other being that does not take part of κοινωνία, such as a beast or a god. Conversely, it is important to notice just why beasts and gods are not part of κοινωνία: they are no part of a *polis*. At this point, therefore, Aristotle has made a three-point identification: human = participant in a polis = κοινωνία. Moreover, he says, body-parts are always what they are *only* in virtue of being related to the whole and so to the other members. Thus the way that the items in the threefold identification mutually define one another is itself internal to the body-polis discourse with which he began.

But there is one more important item in the equation, as we might expect from our discussion of the *Ethics*, and that is virtue. Aristotle continues:

> Man, when perfected (τελεωθέν), is the best of all living things, but, when separated from law and justice, he is the worst of all; since injustice that has weapons is most troublesome, and man has weapons, born with wisdom and virtue (φύεται φρονήσει καὶ ἀρετῇ), which he may use for their opposite ends. So if he is without virtue (ἄνευ ἀρητῆς), he is the most unholy and the most savage of animals, and the most full of lust and gluttony. So righteousness has to do with the polis (or: is political—ἡ δικαιοσύνη πολιτικόν). For justice is a particular ordering of life-together in the polis. Justice is a decision about what is just. (ἡ γὰρ δίκη πολιτικῆς κοινωνίας τάξις ἐστιν, ἡ δὲ δίκη τοῦ δικαίου κρίσις.).[13]

This is a dense paragraph that is much more coherent in Greek than in contemporary English. The central point for our purposes is that to speak of the nature of a polis' κοινωνία is to treat of the virtues and vices. This is because, as we saw above, one's function vis-à-vis the polis is spoken of in terms of either fulfilling that function or failing to do so. To fulfill it is to practice virtues and to fail is to practice vices. But this is also, of course, part and parcel of what it is to be human, since to be human is to be a participant in the polis. So, says Aristotle, man is born with a great potential to be either the best of animals or the worst. His point in this paragraph is that virtue is a political matter, for all that comes before leads up to his conclusion that "righteousness is political." What he means, we can tell by the context, is that the matters of wisdom and virtue or their lack have everything to with the way the polis is run, not least because vice and virtue are weapons (ὅπλα), that presumably will either fight for or harm the city. The polis both trains men into their virtues and is composed of the collection of those virtues that simply are the polis's nature, since each of its embodied virtues are part of the "work" or "function" (ἔργον) of that polis. A man's δικαιοσύνη, therefore, or the nature of his "wisdom and virtue" are all matters for the polis. This means further that δίκη, or the practice of administering justice within the polis, is concerned with the order of the life-together of the polis, for the nature of that life simply is the constitution of its vices and virtues.

Taking a step back from these texts, then, we can discern the basic structure of Aristotle's body-discourse and see that it stands firmly within a classical account of action. We can trace the movement from the nature of the polis as body to the functioning of its virtues. The body is a microcosm of the polis, and the latter gives sense to the former. This observation

---

13. *Pol.* 1253a30–40, AT.

means that *Aristotle is not calling on the human body as a metaphor to "explain" the polis*—at least not a metaphor in the usual sense. Rather, the polis and the human body are so tightly bound up in one another as to be mutually dependent upon (what we think of as) "each other" for description. Body and polis form a single grammatical concept, a sort of body-polis (which of course comes close to coming into English in our logism "body-politic"). The human body and the polis have certain functions only in relation to the functioning of the whole. These "functions" are the virtues of the respective body-parts, reflecting the communal and political nature of the body-polis. The virtues and vices, as actions, are therefore the practices or actions that make up the κοινωνία that *is* the body-polis. In other words, without those actions the body-polis simply would not exist.

Aristotle is probably the most theoretical and abstract thinker who wrote on the "body." I have no wish to claim that Paul knew Aristotle. Rather, Aristotle serves as a convenient point of entrance into several other thinkers whose work is less systematized and complete. Chief among these for our purposes is Cicero in his work *De Officiis*:

> Well then, for a man to take something from his neighbor and to profit by his neighbor's loss is more contrary to nature than is death or poverty or pain or anything else that can affect either our person or our property. For, in the first place, injustice is fatal to social life and fellowship between people. For, if we are so disposed that each, to gain some personal profit, will defraud or injure his neighbor, then those bonds of human society, which are most in accord with Nature's laws, must of necessity be broken. Suppose, by way of comparison, that each one of our bodily members should conceive this idea and imagine that it could be strong and well if it should draw off to itself the health and strength of its neighboring member, the whole body would necessarily be enfeebled and die; so, if each one of us should seize upon the property of his neighbors and take from each whatever he could appropriate to his own use, the bonds of human society must inevitably be annihilated. For, without any conflict with nature's laws, it is granted that everybody may prefer to secure for himself rather than for his neighbor what is essential for the conduct of life; but nature's laws do forbid us to increase our means, wealth, and resources by despoiling others.[14]

Cicero here works within the same framework we saw in Aristotle, but, again, less theoretically. He makes the point that the laws of nature bind

---

14. Cicero, *Off.* III.V.21–22.

human beings together in the same way that a body is bound together. To break the natural law of society is to put it at risk in the same way as a body should become sick and die if its members started attacking each other. The purpose of the passage is to ground human relationship in nature on both "sides" (polis and body). Nature has laws of human interaction that must be kept if society is not going to be "sick," and the human body is simply made by nature in such a way that its members must live in harmony.

This paragraph is foundational for the whole project in De Officiis: it serves the purpose of grounding all that comes after. This includes, of course, the virtues. Thus, the duties that nature dictate are explained by reference to the broader concept of justice, which is famously defined as giving to each his due. The tendency so to do in each situation is called a virtue, and Cicero divides the virtues, just slightly later in the passage above, into four mutually overlapping sections:

> All that is morally right rises from one of four sources: it is concerned either (1) with the full perception and intelligent development of the true; or (2) with the conservation of organized society, with rendering to every man his due, and with the faithful discharge of obligations assumed; or (3) with the greatness and strength of a noble and invincible spirit; or (4) with the orderliness and moderation of everything that is said and done, wherein consist temperance and self-control.

Into the first category fall the virtues of "wisdom and prudence," and into the final three all those virtues that are concerned with the proper maintenance of the Republic, such as magnanimity, consistency of demeanor, rectitude, dignity and self-control.[15] The discourse on the body is thus a moral discourse and moral discourse is talk about the virtues.

Further texts show just how normal such a connection between the body and human action described in terms of the virtues actually is. In his 95th Moral Epistle, after describing in detail how we should behave towards the gods, Seneca comes to a principle out of which all can be deduced: "Would you winover the gods? Then be a good man. Whoever imitates them, is worshipping them sufficiently."[16] Seneca then asks about inter-human relationships:

> Here is the second question: How we should behave toward people? What should we do? Which principles should we give? That we avoid shedding human blood? How small a thing it is

15. Ibid., III.V.16–17.
16. Seneca, Ep. 95.51.

> not to harm one whom you ought to benefit! Of course it is a great praise if one is gentle with another. Shall we take it upon ourselves to lend a hand to the shipwrecked, to show the way to the lost, to share our bread with the starving? Why should I ask all these things, the things to be desired and to be avoided, when I am able to hand down briefly to someone this formula for human duty (*humani officii*): all this which you see, in which both things human and divine are confined, is one. We are all members of a large body (*corporis*).[17]

Seneca here draws conclusions for human action from the fact that there are not really many bodies but one body. There should be no question for him about sharing one's bread with the hungry or of committing murder since all are one body and so to feed others is to feed oneself and to murder is to commit suicide. This is the *formula humani officii* ("the formula of human duty") in which all virtuous actions are grounded, and which produces a certain form of life. Seneca continues:

> Nature produced us related to one another, since she created us from the same source and to the same end. She engendered in us mutual affection, and made us prone to friendships. She established fairness and justice; according to her ruling, it is more wretched to commit than to suffer injury. Through her orders, let our hands be ready for all that needs to be helped. Let this verse be in your heart and on your lips: "I am a human; and nothing in the human lot do I deem foreign to me." Let us possess things in common; for birth is ours in common. Our relations with one another are like a stone arch, which would collapse if the stones did not mutually support each other, and which is upheld in this very way.

The reference to the arch highlights the fact that for Seneca the "body" is not a *mere* metaphor, but the very way of talking about human relations. The arch *is* such a metaphor, wherein each piece is held together and supported by every other piece. We can tell that the arch is metaphorical since it appears as a way of explicating the nature of society, *which simply is a body*. Thus the "body" and "society" are grammatically interdependent in a much stronger way than the body as an arch. Humans are to behave in a certain way toward each other because they have a common birth, just as the parts of the body share a common birth. Once again the explanations of body and society are mutually involving.

---

17. Ibid., 95.52–53.

Romans 12–15 as the Practice of the Body of Christ

"Now then, since we have considered the gods and men, let us see how we should make use of things." For this, Seneca tells us, "there must be a consideration of the virtues." There will have to be a fairly lengthy discussion of this, he says, since there are so many divergent opinions on the matter:

> Some persons will advise us to rate prudence very high, to cherish bravery, and to cleave more closely, if possible, to justice than to all other qualities. But this will do us no good if we do not know what virtue is, whether it is simple or compound, whether it is one or more than one, whether its parts are separate or interwoven with one another; whether he who has one virtue possesses the other virtues also; and just what are the distinctions between them.

So the same basic structure is visible in Seneca as we've seen previously. A discussion of the nature of human relationships and society as grounded in the nature of the body is made the foundation for speaking of proper conduct in the world in terms of the nature and content of the virtues.[18]

There are many other texts that we could look at, but the key characteristics of the discourse are clear enough to help us read Paul. Most basically, in classical discourse the body-as-society grounds the bonds that tie humanity together and require certain actions and prohibit others. Second, in our terms, body-discourse is action-discourse. Third, though, because body-discourse was used to talk about and ground discussions of law and the welfare of the polis, even if the polis has swollen to engulf the whole world (as in Seneca's cosmo-polis), it remains a political discourse.

Three Pneumatic Bodies

INTRODUCTION

Our second study preliminary to Rom 12:3–8 also concerns the body. Recently Stanley Stowers, in some ways following Dale Martin, has argued that understanding what Paul says about the body of Christ requires that we realize that for him πνεῦμα is a type of physical "material."[19] Stowers

---

18. As Margaret Mitchell points out in *Paul and the Rhetoric of Reconciliation*, 162, this is part and parcel of some Greco-Roman practice of speaking about the body: see Dio Chrysostom *Or.* 3.108–9, Isocrates, *Or.* 4.168, Plato *Resp.* 5.462b–e, Plutarch *Sol.* 18.5.

19. Stowers, "Pauline Participation"; Martin, *Body*.

draws on Hellenistic philosophy wherein πνεῦμα is the basic "stuff" out of which the world is made. Accordingly, those "in Christ participate in him because they share with him the most sublime type of pneuma, divine pneuma that he received in being raised from the dead."[20] To claim that the Spirit and the body of Christ share a physicality is but to try to work out the insight of Albert Schweitzer (he called it *Leiblichkeit*),[21] and J. A. T. Robinson has forcefully argued in this vein as well (without reference to Hellenistic philosophy).[22] I think the very grammar of Paul's letters demands something like such a reading, and so here I want to expound and critically nuance such an account, (giving some details that are sometimes lacking). To do this I draw largely on 1 Corinthians, suggesting that Robinson, Stowers, and Martin point us in the right direction, and that following their work we are led to see that Paul's account of the body of Christ is essentially sacramental and pneumatological (though only Robinson really presses things this far). This opens up our understanding of Paul's theology in Romans 12–15 in important respects. We will see below that I do not think this account of participation is incompatible with the sort of participation by practice I follow Hays in advocating. Indeed, I think understanding the Spirit in Paul demands that we hold both together.

Three Instances of Christ's Pneumatic Body

Paul says that baptism and the Eucharist are the ways that the church is the one body, which is Christ: "For you were baptized into one body by one πνεῦμα . . . and we all *drank* one πνεῦμα" (1 Cor 12:13). I suggest that here Paul names a two-part mechanism that leads to in-corporation: the spirit and the sacraments (ἐποτίσθημεν, ἐβαπτίσθημεν).[23] How does this work?

Christ has (or is), in his resurrected and ascended state, a σῶμα πνευματικόν. This conclusion arises from the fact that when in 1 Cor 15:44 he names the future resurrection body σῶμα πνευματικόν, he immediately grounds this claim in *Christ's* resurrection by saying that Ἐγένετο ὁ ἔσχατος Ἀδὰμ εἰς πνεῦμα ζῳοποιοῦν (15:45; cf. Gen 2:7). Christ's σῶ

---

20. Stowers, "Pauline Participation," 356. Cf. Martin, *Corinthian Body*, 104-36.
21. Noted by Stowers, "Pauline Participation," 354.
22. Ibid., 354; Robinson, *Body*.
23. On these two rituals as foundational in Paul's churches see Horrell, *Solidarity*, 110. By "sacraments" I refer to baptism and the Eucharist, whatever exactly those events looked like for Paul. See Horrell, 102-4; Marshall, *Last Supper*, 107-40.

μα πνευματικόν is not a "spiritual body" but a "body-made-of-πνεῦμα."[24] As Martin says, this is a "pneumatic body—that is a body composed only of pneuma with [the lower elements] sarx and psyche having been sloughed off along the way."[25] To say "spiritual body," as Martin shows, is to invite many anachronistic misunderstandings.[26] That Christ has a σῶμα πνευματικόν, on the other hand, affirms that Christ actually has a *body*, but that this body is made out of God's special material, πνεῦμα.[27] Of course the body that Christ is made up of for Paul is not just any old πνεῦμα, not the πνεῦμα that is the ancient analog to the "atom"—that which undergirds everything as its smallest component part—but God's very own πνεῦμα (cf. Rom 1:4, 8:9), holy πνεῦμα. It is this material with which the church communes in order to become united to Christ, precisely because Christ is currently made up of this πνεῦμα. "The same *stuff* makes Christ and believers contiguous."[28] And, I argue, for Paul, the church communes with Christ's σῶμα πνευματικόν through the means of baptism and the cup and bread.

First, baptism. 1 Cor 12:13 is usually translated "we were all baptized in one spirit into one body." This rendering is problematic, however, since it spiritualizes the one succinct, unitary action Paul names. "We were all plunged in one Spirit into one body" is closer to the sense of the Greek ἐβαπτίσθημεν.[29] This "plunging" or "dipping" is the initial act of incorporation, an assumption into the one πνεῦμα that is Christ's body.[30] In other words, the water in the sacrament symbolizes the πνεῦμα *that is, materially, Christ*.[31] This makes symbolic sense if for Paul, as Martin and Stowers emphasize, πνεῦμα would not have been incorporeal, but rather the fine, fluid material that gives form to other, more solid bodies. What Paul seems to be saying is that in baptism the convert is subsumed into Christ's

24. The foremost proponent of the usual rendering as "spiritual body" is Thiselton, *First Corinthians*, 1278-9, who thinks that this is a body whose "desires" and "character" are in line with the Holy Spirit. While this is no doubt true, Paul is saying nothing so mundane, not least because it is unclear how this would advance his argument at all in 1 Cor 15.

25. Martin, *Corinthian Body*, 126.

26. Ibid., 7-37.

27. So Lee, *Paul*, 49-58, Martin, *Corinthian Body*, 7-37. Both these contain extensive reference to ancient physics.

28. Stowers, "Pauline Participation," 358.

29. Oepke, "βάπτω, βαπτίζω, κτλ" in *TDNT* 1:529-30.

30. On being added to Christ by baptism see Best, *One Body*, 97.

31. Ibid., 97.

σῶμα πνευματικόν as she is taken into a body of water. Thus, Schweitzer is right: the "Spirit comes to the believer from Christ *as* the Spirit of Christ."³²

But this is not all. After baptism there is another, ongoing communion with the πνεῦμα that happens in the reception of the body and blood of the Lord: we all "were given one Spirit to drink" (ἓν πνεῦμα ἐποτίσθημεν). This meal is the κοινωνία τοῦ σώματος τοῦ Χριστοῦ (1 Cor 10:17). I infer from these texts, therefore, that in the κυριακὸν δεῖπνον (1 Cor 11:20) the church consumes the very πνεῦμα in which the risen body of Christ consists (1 Cor 10:3-4: τὸ πνευματικὸν βρῶμα καὶ τὸ πνευματικὸν πόμα; cf. 1 Cor 15:45: Ἐγένετο ὁ ἔσχατος Ἀδὰμ εἰς πνεῦμα ζῳοποιοῦν): Christ is passed on to the church in the material substance of his crucified and resurrected being and in this way the church is constituted as Christ.³³ The Eucharistic meal consists of pneumatic bread and pneumatic cup, because Christ's resurrected body is pneumatic and the meal is for consumption of and communion (κοινωνία) with Christ himself (τοῦτό μού ἐστιν τὸ σῶμα).³⁴ In a physical sense then, the church materially participates (μετέχομεν; 1 Cor 12:13) in Christ's pneumatic body through the Lord's supper (cf. 1 Cor 6:17: ὁ δὲ κολλώμενος τῷ κυρίῳ ἓν πνεῦμά ἐστιν).

The further point can be pressed that if Christ is πνεῦμα, and if the church receives that πνεῦμα by the bread and cup, the *bread and cup* can be called both πνεῦμα *and* the body/blood of Christ himself. We've already cited the Apostle saying τοῦτό μού ἐστιν τὸ σῶμα (1 Cor 11:25), πάντες ἓν πνεῦμα ἐποτίσθημεν (1 Cor 12:13), and τὸ πνευματικὸν βρῶμα καὶ τὸ πνευματικὸν πόμα (1 Cor 10:3-4). Though of course saying nothing of later technical discussions about the "nature" of the "elements," Paul's grammar of the bread and cup urges the conclusion that they too might be properly called σῶμα πνευματικόν, as τὸ πνευματικὸν βρῶμα καὶ τὸ πνευματικὸν πόμα comes quite close to doing.³⁵ Thus, Robinson thinks that we have

---

32. Schweitzer, *Mysticism*, 165. This particular aspect of baptism certainly need not exclude the other important aspect of dying and rising. In fact, this reading makes that sense even a bit sharper. Rom 6:3 says that ὅσοι ἐβαπτίσθημεν εἰς Χριστὸν Ἰησοῦν, εἰς τὸν θάνατον αὐτοῦ ἐβαπτίσθημεν: "as many of us as were dipped into Christ Jesus were dipped into his death." Thus, the union with the πνεῦμα that is Christ means union also with the story of his death and resurrection. See Tannehill, *Dying*, 55-70.

33. The strongest emphasis on this, though without the proper focus on the pneumatic nature of the sacrament, comes from the Catholic Cerfaux, *Church*, 265: "We must remember, and emphasize strongly that . . . ἓν σῶμα refers to the body of Christ, his real and individual body, become present in the Eucharist."

34. On the Lord's Supper and the Spirit see Schweitzer, *Mysticism*, 171.

35. Some may want to contextualize the identification of this reference to the Eucharistic elements since Paul is using a typology from the OT, but he weaves the

to "bring together under a single treatment the Pauline doctrine of what is usually differentiated as the glorified, the mystical and the Eucharistic body of Christ, along with the Christians' hope of the resurrection and the renewal of his own body. The clue to the unity of Paul's thought at this point lies in the connection . . . of all this with the flesh-body of the incarnate Jesus. For [Paul's] whole doctrine of the Church is an extension of his Christology."[36]

We would not be wrong, therefore, in seeing in Paul's statements the traditional doctrine of the threefold instance of the body of Christ: the body of Christ the Ascended Lord in heaven, the body of Christ that is the Eucharist, and the body of Christ that is the church. That Christ has a σῶμα πνευματικόν explains the consistent connection which exists in Pauline texts (like these) between the Spirit and the body. To be "in the Spirit" is to be incorporated, and to be the body of Christ is to "have" the Spirit. Christ's-resurrected-and-ascended-body-made-of-πνεῦμα communes with and is part of Christ's-body-the-church-that-is-made-of-πνεῦμα by baptism into the one body of the πνεῦμα, and the church is nourished *with* Christ's own body—a pneumatic food—Christ's-Eucharistic-body-made-of-πνεῦμα, which imparts the Spirit of the risen Christ (cf. Eph 4:4: ἓν σῶμα καὶ ἓν πνεῦμα).[37] So, again Robinson is right that "to say that the Church is the body of Christ is no more of a metaphor than to say that the flesh of the incarnate Jesus or the bread of the Eucharist is the body of Christ. None of them is 'like' his body (Paul never says this): each of them *is* the body of Christ, in that each is the physical complement and extension of the one and the same Person and Life."[38]

---

two stories (of the Israelites and the Corinthians) together so seamlessly that such a separation is hard to make. In any case, it is clear that Paul makes the analogy in the first place *because of* the cup and bread used in the Lord's Supper (cf. 1 Cor 10:4: ἡ πέτρα δὲ ἦν ὁ Χριστός).

36. Robinson, *Body*, 49.

37. Lee, *Paul*, 131, makes gestures in this direction: "Paul refers to the result of the Spirit's work ontologically, citing the Spirit's agency in causing the believers to becomes parts of the body. This ontological implication is similar to that in Stoic physics, where only those bodies held together by a pervasive pneu/ma can rightly be called unified bodies."

38. Robinson, *Body*, 50.

The Practice of the Body of Christ

Sacramental Reception of the Spirit

At this point we can nuance our analysis further. Against the usual understandings of the Spirit in Paul, it is possible to argue that the *only* way that God gives the church this Spirit is through baptism and the Eucharist. It is usually assumed that there was a "charismatic" element of Pauline Christianity—that the Spirit was made available to those present at (something generically called) "worship" in a general way regardless of participation in the elements of the Love Feast. This picture is of the Spirit penetrating or invading the body from outside, from the atmosphere or air outside of the body (as it were), through the skin and into the relevant centers of behavior, emotion or intellect. This is the unspoken assumption undergirding every work on the Spirit that I am aware of.[39]

But it is hard to construct such a picture from Pauline texts. I do not wish to deny that the Spirit *functions* or *acts* in the church outside the sacramental context. I am concerned here with the way it is *received*, both initially, and in terms of ongoing communion. The only way one has the Spirit, I am claiming, is by receiving it at baptism and feeding on it at the Eucharist. Paul *simply does not indicate that Christians receive it in any other way*. Several important texts deserve treatment to substantiate this observation.

The most obvious is 1 Cor 10–14, as this undeniably addresses the liturgical, Eucharistic assembly. This may be evidence that Paul thought that the gifts function *mainly* in liturgical contexts. The reason Paul gives that the Corinthians have the Spirit is not that they have been invaded by

---

39. Good surveys of NT scholarship on the spirit through the 1960s are available in Jewett, *Paul's Anthropological Terms*, 56-88, and Vos, *Paulinischen Pneumatologie*, 1–15. (This note is based largely on these two works; I refer the reader to their extensive bibliographies. Significant works subsequent to about 1970 are cited below.) There are five major "schools" as far as I can make out: (1) *Spirit as principle of Christian life*. Pleiderer and his followers argued that the spirit was a natural part of the Pauline development of the concept of spirit in the early church, and that it slowly became the dominant principle of Paul's theology. 2) *Spirit makes present God's eschatological reign*. Gunkel inaugurated what is today the most common position: the spirit makes present God's eschatological reign, and so "life in the spirit" naturally involves an eschatological ethic. More recently see Fee, *Presence*. (3) *Spirit as cosmic power*. Everling's work, and most famously that of Deissmann, argues that the spirit is at war with the flesh in a cosmic battle that determines behavior. (4) *Spirit as OT ethic*. This position holds that Paul's ethic draws on the work of the spirit in the Old Testament, perhaps most convincingly with reference to Jeremiah's renewed hearts. Horn, *Angeld*, extends this view in some interesting directions. (5) *Spirit as Hellenistic ethic*. Scholars all the way back to Pfleiderer have noted "Hellenistic" elements in Paul's use of the Spirit.

the Spirit from the outside, but because they have been "plunged in one Spirit," and because they have received it in the cup and the bread (1 Cor 11:32, 12:13). There is no indication that the Spirit enters members of the church from outside by penetration or osmosis.

But must this not surely be an overstatement? Are there not many other texts that speak differently? There are, of course, numerous texts that deal with various other aspects of the Spirit, but the specific topic of the manner of its *reception* only shows up in two others. There Paul seems to explicitly make the reception of the Spirit dependent on πίστις:

Gal 3:2   ἐξ ἔργων νόμου τὸ πνεῦμα ἐλάβετε ἢ ἐξ ἀκοῆς πίστεως;
Gal 3:13 ἵνα τὴν ἐπαγγελίαν τοῦ πνεύματος λάβωμεν διὰ τῆς πίστεως.

Happily, we need not delve into debate about the various translation values of πίστεως here.[40] I need its meaning only in so far as it is something other than baptism and Eucharist. But the mention of πίστις in this connection raises a potential difficulty for my theory. Paul seems to indicate two different ways of receiving the Spirit: baptism and the Eucharist in 1 Cor on the one hand and πίστις in Gal on the other. What are we to make of this?

While realizing that neither the context of Gal 3 nor 1 Cor 12 give us as much information as we would like, the simplest interpretive solution is that the reception of the Spirit at baptism and its reception on the basis of πίστις are the moment: being baptized and gaining πίστις (however rendered) happen at the *same time*. However such a theological alignment might work out specifically (which comes first, etc.), the details we do have regarding these two events are usually held, and with good reason, to bear somehow on initiation into the church.

This is so in what must have been an early baptismal saying that aligns τὴν ἑνότητα τοῦ πνεύματος with εἷς κύριος, μία πίστις, ἓν βάπτισμα, εἷς θεὸς καὶ πατὴρ πάντων, ὁ ἐπὶ πάντων καὶ διὰ πάντων καὶ ἐν πᾶσιν (Eph. 4:3-6).[41] Galatians itself, in its one reference to baptism, makes it apposite to πίστις in the chiasm: Πάντες γὰρ υἱοὶ θεοῦ ἐστε διὰ τῆς <u>πίστεως</u> ἐν Χριστῷ Ἰησοῦ· ὅσοι γὰρ εἰς Χριστὸν <u>ἐβαπτίσθητε</u>, Χριστὸν ἐνεδύσασθε

---

40. I mean, of course, the various translation values of πίστις current in modern scholarship, ranging from "faith" to "belief" to "trust" to "faithfulness" to "fidelity" to "loyalty," and the various referents of the term, ranging from the Christian's πίστις to Christ's πίστις to πίστις as "the Faithful One."

41. Thus, rightly, Meeks, *Urban Christians*, 150-57.

(3:26-7). Thus, at the end of the same argument that Paul begins in Gal 3:2 with the reference to receiving the Spirit through πίστις, he is able to *predicate* πίστις on baptism: "*Because* (γὰρ) as many of you as were dipped into Christ have put on Christ, you are all sons of God διὰ τῆς πίστεως ἐν Χριστῷ Ἰησοῦ." Thus, not only are baptism and πίστις mutually inclusive parts of the same sacramental act of initiation, but the latter is actually *dependent upon* the former. Though of course we know next to nothing about what the Pauline baptismal rite involved (surely to name it Pauline must be wrong), from this text we might surmise that being dipped into Christ is the primary act of initiation, an act which shows or vows πίστις.[42]

But if this is the case, and Paul thinks of the Spirit as primarily being received in baptism, why in Gal 3 does he not just oppose *baptism* to the works of the Torah and not πίστις? I suggest the answer lies in the specific argument of the letter to the Galatians, in which Paul for the first time (and perhaps the first time in Christian history) highlighted πίστις as an essential part of the Christian life. He was forced to this by his opponents, who, Martyn and Campbell *inter alia* suggest, were using the texts from Genesis 17 about Abraham to convince Paul's converts that in order to be a part of God's covenant they needed to take up the Torah, including circumcision. In this familiar line of argument, Paul turned to Gen 15:6 to show that even in the Abraham-cycle God did not require circumcision for "righteousness."[43] Rather, God required only that one ἐπίστευσεν or could be said to have πίστις. He then found Hab 2:4 to back this up, which predicated eschatological life not on works of the Torah but on πίστις: ὁ δίκαιος ἐκ πίστεως ζήσεται.

So far most are in agreement. But the further conclusion that has not been adequately appreciated is that it is this exchange with the Teachers that first brings out πίστις as central to Pauline theology.[44] Outside of Galatians and Romans Paul uses the word sparingly. But in Gal 3 πίστις becomes a central characteristic of his position because he has found it in a counter-text (Gen 15:6) to defend his claim that Gentiles need not be circumcised. Finding it appropriate to place πίστις alongside baptism as activities of initiation, he speaks of πίστις as the time when they received the Spirit. In Gal 3:2, in other words, Paul is asking the Galatians to decide whether their *way of life* in the reception of the Spirit at their conversion

---

42. Again we need not decide for our argument if this is the πίστις of the convert or of Christ.

43. Martyn, *Galatians*, 302–5, 457–66. Campbell, *Deliverance*, 495–510.

44. My thanks to Professor Campbell for pointing this out to me.

was characteristic of their practice of πίστις, or alternatively of ἔργα νόμου, and in so doing he is asking them to decide between the Teacher's proof text(s) and his.[45]

We can go further. If it is true that Paul develops πίστις as characteristic of Christian conversion at this point in a manner that surpasses its importance in his theology at any previous point, then it is likely that Paul thought of πίστις as *one characteristic* of the baptizand, and not as a sort of second entrance requirement. Nor does it appear to be the case that baptism is the *expression of* πίστις, or that πίστις is "required" for baptism. Nowhere in the other passages that mention baptism is πίστις part of the equation (Rom 6:1-14; 1 Cor 1:13-17, 12:12-13, 15:29-30): Gal 3:26-27 is the *only* passage where they come into any sort of relationship with one another, and there πίστις is dependent upon baptism.

I suggest, therefore, that the impression that we get from 1 Corinthians is substantially correct, and that for Paul the two primary, and, from what we have in his letters, the *only* vessels of communion with the πνεῦμα of Christ are the dominical sacraments. What this means is that there is a two-fold contact of the church with the πνεῦμα: the first at the time of baptism which provides the initial incorporation into Christ's body, and the second, providing ongoing communion with Christ's body in the consumption of the Eucharistic elements.

Sacraments and Spirit in Pauline Theology

Two further observations. First, this way of construing the church's relationship with the Spirit is at least as theologically coherent as the usual "osmosis" theory. For the latter, usually the sacraments for Paul have very little or nothing to do with the communion of the Spirit.[46] This, coupled with the fact that the Spirit is undeniably central to Paul's theology in general, means that the sacraments are relegated to a secondary status (ironically, displaced by the Spirit). They appear as *ad hoc* actions having something to do with "identity" or "initiation" or "worship," but they are not central to Paul's ecclesiology or soteriology.[47] In other words, because of the incontestable centrality of the Spirit in Paul, a non-pneumatic read-

45. Martyn, *Galatians*, 328-33.

46. So, in addition to the works listed above, Furnish, *Theology*, 203. Cerfaux, *Church*, somehow manages to not even take up the Pauline sacraments *at all*.

47. Lee, *Paul*, 131-33, recognizes rightly that the sacraments must be important for Paul, but, following Meeks, *Urban Christians*, 150-62, gives them no part in his soteriology or ecclesiology apart from being "boundary markers."

ing of the sacraments ultimately obviates them. Pauline scholarship as it currently stands does not have any coherent place for the sacraments, so most studies fail to explain (e.g.) why Paul would quote a Eucharistic tradition in the first place (1 Cor 11:23–6).

Second, I contend that my sacramental reception theory is at least as cogent as a theory that sees the Pauline sacraments as pneumatic, but allow that the Spirit is received outside of them. For, again, why should the Spirit be mentioned constantly in such connection with baptism and the Eucharist if it is available outside of them? Current Pauline scholarship sees the *primary* reception of the Spirit in Paul as occurring outside the sacraments. But, if this is the case, why is any other further communion with it necessary?

Finally, this sacramental reception theory provides a much clearer rationale for why Paul discusses the gifts of the Spirit only and always in his discussions of the body of Christ (Rom 12:3–8, 1 Cor 12, Eph 4:1–16). Pauline charismata are given at the Eucharistic meal precisely because they depend on the Spirit's action for their functioning, and the Eucharistic meal is the only means post-baptism by which one consumes and receives the Spirit. This is why, in Corinth, problems having to do with the Spirit, whatever their exact nature, fall within the context of the Agape.

Most of this section has been dependent upon 1 Cor 10–14, and we are interested in Rom 12:3–8. So I want to be clear that I am not claiming that we should simply read the former into the latter, but rather that the former helps us to see possible connections in the latter that may be there already. Specifically, this discussion functions to further contextualize Rom 12–15 and 12:3–8 in particular. Paul does not talk about the pneumatic elements of the Eucharist: he presumes it—just as he presumes that his letter will be read the context of the Agape in the first place.

Η ΑΓΑΠΗ ΑΝΥΠΟΚΡΙΤΟΣ

Before coming to treat Rom 12:3–8 itself it is important to establish that the instruction given there concerns the church's worship and has to do specifically with the central act of communal worship for Paul's communities, the "Lord's Supper" or "Love Feast." One substantial anchor for such a claim is the relative plausibility with which we can translate ἡ ἀγάπη ἀνυπόκριτος in Rom 12:9 as "The Unhypocritcal Love Feast." To establish this I set out the evidence for such a translation in the history of earliest Christianity, from Paul's other letters, and finally from the context of

Romans, suggesting that this is a better reading than the traditional one. At that point I can read Rom 12:3–8 as enumerating gifts that have their proper setting in the Love Feast. In other words, I will argue that there is good reason to think that the roles Paul sets out are *liturgical* roles played at the Lord's Supper. That the gifts appear to fit well into such a ritual setting ends up, therefore, not just being a re-reading of 12:3–8 but also adding a degree of support for the case that the material that follows is predicated upon the Eucharist.

The Agape in the Early Church

The history of the use of ἀγάπη in reference to a liturgical meal has been written elsewhere and so here I merely give an overview of the evidence to emphasize how widely spread this linguistic practice was.[48]

First, within the NT corpus, Jude 12 speaks negatively of those who are "blemishes in your Love Feasts (ἐν ταῖς ἀγάπαις), feasting with you (συνευωχούμενοι) fearlessly." Of course, the date of Jude is notoriously difficult to establish, given so little material to work with, but it could be quite early and so attest to a usage not long after the time of Paul.[49] Second, the parallel passage in 2 Peter 2:13 speaks equally of the unsavory who "take pleasure reveling in the daytime . . . reveling and feasting at their Love Feasts (συνευωχούμενοι ἐν ταῖς ἀγάπαις) with you."[50]

Third, moving move outside the NT, Ignatius of Antioch writes in his *Letter to the Smyrneans* 8:2 that "it is not lawful either to baptize, or to hold a Love Feast (ἀγάπην ποιεῖν) without the consent of the bishop." That this sentence comes within a discussion of the Eucharist suggests that Ignatius does not distinguish the Love Feast from the Eucharist, the latter being so central and prominent a theme for him.

Jumping with the evidence from the beginning to the end of the second century, Tertullian says in his explanation of the Christian practice that "it is the practice of the Love Feast (*operatio dilectionis*) which makes some brand us with a mark of evil . . . Our Feast (*Coena nostra*) shows its nature in its name. It is named by the word which Love is among the Greeks (*Id vocatur quod dilectio penes Graecos*)."

---

48. On the nature of the earliest celebration of the Eucharist see Schweitzer, *Mysticism*, 251–58, and especially Horrell, "Pauline Churches," 185–203; more broadly McGowan, *Ascetic Eucharists*; Reicke, *Diakonie*.

49. Cole, *Love Feasts*, 55–56.

50. This is the reading to be preferred as found in A and B, as proposed by Cole 56–57. "Love Feasts" is an early reading even if it turns out to be secondary.

The Practice of the Body of Christ

Clement of Alexandria has much to say about the relation of the Love *Feast* to love itself as a virtue. He in fact seems to be concerned that his audience might conceive of love *only* in terms of the Feast, and not in terms of the virtue. For our purposes his discussion shows how common it was in the late-middle second century to call the Christian gathering the Love Feast:

> The Love Feast (ἡ ἀγάπη) is in truth celestial food, the banquet of reason. "It bears all things, endures all things, hopes all things. Love never fails." "Blessed is he who shall eat bread in the kingdom of God." But the hardest of all cases to make is for agape itself, which fails not, to be cast from heaven above to the ground into the midst of sauces. And do you imagine that I am thinking of a supper that is to be done away with? "For if," it is said, "I bestow all my goods, and have not agape, I am nothing." On this agape alone depend the law and the Word; and if "you shall love the Lord your God and your neighbor," this is the celestial festival in the heavens. But the earthly is called a supper, as has been shown from Scripture. For the supper is made for agape, but the supper is not agape itself, but only a proof of mutual and reciprocal kindly feeling. "Let not, then, your good be spoken of as evil; for the kingdom of God is not meat and drink," says the Apostle, in order that the meal spoken of may not be conceived as ephemeral, "but righteousness, and peace, and joy in the Holy Ghost." He who eats of this meal, the best of all, shall possess the Kingdom of God, fixing his regards here on the holy assembly of agape, the heavenly Church. Agape, then, is something pure and worthy of God, and its work is communication (ἡ μετάδοσις). "And the care of discipline is agape," as Wisdom says; "and agape is the keeping of the law." And these joys have an inspiration of agape from the public nutriment, which accustoms to everlasting dainties. Agape, then, is not a supper.[51]

Clement's concern is that because ἀγάπη was in fact lacking at ἡ ἀγάπη, the latter should not be used for the supper but for the virtue. What this means, of course, is that the central Christian meal was widely known as ἡ ἀγάπη.

Parallels Between Rom 12–15 and 1 Cor 8–14

Another reason for the proposed translation in 12:9 is that the material in Rom 12–15 is in some ways parallel to material in 1 Cor 8–14, where the

---

51. Clement of Alexandria, *Paed.* II.1.

context *is* demonstrably Eucharistic. Fortunately we do not need to solve all of the troublesome exegetical issues that surround these Corinthian chapters in order to make the relevant connections.

All of 1 Cor 10–14 (and we can include 1 Cor 8 in some ways too) concerns the Corinthian "worship assembly" in one way or another, and at its heart is the Eucharist. Hays sees this clearly.[52] 1 Cor 10 brings to a close the discussion of idol meat begun in 1 Cor 8 by connecting it with the Eucharist: "You are not able to drink the cup of the Lord and the cup of demons" (1 Cor 10:21). 1 Cor 11:2–16 urges women to cover their heads, unlike men, "while praying or prophesying" (11:4, 13).[53] The Lord's Supper itself is of course directly under discussion in 11:17–34. A few have held that this discussion is separate from the following one concerning gifts (1 Cor 12–14), but there is no basis for this distinction in the text.[54] It is simpler to imagine, not least on the grounds already set forth, one single assembly where the Spirit is received in the Eucharist (1 Cor 10–11) and practiced in the gifts (1 Cor 12–14). What this shows is one sure instance in which Paul treats all these related liturgical issues in a single stretch of text. I suggest he does the same in Romans.

Broadly, discussion topics in 1 Cor include kinds of food (1 Cor 8, 10), issues surrounding the Eucharist (1 Cor 10, 11), the body of Christ (1 Cor 12), the gifts of the Spirit (1 Cor 12, 14), and agape (1 Cor 13). Of course all of these topics are intertwined in complex ways, but they are all united under a discussion of the Corinthian assembly. But what has not been noticed is the parallelism of these topics with the discussion in Rom 12–15. There we also find a discussion of food (Rom 14:1—15:7), of the body of Christ (Rom 12:3–5), of the gifts of the Spirit (Rom 12:6-8), and of agape (Rom 13:8–10). Of course there are many differences in details and in the way that each of these subjects is treated. Nevertheless the parallels deserve to be considered. If we look at this comparison as an algebra problem for a moment, I suggest that the solution presenting itself is that in Rom 12–15 we should also expect to find the Eucharist.

---

52. So Hays, *First Corinthians*, 182–83. Also here with notes Fee, *First Corinthians*, 568: "Since chapter 8 Paul has been dealing with matters related to worship. [Chapters 8 and 10 are] followed by three issues involving [the church's] gathering for worship."

53. So, Fee, *First Corinthians*, 505, cites Bachmann as one of a minority of scholars who would contest that this refers to the assembly.

54. So, completely convincing is the argument of Mitchell, *Paul and the Rhetoric of Reconciliation*, 258–79; also Martin, *Corinthian Body*, 163–67.

The Practice of the Body of Christ

	1 Corinthians 8–14	Romans 12–15
Food	X	X
Body of Christ	X	X
Gifts	X	X
Agape	X	X
Eucharist	X	?

We might make this conclusion even without the direct verbal attestation I suggest for Rom 12:9.

Moreover, there is good historical reason for supposing Paul might write two letters treating comparable subjects, and specifically that of the liturgy of the church, since he likely wrote Romans within a year of 1 Corinthians, and this probably *from Corinth*.[55] Writing to a congregation (in Rome) he had never visited but about which he had informants, it is reasonable to suppose that Paul wanted to preempt issues in one church that had plagued him elsewhere. The matter can be put conversely as well: it would be odd for Paul to connect so many themes to the Eucharistic gathering in one place and then turn to another church and completely, treat the same themes, but not say anything about the Eucharist. Are we really to suppose that the gifts functioned in the Eucharistic context at Corinth but that the practice was different at Rome and that Paul had nothing to say about this this? I would contend that there is every reason to seek references to the Eucharist in Rom 12–15.[56]

Rom 14:1—15:6 and Food at the Agape

I now want to argue that Rom 14:1—15:7 is a discussion of food eaten at the Eucharist or Love Feast. As Jewett says, that very few read the passage this way is understandable, since it is assumed that Paul is not concerned with worship in Romans in the first place.[57] But, in fact, such a reading

---

55. This based on a Knoxian reconstruction of Pauline chronology: Knox, *Chapters*, 53–73; cf. in the same vein Lüdemann, *Chronology*, 262–64; Käsemann, *Romans*, 421; Jewett, *Romans*, 21–22.

56. We can also note the fact that Watson, *Judaism and Gentiles*, 182–88, has argued that the catalog of names in Rom 16 reveals that the congregations in Corinth and in Rome overlap significantly. It appears, in other words, that many people that Paul knew from Corinth and the east had migrated to the capital by the time he wrote a letter there.

57. "Scholars have long been conscious that one of the main impediments against

makes good sense of the passage.⁵⁸ To establish this I do not need to solve the intractable riddles about who exactly the historical actors are that stand behind this text. I can simply point out that there are several indications that this is a faithful reading.

First, the issue discussed is pressing on the community significantly, such that some are despising the practices of others: ὁ ἐσθίων τὸν μὴ ἐσθίοντα μὴ ἐξουθενείτω, ὁ δὲ μὴ ἐσθίων τὸν ἐσθίοντα μὴ κρινέτω (14:3). Of course it might just be that the church in Rome is particularly concerned about what is proper to eat on *any* occasion and specifically whether all, like the "weak," are required to be vegetarians or not (ὁ δὲ ἀσθενῶν λάχανα ἐσθίει) (14:2).⁵⁹ But the deep division in the church is more easily explained if we presume a liturgical context where the community is concerned with presenting itself properly to God. Were this the case, it would make sense for Paul to point out regarding the one who does not eat that, by his very ability to be present at the table and receive the Spirit, regardless of what he eats, still "God has received him" (ὁ θεὸς γὰρ αὐτὸν προσελάβετο) (14:3). Because of this the strong must too *receive* the weak in the same way (14:1: τὸν ἀσθενοῦντα προσλαμβάνεσθε, cf. 15:7: προσλαμβάνεσθε ἀλλήλους, καθὼς καὶ ὁ Χριστὸς προσελάβετο ὑμᾶς).

Second, and central for my argument, we come to 14:6, where Paul, I suggest, speaks directly of the Eucharist: "The one who eats, eats in the Lord, for he εὐχαριστεῖ τῷ θεῷ, and the one who does not eat abstains in the Lord and he too εὐχαριστεῖ τῷ θεῷ." This is, I suggest, Paul's central contention in this section. Both groups, weak and strong, eating and not eating, "celebrate the Eucharist unto God" (εὐχαριστεῖ τῷ θεῷ).⁶⁰ It is well known that the earliest texts relating the name of the Christian gathering call it εὐχαριστία, and the verb signifying the practice is common along

---

the idea of Romans as a comprehensive doctrinal treatise is that it allegedly has no discussion of the sacrament. If we are right in discerning the love feast as explicitly mentioned in 13:10, then the entire discussion in the last three chapters deals with a crucial sacramental issue: who is welcome to take part in the breaking of the bread and the drinking of the cup?" (Jewett, "Love Feast," 277).

58. Thus Jewett, *Romans*, 831–85, esp. 835, reads the passage this way. Of course all depends on finding a liturgical context to begin with. If this is done, these paragraphs fall nicely into place as a coherent part of the argument and not as one more piecemeal issue.

59. This is the majority position, and it usually involves, of course, the Jews being the weak and the gentiles as the strong. See Byrne, *Romans*, 404–7 for good bibliographic information. Also Wright, "Romans," 730–73.

60. Surprisingly Jewett, *Romans*, 846, does not make this move.

with the noun.⁶¹ Moreover, this translation makes the sense of what Paul is saying much less abstract and shows that he is offering concrete pastoral advice and not spiritual platitudes. Specifically, he is making a judgment about the conditions under which the Eucharist is valid. It is not just that in the Lord the sort of food that is eaten is immaterial to "giving thanks" in a general way. Paul's point is much less mundane: the sort of food that one eats at the Eucharist does not invalidate the sacramental act of worship. This is the basis on which Paul's injunction not to judge or despise one another rests.

Third, the language of "building up" appears in 14:18 (τὰ τῆς εἰρήνης διώκωμεν καὶ τὰ τῆς οἰκοδομῆς) and 15:2 (τῷ πλησίον ἀρεσκέτω πρὸς οἰκοδομήν). This language shows up in Paul most pervasively in the context of the discussion of the body of Christ and of the "gifts" in 1 Cor 12:1-28, 14:3-5, 17. There, the gifts are the manifestation of the Spirit that is received at the Eucharist and practiced in the Eucharistic assembly (cf. also Eph 4:11, 16). This lends credence to the suggestion that the eating we are talking about here is liturgical in nature and concerns the Love Feast.

Fourth, in 14:23 Paul says ὁ δὲ διακρινόμενος ἐὰν φάγῃ κατακέκριται, ὅτι οὐκ ἐκ πίστεως. It is significant that only other place in the letters where the language of "discerning" and "judging/condemning"—both linguistically connected by the root κρι—are used in close conjunction is in 1 Cor 11:19-34, which deals with the Lord's Supper. There, Paul has just given the *verba Christi* and he says that "the one who does not discern (διακρίνων) the body eats and drinks judgment (κρίμα) on himself . . . . But if we discern ourselves (διεκρίνομεν ἑαυτούς) we shall not be judged (ἐκρινόμεθα). But being judged (κρινόμενοι) by the Lord we are disciplined in order that we not be condemned (κατακριθῶμεν) with the world." The obvious point is that the context of 1 Cor 11 is liturgical and so, taken with the other evidence I have amassed, Rom 14-15 might well be too.

Specifically, this linguistic connection might mean that Paul often used the language of discernment and judgment, with their common κρι-roots and audible connectedness, to describe things that should, or at least potentially could, go on at the Eucharist. The latter is a time for "discernment" of the body and "judgment" on the faithful (either by the faithful themselves or by God), for the purpose of avoiding the judgment of the

---

61. See especially Justin Martyr, 1 *Apol.* 65-67 (PG 5, 429-32) where this language shows up, significantly, in our earliest full description of the liturgical rite. See also the passage from Ignatius of Antioch above.

Romans 12-15 as the Practice of the Body of Christ

world by undergoing God's discipline. All this of course is set in 1 Cor 11 specifically in the context of the exclusion, of some type, of the poor from the meal (1 Cor 11:20-22, 33-34), which parallels the exclusion apparent in Rom 14-15.

Playing the Hypocrite

Another circumstantial reason to translate ἡ ἀγάπη ἀνυπόκριτος as "the unhypocritical Agape" is that the only other place Paul uses the language of hypocrisy, Gal 2, definitely involves a meal and, I suggest, may concern the Eucharist. This is the so-called Antioch Incident.[62] The thorny details of this difficult text thankfully do not obscure the simple connection we are interested in making. After relating the slim connections he had with the churches in Judea prior to the "Jerusalem Council," Paul goes on to tell of a fateful incident in Antioch which either precipitated or followed upon the Council.[63] Paul recounts that Cephas used to eat with the gentiles in the congregation until some men came down from Jerusalem, at which point he withdrew from them in fear (Gal 2:11-12). What proceeded was that "the remaining Jews also played the hypocrite, so that even Barnabas was lead away in their hypocrisy" (καὶ συνυπεκρίθησαν αὐτῷ οἱ λοιποὶ Ἰουδαῖοι, ὥστε καὶ Βαρναβᾶς συναπήχθη αὐτῶν τῇ ὑποκρίσει) (Gal 2:13). The language of "hypocrisy" is undoubtedly used here in connection with a meal of some sort.[64] Admittedly, Paul does not say that this was a Eucharistic meal, but I think there are strong considerations that point in this direction.[65]

The first is that Paul makes "the truth of the Gospel" (2:14) rest on this occasion. This is more understandable if the context is central to the very liturgical life of the church.[66] Second, a Eucharistic meal explains the

---

62. My thanks to my colleague Hans Arneson for pointing this out. Also making this connection is Esler, *Galatians*, 93-116.

63. Cf. Martyn, *Galatians*, 222-24; For the extensive bibliography and good outlines of the issues see Georgi, *Remembering the Poor*; Overbeck, *Über die Auffasung*.

64. "The fight develops in such a way as to be focused on the arrangements for the church's common meals" (Martyn, *Galatians*, 241).

65. The only author besides Esler, *Galatians*, 93-117, I can find who thinks the meal is Eucharistic is Schlier, *Galatierbrief*, 83.

66. Martyn, *Galatians*, 246, thinks, plausibly, that this violation of the truth of the gospel lies in Peter's compelling the gentiles to live in a Jewish manner. This is part of my answer, but as we will see, it does not penetrate far enough in the problems. For what Paul is really worried about is *why* this specific way of living like a Jew is

connection of this incident to the issue of circumcision that is so central to the rest of the letter.[67] Paul is not just concerned that the Gospel means that Jew and Gentile should eat any old meal together—that occurrence was common enough, both in and outside the Christian movement.[68] Concern for the very truth of the Gospel is better explained if it is due to the fact that it was precisely *from the worship of the church* that Cephas had withdrawn. Gal 2 then concerns not just who is allowed to eat together, but the kind of life required to approach the body and blood of the Lord. Because worship in the church is centered on a shared meal, the boundaries of the community are drawn by who eats together.

The common supposition that those from James merely thought that the church should be divided for the sake of the purity of the Jews contains within it a supposition that they saw two groups who were both equally "in" but which they thought needed to be separate for occasions such as meals.[69] But the issue seems to be more pressing. The "truth of the Gospel" that Paul is concerned about (and this why it concerns the *Gospel*) is that Gentiles were included in the worshipping community without being circumcised (Gal 1:23; 2:21; 3:4, 6:15). And if the Eucharist was for Paul, as I have argued, the means by which the communion with the Spirit begun in baptism was maintained—in short that the Sacrament was soteriologically central—then excluding some from it would not just be to draw "community boundaries" but to claim that the Gentiles were not part of the body of Christ.

Finally, conceiving the "eating" in Gal 2 in this way makes good sense out of the various parts of the letter as a whole—parts which can be hard to fit together.[70] On my reading, the report about the Jerusalem Coun-

---

problematic.

67. Esler, "Making and Breaking," 305–6, intuits this problem and tries to solve it by making ἰουδαΐζω (2:14) mean "to become Jews *through circumcision*." While this would solve the problem of the connection of the Antioch Incident with the broader issue of circumcision, it is certainly speculative.

68. Sanders, *Judaism*, 213–41.

69. This is the default position of Matera, *Galatians*, 89, and also of Dunn, "Incident at Antioch," 95–122.

70. I have already suggested that Martyn's approach, while on the right track, does not take us far enough and so does not actually give a rationale for the unity of the letter's theme. Giving such a rationale, however, is vital, and is usually neglected. When it is attended to, the most popular, if unspoken, line is amazingly still to unite all that Paul opposes (kosher law, circumcision, "works") under "the Law" in general, or even worse "Judaism" in general. The former track seems to be implicitly taken by Martyn while the latter is still present as late as Betz, *Galatians*, 104.

cil is important because it sets out Paul's claim that there is (or at least was) consensus and cooperation among the Apostles regarding the fact that circumcision is not necessary to be a part of the body. Then comes the incident in Antioch illustrating that in fact "the truth of Paul's proclamation" hinged on a Eucharist celebrated by all the baptized—even the uncircumcised. This flows into the argument begun at 3:1 that the Gentiles themselves have manifestly received the Spirit. I presume, following upon what I have said above, that the Spirit is received and exercised precisely in the shared Eucharistic meal, so that the mention of the Spirit in 3:1 is *not* a fresh argument but a continued meditation on the Eucharist and the inclusion of the Gentiles. Finally, there is the long, extended argument of chapters 4–5 to the point that Gentiles are also children of Abraham and Sarah.

We have therefore good reason to think that the context we are to imagine for the Antioch Incident is the Eucharist, in which Paul employs the language of hypocrisy. This corroborates my reading of Rom 12:9 since it reveals the likelihood that Paul specifically used such language in reference to the type of life that was necessary for the celebration of the Agape.

The Agape in Rom 13:9-10: Jewett's Thesis

Zeroing in even closer to 12:9, Robert Jewett has argued in an article and in his commentary that there is an allusion to the Love Feast in Rom 13:9-10: εἴ τις ἑτέρα ἐντολή, ἐν τῷ λόγῳ τούτῳ ἀνακεφαλαιοῦται [ἐν τῷ] Ἀγαπήσεις τὸν πλησίον σου ὡς σεαυτόν. ἡ ἀγάπη τῷ πλησίον κακὸν οὐκ ἐργάζεται· πλήρωμα οὖν νόμου ἡ ἀγάπη. In the commentary, Jewett says that it "is not love in general, or in the abstract, but rather love in the every-day experience of the love feast and other intense interactions of small groups of urban believers that is in view here."[71] The "desire" that the commandments prohibit is problematic in that "the desire for possessions under one's control" is a "threat to the agapaic sharing."[72] In his (earlier) article Jewett posits a chiasm in 13:10 that explicitly references the meal itself: "The *agape* does no evil to the neighbor; the law's fulfillment is therefore the *agape*."[73] The commentary appears to have backed off such a liturgical translation the commentary. There is still a close connection, however. The result, as I read the later Jewett, is not so much that

---

71. Jewett, *Romans*, 809.
72. Ibid., 812.
73. Jewett, "Love Feast," 274. See also his "Tenement Churches," 43–58.

we should translate these verses with "the Agape," but that the language of agape would naturally lead readers to define what agape is in reference to the Agape.

Admittedly, Jewett nowhere spells things out that clearly, but I think this is what he means, and for good reason. For, what Jewett points to is the threefold place that agape holds in Paul's grammar. These three grammatical positions bounce off one another dynamically in different directions. First, there is the Love Feast itself, which consists in shared commensality, sharing of possessions (as we will see), and sharing in the body and blood of Christ. If Jewett and I are right about the Love Feast holding a place in Paul's theology and practice, this is one dimension of agape. This Agape Feast is rooted in, but also gives light to, the act of God in giving Christ for the redemption of sinners, which "showed God's agape for us" (Rom 5:6-8)—the second instance. This is perhaps the most immediately apparent use of agape in Paul—agape defined as the kenotic, selfless action of Christ. But of course this opens up onto what we might call agape the Christian virtue—the third instance. *Imitatio Christi* in Paul (Phil 2:5–11, etc.) is a call to agape as a way of life (1 Cor 13) *defined as* the same humility and obedience unto death embodied by Jesus (Rom 8:17, 12:2).

But, although Jesus' kenotic act does causally "found" the other two instances of agapaic practice, this is not to say that the church only subsequently embodies that act "metaphorically" in its meal and virtue. Each instance is theologically and practically illuminating of the other. The church learns from the Agape Feast what it means to embody the virtue of agape: sharing possessions, bearing one another's burdens, crying with those who cry, et cetera. And by so learning how to be church the church learns about the agape God showed in the giving of the Son, and the Son showed in his humiliation and death. In the latter the church sees the gratuitous agape of God in Christ which is embodied in the practices of Eucharist and common life.

If this is anywhere near the mark for Paul, then it would shed much light, both Christological and ecclesiological, on texts like 1 Cor 13 and, for our purposes, Rom 13:8–10. Like the later Jewett, I do not want to argue that Paul means to refer to the Love Feast *itself* in these verses, but I have no problem seeing here an *allusion* to it, since the church learns the virtue of agape by enacting God's agape in *the* Agape.

In other words, Jewett has shown just how ripe Rom 12–15 is for being read as liturgical instruction. In particular, his work shows just how precarious and over-determined are the usual renderings of agape in Rom

12–15 simply as "love" in a general sense. There is nothing in the text to suggest that such a reading should be *prima facie* preferred. To the contrary, we find good reasons that such a general reading of the word should be *prima facie* doubted, if not bearing the burden of proof over against the eucharitic view.

Finally, I simply point out that the supposition of a Eucharistic context is not more speculative than the common supposition that this passage concerns food in general. That this has been the default interpretation does not place the burden of proof on alternative proposals. The presumption of a context of general exhortation is still a presumption. Those who would argue *for* a general context have to be able to point to things that indicate this in the text—a difficult task (as trying to prove a negative usually is).

So I submit that the case I have made for the translation "The Unhypocritical Love Feast" is cumulatively stronger than the general translation "love is sincere" or "let love be genuine." The reasons to prefer this reading are multiple, though Jewett is the only interpreter that I know of who advocates anything like this sort of move.

Exegesis of Rom 12:3–8

After a good deal of exploration of Paul's broader grammar, we are finally ready to come back and work out what he says in Rom 12:3–8.

Paul starts off right away in v. 3 with the language of virtue, exhorting the church: "do not be arrogant—beyond what wisdom requires—but behave wisely with temperance" (μὴ ὑπερφρονεῖν παρ' ὃ δεῖ φρονεῖν ἀλλὰ φρονεῖν εἰς τὸ σωφρονεῖν).[74] This is to begin right in the middle of a discussion of two of the cardinal virtues (φρονεῖν and σωφρονεῖν).[75] My translation brings out what is lost in most, for, as we have seen, φρονεῖν is not just "think" or "consider" in the sense of modern instrumentalist reason. Paul is not counseling against "thinking too much" or against "philosophy" in a general sense. Rather, φρονεῖν means "to be wise" or "prudent." Thus οἱ φρονοῦντες are commonly "wise men" and φρονεῖν is the verb corresponding to the virtue φρόνησις. Thus φρονεῖν names a tendency to wise *action*. Recall that Aristotle replaces Plato's σοφία with φρόνησις as among the four cardinal virtues. For Aristotle, therefore, φρόνησις is πολιτική (revealing how inadequately "think" or "be minded" renders this

---

74. On ὑπερφρονεῖν as arrogance and akin to ὕβρις see Furnish, *Theology*, 81–82.
75. See Aristotle, *N.E.* 6.7.4–8.9.

word).⁷⁶ Likewise σωφρονεῖν is universally one of the cardinal virtues, for it is impossible to be virtuous at all if one is unable to control one's appetites.⁷⁷ What Paul is doing, therefore, is opening up the discussion of the virtues of the church at a very general level.⁷⁸ He will go on in this section, and through the rest of chapters 12-15, to fill out this basic sketch.

The virtues of prudence and temperance are to be manifested in each person, he then says, "as God has given a measure of fidelity." The practice of virtue is closely involved in the fidelity that characterizes the church. This raises the point that for Paul, the root πιστ- denotes primarily a way of *acting*, a particular *practice*. Thus he can write that ἐλάβομεν χάριν καὶ ἀποστολὴν εἰς ὑπακοὴν πίστεως (Rom 1:5; cf. the phrase also in 16:26). Moreover, that πίστις opens up a discussion of Christ's body is appropriate since, for Paul, πίστις is defined by the πίστις of Jesus, understood as the latter's *loyalty* or *faithfulness* to the Father even unto death. This has of course come out in the famous *Pistis Christou* debate spurred by Hays' book *The Faith of Jesus Christ*.⁷⁹ I have no intention of delving into that debate, but one firm conclusion that has emerged from it is that when Paul does talk about the *Christian's* πίστις, it is πίστις modeled on the πίστις Χριστοῦ γενόμενου ὑπήκοου μέχρι θανάτου (cf. Phil 2:8, Rom 1:5, 5:8, etc).⁸⁰ We have seen this below in Rom 5. So Paul says that God imparts each a certain measure of this Christic character that leads to a particular manifestation of Christ.

This Christological dimension of πίστις is essential to a proper understanding of 12:4. Without this nuance the force of this word is ambiguous, since we would in that case move right from "to each as God has imparted a measure of faith" to "*for* just as in one body we have many parts." In that case it would remain unclear how the notion of a measure of faith is related to the notion of the body. That God is, as it were, imparting a measure of Christ's fidelity, however, means that vv. 4-5 actually *explain* 3b. It looks, in other words, as if Paul says that the fidelity God has given us is intimately bound up with being Christ's body. Furthermore, we can now establish a three-part connection between the virtues of wisdom and

---

76. Cf. also Cicero, *Resp.* I.XX: "I consider the knowledge of those arts which can make us useful to the state (*usui civitati*) to be the noblest function of wisdom (*sapientiae*) and the hightest duty of virtue (*virtutis*)."

77. See also Plato, *Leg.* I.631; Cicero, *Fin.* V, xxiii, 67; *Off.* I, ii, 5; and in biblical material see Wis 8:5-7; 4 Macc. 5:22-23.

78. So agrees Sharp, *Epictetus*, 218.

79. Hays, *Faith*.

80. See ibid., 119-62.

Romans 12-15 as the Practice of the Body of Christ

temperance (v. 3a), fidelity (v. 3b), and being Christ's body-parts (v. 4). Wisdom and temperance are at least part of the content of the Christic fidelity the church practices *precisely because* (γὰρ) it is Christ's body.

Strictly speaking, Paul does not say here that the church *is* Christ as he does in 1 Cor 12:27, but rather that it is one body "in Christ." While most have recognized that this amounts to the same relation, our study of the nature of Christ's three pneumatic bodies helps us to see why.[81] "In Christ" is not just a convenient way of naming the members of the church but is rather a phrase that has its place in the sacramental nature of the church. In baptism the movement is literally from a position outside the pneumatic body to inside, such that the position is now literally "in" instead of "out" in relation to Christ. We have seen of course likewise that this relationship is maintained by means of constant ingestion of the πνεῦμα of Christ in the Eucharist.

With this background it becomes apparent that in vv. 3-5 Paul is giving a particular account of the relationship between Christ's pneumatic body and the church. He tells us, in other words, that the church becomes and so *is* Christ (οἱ πολλοὶ ἓν σῶμά ἐσμεν ἐν Χριστῷ). Specifically, God gives each person in the church a particular "measure" of Christic fidelity (ἑκάστῳ ὡς ὁ θεὸς ἐμέρισεν μέτρον πίστεως)—a particular way of acting like Christ. This gifted practice (χάρισμα) is one particular practice (πρᾶξιν) that is a part (μέλη) of Christ's body (ἐν ἑνὶ σώματι μέλη).[82] Each person (καθ' εἷς) therefore is a particular body-part (μέλη) of Christ on earth, and the whole church is the body (ἓν σῶμά ἐσμεν) of Christ himself.[83] This gift, I suggest, is given by means of the Holy Spirit that is received in the Eucharist in the way that I indicated above (but Paul does not spell things out that fully in this letter).

We now come to Rom 12:6-8 and the list of seven χαρίσματα. So far in this paragraph Paul has spoken of the nature of the church as a body. But, as we saw above, body-polis discourses usually include a discussion of the actions of the polis, conceived in classical terms as a discussion of virtues and vices. So, with classical readers like Origen, Chrysostom, Pelagius, and Thomas Aquinas, we can read vv. 6-8 as a list of virtues of the

---

81. There is wide agreement that "in Christ" refers to the church's existence as the Body. So Bultmann, *Theology*, 311; Best, *Body*, 44-82; Schweitzer, *Mysticism*, 122.

82. So, correctly, Horrell, *Solidarity and Difference*, 122, identifies the carisma with each member's πρᾶξις.

83. See here Bosch, "Le Corps," 51-72.

body.⁸⁴ These χαρίσματα are *a list of Christ's virtues*, given to the church by God, that are to be performed by the church since the church is Christ. God makes the church Christ by making it act like Christ by acquisition of his virtues through the Spirit in baptism and the Eucharist. Why has this not been more widely noted?

Primarily because, though these are virtues, these are unusual virtues. Paul has taken up the body-action discourse and overlaid it with much that was not common to it. Thomas recognized this aspect of the gifts in our passage: they are functioning in the place that virtues do and must be recognized as such; on the other hand, these are a special kind that God has given especially to equip the action of the church.⁸⁵ Pelagius calls them charismatic virtues.⁸⁶ Thomas himself says that they are "abiding habits of the Holy Spirit."⁸⁷

But I think these gifts also have another aspect; while virtues—that is, capacities and skills exercised in roles more or less well played—they have their function in *liturgical* roles. Virtues always have a certain arena in which they are imagined to be practiced, they perform a certain function, classically, within the economy of the polis, and the sum total of them makes up the character of the city. Each virtue within the city is dependent upon and gives rise to the other virtues. The same is true for these gifts. They are virtues that corporately make up Christ and they have their particular function in the concrete situation that is the agapaic liturgical life of the community. The difference from the classical virtues is in kind; these virtues are *gifted* and when they are received their recipients are transformed corporately into Christ.

What exactly are these gifted liturgical roles and how do I imagine them functioning at the Agape? The evidence does not allow anything like a comprehensive picture, but there are some indications, and treating the gifts one by one ends up further supporting the liturgical nature of this material.

---

84. So Origen *Comm. Rom.* 9.1.2; Chrysostom, *Homilies on Romans* 21 (*NANF* 8: 502); Pelagius: "And to each one, as God has appointed a charismatic virtue (*gratia virtutum*) which none but the faithful receive, is to be called a measure... They could not all have the same gift, so the likeness of the body of Christ may be evidence among us... to him who has a heart so pure that he deserves it receives even in this life the *gratia virtutum*." See De Bruyn, *Pelagius' Commentary*. See Thomas Aquinas *ST* I.II q. 68.

85. See, e.g., *S.T.* I.II.68.1.

86. The Latin is *gratia virtutum*; see above note 84.

87. *S.T.* I.II.68.3.

Προφητεία is of course mentioned in 1 Cor 12:28 as the second among the gifts, and in 1 Cor 14 it is part of a long discussion regarding tongues. If I am right about the Eucharistic setting supposed for that instruction, there is good reason to see the same in Romans.

Few will doubt that ὁ προιστάμενος is to be translated "presider" or "celebrant." What we do not know is whether this was an "office" or a "function" in Paul's time. But whether "ordained" or "lay" (to anachronize?), there seems to have been an appointed leader at the Feast. This title is quite well attested later of the Eucharistic celebrant, particularly the bishop and then later the priest. The very earliest outline of the Eucharistic celebration that we have after Paul and the *Didache*, in Justin Martyr, calls the Eucharistic president ὁ προεστώς five times in the span of three chapters.[88] Of course, there Justin describes the president as celebrant in a rather complex liturgy that we have no way of anchoring back to the middle of the first century. However, it appears that the *basic* function is the same as in Paul's case. This is not just a "community leader" in general (what would that mean?) but, given 12:9, the leader of the Agape. After all, there is every reason to think that Justin describes a well-established practice of the church, elements of which *could* go back into the earliest days of the church.

The second named gift, διακονία, of course is later attested to as a full-fledged ecclesiastical office.[89] But there is no reason to doubt that something like a specific function obtained for this gift at the Agape that had something to do with serving the meal or distributing the Elements. Thus Jewett says that "the diaconal role in early Christianity developed from functions related to the common meal . . . The eucharistic celebration, probably celebrated as a daily, common meal was the center of their common life."[90] This means that the later diaconate developed out of a liturgical role that was already centered on the distribution of the Eucharist and the common food rather than being only later placed into that function from a more general practice of "service." So Reicke thinks that this liturgical use is the foundation for Paul's more general use of διακον- cognates and not vise-versa.[91] Thus the contention that even in Paul's time there was something of a diaconate need not be ruled out, and Phil 1:1 and

---

88. Justin Martyr, 1 *Apol.* 65–67 (PG 5, 429–32).
89. E.g., Chrysostom, *Hom. Rom.* 21 (*NPNF* 11: 501–2). See Jewett, *Romans*, 750.
90. Jewett, *Romans*, 750.
91. Reicke, *Diakonie*, 31-8. On the diaconate see also Richard Pervo, "PANTA KOINA," 187–94.

Rom 16:1 would seem to point in this direction.[92] Such an office exists, after all, if in some kind of nascent form, by the time of 1 Tim 3:8–10 and Acts 6.[93]

Next, the "teacher" and the "exhorter/comforter" both read well as functions or offices fulfilled at the Agape. Both παρακαλῶν and διδάσκαλος probably can be best understood with reference to the ancient philosophical school.[94] The church gathers not just to do certain common things but also to learn about what they are doing and why they are doing it. They are being trained into a particular way of life and part of that discipline is instruction.[95] The exhorter, specifically, is connected in such situations with "soul craft," and what we would name "pastoral care" is probably to be found under this heading (though of course in a different mode than modern therapeutics).[96] The Agape then is not unlike a symposium where philosophers gather to teach, learn and discuss the good life over common food and drink.

Ὁ μεταδιδούς is not just the one who "shares" in a general sense, but one who "distributes" the Eucharistic elements. Justin reports that at the Eucharist ὁ προεστώς repeats Jesus' words of institution and reminds the church that Jesus distributed (μεταδοῦναι) the meal to his disciples alone.[97] For Justin this word denotes the giving specifically of the Eucharistic elements and not the general sharing of needs by the community, for which he uses ἐπικουρεῖν and προσφέρειν.[98]

A similar variety can be seen in Paul's terms. The μεταδιδούς is not simply the one appointed to wait on tables at the Agape. This is the job, as we have seen and as is lexically most appropriate, of the deacon. Nor is the μεταδιδούς "sharing" in the sense of *providing* the Agapaic food for others

---

92. This realization has popped up from time to time in the history of scholarship, despite the discipline's tendency to be determined by Weberian (and of course Protestant) sociological models. So see Lietzmann, *Römer*, 109; Murray, *Romans*, 124; Brockhaus, *Charisma*, 98–100.

93. Cf. also Romans 15:25: νυνὶ δὲ πορεύομαι εἰς Ἰερουσαλὴμ διακονῶν τοῖς ἁγίοις.

94. Jewett, *Romans*, 750–51.

95. Hadot, *Philosophy*, 49–70.

96. Schmitz, "παρακαλέω, παράκλησις," 773–74, 779–88.

97. Justin Martyr, 1 *Apol.* 66-7 (PG 6, 429).

98. In 1 *Apol.* 67 (PG 5:429) Justin says that the "distribution" (ἡ διάδοσις) of the Eucharistic elements (ἀπὸ τῶν εὐχαριστηθέντων) is given to each member. Those called deacons distribute (διδόασιν) the Eucharistic bread, wine and water, to all those present, who "receive" (μεταλαβεῖν, λαμβάνειν, μετασχεῖν) it.

who do not have much or anything to contribute to the meal; Paul names this contributor the "one who performs works of mercy" (ὁ ἐλεῶν).⁹⁹ This person or persons (I do not assume the congregation is too big) are also probably responsible for providing any goods that are distributed to the poor outside the community, as Jewett avers.¹⁰⁰

We may therefore be able to see with slightly more precision a variety of liturgical functions being performed at the Agape. If the food for the meal is provided by ὁ ἐλεῶν and brought to the table by ὁ διάκονος, it seems plausible that in such a liturgical context ὁ μεταδιδούς names the one who hands out the body and blood of Christ. The latter is the one who distributes, as it were, the special food, the former the common. If Scripture (the Septuagint and some of Jesus' words?) was read at these Feasts, as Paul's assumption of a certain level of scriptural knowledge would allow, it would seem that the παρακαλῶν and διδάσκαλος performed their duties in some connection with such reading. In Justin's description, indeed, it is the προεστώς who also teaches and exhorts, and we cannot rule out the possibility that one person performed more than one of these functions. Where exactly we are to imagine προφητεία fitting in the liturgy is impossible to determine, but in Corinth at least there seems to have been a time set aside for speaking in tongues and prophecy (cf. 1 Cor 12–14).

In sum, the specific place of each gift remains speculative, but my liturgical construal has the advantage of giving the otherwise (and on most readings) fairly random list a certain rationale. What I hope to have shown is that these gifts can best be thought of as liturgical practices, whatever specific function they may have had at the liturgy itself and however the gift may have been put into service outside of the Agape.

Furthermore, I have argued that Rom 12:3–8 presents God's gift of the virtues of Christ's body to the church. These gifts are specifically exercised at the Love Feast where participants receive the Spirit in the Eucharist. This Spirit imparts the gifts as Christ's charismatic virtues, which make the members of the church into his body-parts. Thus the reception of Christ's body makes the church into Christ's body. What sort of agency does this imply?

I pick up this question in the concluding chapter, but we should note the collective sense of agency as we go forward. Paul's emphasis in Rom 12:3–8 is squarely on the fact that the many members, though certainly

---

99. So Jewett, *Romans*, 753–54. Also Chrysostom, *Com. Rom.* 20; Aquinas, *in Rom* 6:3.

100. Jewett, *Romans*, 753.

parts of Christ's body, are also (and thus) parts of *each other*, as the resumptive τὸ that begins v. 5b reveals. Paul does not say that "we who are many are one body in Christ *and* parts individually of one another." Rather, he says that "in this way we who are many are in Christ one body, and that body is parts, each one of another" (τὸ δὲ καθ' εἷς ἀλλήλων μέλη). Thus Paul does not say that each "individual" is part of another and part of Christ. Paul does not know the modern word or concept "individual" with all its moral and philosophical nuance.[101] More precisely, he does not know anything of the independent self which is *even in principle* separable morally, socially, spiritually or religiously from other "individuals." To render καθ' εἷς ἀλλήλων μέλη "individually parts of one another" is to reinstate through the back door precisely what Paul excludes, namely, that that there are any bodies in the church that have any integral individuality to them.

The Ethics of the Agape

Rom 12:1–2: The Martyr as the Sage

We are now in a better position to understand the rest of Rom 12. But before going on to consider the specifics that follow 12:9 we can go back and consider 12:1–2, where we see much of what we have learned of 12:3–8 anticipated, and the ground laid for the critique of honor in 12:9–21.

In Rom 12:1–2, Paul continues the claim that the participation in Christ by the Spirit he treated in Rom 5–8 is marked by suffering (cf. specifically Rom 5:3–5; 6:3–6; 8:17). But in 12:1–2 he makes explicit what has been mentioned in passing. He says "I exhort you therefore, brethren, to present your bodies, through the mercy of God, a living, holy and pleasing sacrifice to God, your logical worship." In light of (οὖν) what he has said in the previous chapters, martyrdom on the model of the crucified Christ is the church's "logical" worship. The image is both cultic and martyrological; because church bodies participate in Christ, and so are Christ by his Spirit, their worship or temple-service to God is to become martyrs—to offer their bodies as a living sacrifice.

There are several items packed into this verse that should not be missed. First, the whole church is viewed as one sacrifice. Paul indicates that there are many bodies (τὰ σώματα) but that there is just one sacrifice (θυσίαν ζῶσαν). He does not say that "bodies" are "living sacrifices." The

---

101. Taylor, *Sources*, 143–76.

church is the sacrifice. The corporate nature of the agency involved in worship and service to God are consequently unmistakable. This anticipates in turn the grammar of the church as the body of Christ: the church worships by embodying that which it is, Christ, who was himself a pleasing sacrifice to God (cf. Rom 3:25, Eph 5:25).[102] The church is thus called, again, as in Rom 8:16-17, to suffer in the same way as Christ did. With regard to agency, the church has differentiated bodies. Even though they have been incorporated "into Christ," they are not only called one body, but each of their bodies cannot be defined as other than (part of) Christ's body (cf. 12:5).

But why does Paul say that the church's corporeal sacrifice is its λογικὴν λατρείαν? We get an idea from elsewhere in his letters. It appears that offering the body as a sacrifice is the only thing church members can do *because* the church is Christ (so cf. 2 Cor 4:10-11 πάντοτε τὴν νέκρωσιν τοῦ Ἰησοῦ ἐν τῷ σώματι περιφέροντες . . . ἀεὶ γὰρ ἡμεῖς οἱ ζῶντες εἰς θάνατον παραδιδόμεθα διὰ Ἰησοῦν, etc.). If, therefore, the church is only the church *as* the body of Christ, it follows that *if* the church is going to be glorified with Christ it will also be sacrificed as Christ was (Rom 8:17).

Moreover, a notion of the corporate nature of Christ *as the church* (i.e., versus the church as Christ) can also be discerned. We are heirs of God, but *fellow* heirs *with* Christ (συγκληρονόμοι δὲ Χριστοῦ). The church stands *with Christ* as heir of sonship (as we saw above). Indeed, because Christ's body is made up of the church which suffers with (συμπάσχει) him, Christ himself is an heir of God *with us*. Christ inherits what the church does (cf. Rom 8:29). This is part of the Spirit's work qualifying us as Christ: it is this Spirit that makes us "co-heirs," "co-sufferers" and "co-glorifieds" with Christ (Rom 8:17).

This is why Paul says that suffering is their λογικὴν λατρείαν. λογικὴ belongs squarely in the middle of classical accounts of action, from Plato and Aristotle to the Stoics. In this sort of context, an action is λογική if it "fits" the λόγος,[103] that is, if it "meshes" with the way the world really is, or, to borrow Yoder's phrase, if it is "with the grain of the universe."[104] As such, to live "logically" is to live "according to nature." This appears to be the way that Paul is using the word here. Anticipating his definition of the

---

102. So Moxnes, "Quest for Honor," 203-30. On Christ as sacrifice see Schweitzer, *Mysticism*, 218-21, and of course Williams, *Jesus' Death*, 5-56; see too the more recent treatment of Brandos, *Paul on the Cross*, 103-49.

103. Paul certainly uses classical terms often in Romans. See Swancutt, "Sexy Stoics," 42-73.

104. Yoder, "Armaments," 58.

church as the body of Christ (12:3), and recalling that God has poured out the Spirit into their hearts (5:5), qualifying them as Christ and therefore as sufferers with Christ (8:17), it is only "logical," only in keeping with the way things are, that those who are the body of Christ in this way offer their bodies as a living sacrifice. As determined by Christ's own Spirit, not to suffer with Christ would be to live ἄλογος—out of step with the flow of the world.

In Rom 12:2 Paul continues his introduction to Rom 12–15 by taking up the issue of the good life and its attainment: καὶ μὴ συσχηματίζεσθε τῷ αἰῶνι τούτῳ, ἀλλὰ μεταμορφοῦσθε τῇ ἀνακαινώσει τοῦ νοὸς εἰς τὸ δοκιμάζειν ὑμᾶς τί τὸ θέλημα τοῦ θεοῦ, τὸ ἀγαθὸν καὶ εὐάρεστον καὶ τέλειον. The good, the pleasing and the perfect are the ends to which life is directed and every action should be made in reference to these ends. Paul defines these ends in terms of τὸ θέλημα τοῦ θεοῦ. *Discerning* (τὸ δοκιμάζειν) the will of God concerns the nature of the transformation that Paul seeks. What is Paul up to?

First, it appears that the exhortation of 12:2 is dependent upon that of v. 1. Thus, the central way the church is to be transformed is to imitate Christ precisely in his *suffering*. This is, for Paul, as Yoder perceives, the central and perhaps the only (as Yoder would have it) way that the church imitates Christ.[105]

Second, the church is transformed τῇ ἀνακαινώσει τοῦ νοὸς. Not only is the church just *one* sacrifice made by its acceptance of θλίψας (5:3), but it has but *one* νοῦς that is renewed. Thus, just as the one ecclesial sacrifice is the same as Christ's sacrifice, so also this renewed mind is Christ's mind (cf. 1 Cor 2:16 ἡμεῖς δὲ νοῦν Χριστοῦ ἔχομεν.).[106] The νοῦς is one part of the anthropology of classical action discourse used to denote that part of the person that is in charge of reasoning and *acting*. This is a primary difference between the νοῦς Paul names and our modern word "mind." The former is not limited to the ephemeral realm of "thought" as *opposed* to the body or action. The grammar of νοῦς is precisely that it "leads" and controls the body's acts by perceiving the nature (φύσις) of the λόγος.

Thus, Paul exhorts the church to offer worship in conformity with the way the world is because this is what renews the νοῦς, and the νοῦς is the part of the body that is in charge of perceiving the nature of the world and acting accordingly. If it is functioning rightly, the νοῦς leads to knowledge

---

105. Yoder, *Politics*, 112–33.
106. On the mind of Christ belonging to the church see Lee, *Paul*, 155–64.

of the world and action that accords with one's proper end (τέλος). Paul even says as much, for the renewed mind is used εἰς τὸ δοκιμάζειν ὑμᾶς τί τὸ θέλημα τοῦ θεοῦ, τὸ ἀγαθὸν καὶ εὐάρεστον καὶ τέλειον. Paul has therefore embedded in this exhortation an approximation of a practical syllogism: the *telos* of martyrological sacrifice on the model of Jesus defines the good action.[107]

All this leads to an important conclusion regarding agency: for Paul right action requires a "repositioning" of the body. Before one can hope to know and do the good, the perfect, and the pleasing (12:2), that is, one must be transformed into Christ. But this means submitting the physical body to the discipline of making a martyr's sacrifice which makes it possible to act rightly (justly). This has its parallel in what I argued about Rom 5:12–21: Christ's just deed leads to the church's practice of further just deeds which make the church's members just. So too here, the church is to offer its bodies as one living sacrifice in imitation of Christ's paradigmatic offering. In Rom 5 Paul indicates the form of the just life. Here he gives content to that life and exhorts the church to such practice. Yet, as in Rom 5, the church practices the body of Christ only because of God's initiative and only as an always already gifted way of life (cf. 12:1 διὰ τῶν οἰκτιρμῶν τοῦ θεοῦ). Only if we maintain a strict division between Christ and the church (and *so* between divine and human agency) does this become paradoxical. It is fitting then that Paul moves from Rom 12:1–2 to a discussion of the church as Christ. This sort of unity in act and character has been latent in this discussion at least since Rom 5, until at last the two agencies merge.

Rom 12:9–21: The Praxis of Honor and Political Philosophy

At 12:9 Paul moves naturally from naming certain liturgical roles as the specific gifts Christ gives to make up his body to an explicit discussion of various aspects of the life of the church (always understood as united to the liturgical life of the community). Paul starts out with the general condition of the Eucharistic life and then goes on to fill in what that looks like in its details. So I do not think, as many have, that Paul's exhortation here is basically ad hoc. He is not just selecting from a stock of Hellenistic

---

107. Origen (*in Rom* 6.13.2) thinks Paul uses syllogisms often: "That the Apostle Paul makes use of syllogisms accepted and derived from the art of dialectic, both in this passage and in his other letters, is a fact that, in my opinion, does not require expansion..." On the practical syllogism itself see Aristotle, *N.E.* 6.7.9.

maxims.[108] Rather, it appears that for Paul "the good" is the sum total of good actions, defined as the concrete actions of the *church*. This thesis can be demonstrated in detail.

The first exhortation is general: "put away the bad, cling to the good" (ἀποστυγοῦντες τὸ πονηρόν, κολλώμενοι τῷ ἀγαθῷ). "Clinging," or being "united with" (κολλώμενοι) is language taken directly from the church's relationship with Christ himself: ὁ δὲ κολλώμενος τῷ κυρίῳ ἓν πνεῦμά ἐστιν (1 Cor 6:17). This suggests Paul conceives the good in terms of the behavior of the church *as* Christ.

Most immediately, τῷ ἀγαθω draws on the summation in 12:2b of the ends of action as "the good, the pleasing, and the perfect." The good in that context is a martyrological praxis that is the sacrifice of one's own body. Putting off evil and clinging to the good, defined within the way of life of the church that Paul has already begun to set out and in which his audience lives, should not therefore be construed abstractly. What Paul is urging throughout this section is precisely a way of life where the good and the perfect get defined by these specific actions, which are contrary to the life of the world in which the Romans live.[109]

The specifics of the good come right away. The church is to conceive itself in terms of the family—τῇ φιλαδελφίᾳ εἰς ἀλλήλους φιλόστοργοι (12:10)—implying a strong critique of the biological family.[110] In such a familiar context they are to "make haste and not be hesitant to consider each other foremost with regard to honor" (τῇ τιμῇ ἀλλήλους προηγούμενοι τῇ σπουδῇ μὴ ὀκνηροί) (v. 11). With this statement Paul opens his critique of honor. That members of the church are not to seek honor is not a pious platitude. On the contrary, honor was for the Romans (as probably in most societies) tightly tied up with the good, so that honor itself was a primary good to be sought.[111] Paul is therefore tearing at the fiber of the prevailing *Lebensform* by upending a primary motivation for action. Honor is not something to be sought, but rather something to ascribe to others. This means the church does not compete for honor as a good internal to its

---

108. Thus, contra Furnish, *Theology*, 81–94; Cranfield, *Romans*, 2:631; Käsemann, *Romans*, 330; Talbert, "Tradition," 88–91, offers a slightly more nuanced middle path.

109. So, Jewett, *Romans*, xi.

110. Thus the indispensible work by Schäfer, *Gemeinde als "Bruderschaft."*

111. The best and most comprehensive treatment is by Barton, *Roman Honor*, esp. 34–130. See also Lendon, *Honor*, 30–106; Earl, *Age of Augustus*, 1–25.

practice; it is free to cooperatively seek the common good. The critique of honor is an admonition to a kenotic daily existence with one another.[112]

Then follow in vv. 12-13 seven sharp parallel commands, each concluding with participle functioning as an imperative.

5. πνεύματι ζέοντες
6. τῷ κυρίῳ δουλεύοντες
7. τῇ ἐλπίδι χαίροντες
8. τῇ θλίψει ὑπομένοντες
9. τῇ προσευχῇ προσκαρτεροῦντες
10. ταῖς χρείαις τῶν ἁγίων κοινωνοῦντες
11. τὴν φιλοξενίαν διώκοντες

These commands treat behaviors both inside the community and practice toward those outside, suggesting that Paul sees both—the whole of life—as essential to the unhypocritical Agape.

The first five exhortations appeal back to similar themes in earlier parts of the letter. This is important for my case that chapters 12-15 provide the basic content that fills in the more general claims made before. Specifically, commands one through five reach back most directly to Rom 5:2-5 where they are introduced all at once before being developed in the following chapters:

καυχώμεθα ἐπ' ἐλπίδι τῆς δόξης τοῦ θεοῦ. οὐ μόνον δέ, ἀλλὰ καὶ καυχώμεθα ἐν ταῖς θλίψεσιν, εἰδότες ὅτι ἡ θλῖψις ὑπομονὴν κατεργάζεται, ἡ δὲ ὑπομονὴ δοκιμήν, ἡ δὲ δοκιμὴ ἐλπίδα. ἡ δὲ ἐλπὶς οὐ καταισχύνει, ὅτι ἡ ἀγάπη τοῦ θεοῦ ἐκκέχυται ἐν ταῖς καρδίαις ἡμῶν διὰ πνεύματος ἁγίου τοῦ δοθέντος ἡμῖν.

The case that Rom 5:2-5 is a thesis paragraph that is developed broadly in chapters 5-8, and in detail in Rom 12-15 will become clearer as we progress.

"Boil in the Spirit" picks up most obviously on Rom 8:1-11 and the exhortation there to practice the Spirit. Paul therefore signals here that he is explaining exactly what this action looks like, just as in Rom 8 he was indicating more fully how it is that the Spirit allows one to live the just life of Rom 5:12-21 for which the church is given the Spirit (5:5).

This intense action ("boiling") and practice in the Spirit is followed up by another more general command: "Be slaves to the Lord!" This is the one command of the first five that does not have an antecedent in 5:2-5,

---

112. See the extended analysis of Paul's critique of Roman honor in Hellermann, *Reconstructing Honor*, 129-66.

but it is still the climax of several statements in the letter regarding slavery. Paul said in 6:16–23 that the church is either a slave of sin or justice, which picked up and developed the theme of obedience and disobedience from the previous section (5:12–21). In Rom 7:6–25 he argued that the divided selves (of whatever kind exactly we again leave open) are in a condition of "being slaves" (7:25) to both that law and to sin. Finally, in Rom 8, the church is told that they are not slaves but sons of God if they suffer with Christ, which is part of receiving and practicing his Spirit (8:15, 21). This drawn-out description of Rom 5–8, therefore—of God's love through his gift of Christ that enables holy lives of obedience to the Lord Jesus by the practice of the Spirit—is recalled and commanded in these first two exhortations.

The third command is "Rejoice in hope!" The locus of the theme of hope in the letter is firmly planted in 5:2–5 and 8:20, 24–25. In the former it is the result of the church's endurance and testing in which it boasts in the hope of God's glory (καυχώμεθα ἐπ' ἐλπίδι τῆς δόξης τοῦ θεοῦ. ἡ δὲ ὑπομονὴ δοκιμήν, ἡ δὲ δοκιμὴ ἐλπίδα. ἡ δὲ ἐλπὶς οὐ καταισχύνει . . .). In the latter, equally eschatological and involving persecution (and ὑπομονή; cf. 5:3), the church hopes for the revelation of the glory of the sons of God as it groans in tribulation with the rest of creation (τῇ γὰρ ἐλπίδι ἐσώθημεν· ἐλπὶς δὲ βλεπομένη οὐκ ἔστιν ἐλπίς· ὃ γὰρ βλέπει τίς ἐλπίζει; εἰ δὲ ὃ οὐ βλέπομεν ἐλπίζομεν, δι' ὑπομονῆς ἀπεκδεχόμεθα). In both cases the church's hope in God's eschatological action appears to be what grounds its capacity for "endurance."

"Persevere in tribulation!" Suffering tribulation is perhaps one of the most under-appreciated major themes in Romans.[113] References to it abound, especially in chapters 5 and 8.[114] I have noted above just how closely "endurance" and "persecution" are tied in these chapters: καυχώμεθα ἐν ταῖς θλίψεσιν, εἰδότες ὅτι ἡ θλῖψις ὑπομονὴν κατεργάζεται, ἡ δὲ ὑπομονὴ δοκιμήν (5:3–4). The result of these trials is that the church awaits the renewal of creation δι' ὑπομονῆς (8:25).

Prayer (τῇ προσευχῇ προσκαρτεροῦντες) too reaches back to Rom 8:26–27 where the church is assured that even if it does not know how to pray as it ought, the Spirit is praying in them. There, prayer stands in the context of a persecuted church (cf. 5:3, 8:17), which is groaning in the midst of the groaning of creation. We should therefore take the

---

113. This is one thesis of the fantastic work of Pauline biography by Cinera, *Religionspolitik*.

114. Cf. Rom 2:7, 9; 5:3–5; 8:25, 35; 15:4–5.

"intersession" of the Spirit (τὸ πνεῦμα ὑπερεντυγχάνει) as a sort of judicial pleading with God on behalf of the innocent. This is the prayer that they are to persevere in while they endure suffering.

There is not space to explore the internal theological relation of each of these five themes with each other, though Paul certainly thinks that they are so related (judging by 5:2–5, where they are carefully ordered and set in relation to ἀγάπη). My point is rather a structural one: not only do these specific commands bear a thematic unity with the foregoing, but they are also theologically necessary as the fulfillment of the previous chapters. Again, they are anything but randomly chosen exhortations.[115]

The final two commands do not refer back to earlier portions of the letter, but they do further specify conditions of the life in the Spirit. Ταῖς χρείαις τῶν ἁγίων κοινωνοῦντες is not just to "*contribute* to the needs of the saints" (NRSV et alia), but rather to "make common the needs of the saints." In other words, this is an appeal to the church's practice of communal distribution of goods presumed in such a passage as 2 Thess 3:7–12 (and illustrated in Acts 2:43–47, 4:32—5:11), where the admonition to work for one's own living is understood as necessary instruction given to a community in which no one lacks. Paul again refers to such sharing in Rom 15:26 when he says that "Asia and Macedonia were pleased to make some κοινωνίαν for the poor among the saints in Jerusalem." The just life is therefore constituted by some sort of micro-scale communal economic practice.

The final exhortation, to hospitality (τὴν φιλοξενίαν διώκοντες), is unique in the undisputed Pauline corpus, but fits closely with the practice of sharing possessions. Presumably Paul envisions hospitality that extends beyond the bounds of the church. Of course we do not know whether this means a place for guests was provided at the Agape itself, but we cannot rule out this possibility.[116] We can imagine all seven of these introductory exhortations being carried out both at the Agape and outside of it.

This last exhortation in 12:13 is connected linguistically with the following commands in vv. 14–21 (τὴν φιλοξενίαν διώκοντες . . . εὐλογεῖτε τοὺς διώκοντας), which nonetheless break the stylistic parallelism. Turning to these latter verses, we see Paul inverting the received practical wisdom (that is to say moral-political-philosophical wisdom or φρόνησις) and setting out a new program for the church to follow in living the agapaic life.

---

115. So, Jewett, *Romans*, 759.

116. On such hospitality see Konstan, *Friendship*, 37–45; also the good surveys in Pohl, *Making Room*, 16–59.

The Practice of the Body of Christ

This section deals with how the church is to behave toward both its own and those outside.

In Rom 12:14-21 Paul inverts the status of ancient philosophy and politics. But these are of course not two different things. Plato's *Republic* is as much a discourse on epistemology and metaphysics as it is on the concrete practices and virtues of the ideal polis. Likewise the most popular philosophical school of Paul's day, the Stoics, always insisted that their "ethics" were rooted in their "physics" and so in the nature of the cosmos. The "higher sciences" were not any sort of speculative philosophy that was to be avoided because of its futility, but simply any discussion of what we would call ethics or politics or theology done in a philosophical *school* (and so such schools were by nature *political*). In these schools, of course, there was some division of curriculum into (to take the Stoics) logic, physics, ethics and politics, but this was a division of the chronology of study and not of discrete categories.[117]

I say all this because we could be tempted by our modern division of curricula to assume that for Paul talk about how to behave toward one's enemy, the nature of the good, and what sorts of things are worth thinking about, are disparate subjects and so random commands. On the contrary, Paul has in Rom 12:14-21 the specific end in mind of turning the church away from Roman φρόνησις and beginning, *in nuce*, to set out his own ecclesial material.

Paul first excises Roman philosophy itself: τὸ αὐτὸ εἰς ἀλλήλους φρο νοῦντες, μὴ τὰ ὑψηλὰ φρονοῦντες ἀλλὰ τοῖς ταπεινοῖς συναπαγόμενοι. μὴ γίνεσθε φρόνιμοι παρ' ἑαυτοῖς (12:16). I have already emphasized that the φρον- family of words shows up frequently in Paul and in Romans in particularly, and that this places us in the middle of classical discussions of human action. Hellenistic philosophy, which, in a certain way, had its center in Rome and was part of any claim to high status or civility, could be characterized as "being wise about lofty things."[118] At least since Plato, one part of this high-status activity was to know things as they really are and not as they appear to be, which is the lot of the masses.[119] But Paul, drawing on the OT disclosure that God gives preference for the humble,

---

117. For all this see Hadot, *Philosophy*, 47-78, and the bibliographical material on the Hellenistic schools in Vegge, *Paulus*.

118. See Philo, *Congr.* 89; 4 Macc 1:13-17; Cicero, *Tusc.* 4.57; *Off.* 1.16, 2.2; Seneca, *Ep.* 89.4-7.

119. See Plato, *Resp.* 6-7.

poor, and lowly councels them *to be* "led away with the lowly"![120] Here Paul seems to anticipate some modern insights about the epistemic priority of the poor implying that in fact *these* (and not comfortable scholars) are the ones with a line on the heights of wisdom (τὰ ὑψηλὰ φρονοῦντες).

That Paul's church was itself praying the Psalms and so would be aware of the place of the lowly there is likely, not least because the Psalms are the most quoted OT book in the Pauline corpus and the second most quoted in Romans itself (after Isaiah).[121] The radical suggestion that it is in fact the lowly and not the sophisticated philosophers whom God has chosen and who have true wisdom underlines major sections of Paul's other letters (1 Cor 1–2, Col 2:1–8, etc), and is simply in keeping with the tenor of much of NT Christianity.[122] What is necessary to remember (in our time, now that humility has become a virtue) is that being called ταπεινός is *not* a compliment for a pagan in Rome.[123] What *is* a compliment is to be called φρόνιμος ("sage")—one who has an examined life and who is practically wise in the affairs of the state.[124] To those who would seek such honorable status Paul says μὴ γίνεσθε φρόνιμοι παρ' ἑαυτοῖς (a corporate version of Prov 3:7: μὴ ἴσθι φρόνιμος παρὰ σεαυτῷ).

Paul's ecclesial polity continues to undercut accepted norms: bless persecutors instead of cursing them, do not repay evil for evil, and instead perform works of mercy for your enemies (Rom 12:19–20).[125] One of the most well established principles of justice—one that many layman would know—is that justice is giving to each his due.[126] Another commonly accepted maxim is to give good things to friends and bad things to enemies.[127] Assuming, as Plato and Aristotle along with the Roman philosophers after them did, that the gods are on the side of one's own polis and have given it the most virtuous way of life, such principles of justice fit very well into

---

120. This is of course most prevalent in the prophets and especially in the Psalms: κρίνατε ὀρφανὸν καὶ πτωχόν ταπεινὸν καὶ πένητα δικαιώσατε (Ps 81:3).

121. Jewett, *Romans*, 25.

122. Matt 18:4; 23:12; Luke 1:48, 52; 14:11; 18:14; Acts 8:33; 20:19; Jas 1:9; 4:6, 10; 1 Pet 3:8; 5:5.

123. MacIntyre, *AV*, 181–86.

124. Cf. Cicero, *Resp*, I.II.

125. Cf. Cicero, *Resp*. III.XIII: "We must choose one of three things—to do injustice and not to suffer (*accepere*) it or both to do it and to suffer it, or else neither to do it or to suffer it."

126. Plato, *Resp*. 331c, e; Cicero, *Resp*. III.XI.

127. Plato, *Resp*. 32b, d; 334e; also Cicero, *Off.*, I, xvi–xvii. So too MacIntyre's discussion in *WJWR*, 148–49.

an imperial ideology wherein the enemies and friends of Rome are the enemies and friends of the gods. Paul's council in vv. 19-20 strikes at the heart of this. The same is true of the admonition to "speak well of those who persecute you, speak well and do not curse them" (12:14).

Then Paul violates those most famous maxims of justice regarding one's friends and enemies: rather than giving each his due, evil for evil, good for good, the church is to replay *no one* evil for evil. This excludes revenge (12:17, 19), and urges the church rather to have *good* in mind. It is *God* who is in the judgment business, not the church (12:19). But such a principle excludes the very thing that gave Rome its power and rationale: πολευμεῖν ("making war"). The latter is simply the large-scale application of the common Roman principles of distributive justice, and Paul seems to realize this when he says that the church is to instead "be peaceable with all" (12:18).

By the end of the paragraph (12:14-21) Paul has completely disrupted any lingering notion the church might have that it is to run on the traditional principles of justice laid down in Roman law and embodied in its notions of honor. Far from it; the church is to give food and drink to its enemies and in *this* way they *defeat* them (12:20). And, as if the previously prescribed actions were not enough, contrary to the norms of Roman justice, Paul adds μὴ νικῶ ὑπὸ τοῦ κακοῦ ἀλλὰ νίκα ἐν τῷ ἀγαθῷ τὸ κακόν. Evil itself is to be defeated, not by waging war against it and so defeating it with more evil (the principle of giving to each his due), but by "the good."

With this last sentence Paul has tied up the section. The reference to the good and the evil forms a ring with the introductory admonition ἀποστυγοῦντες τὸ πονηρόν, κολλώμενοι τῷ ἀγαθῷ of 12:9 and again with the statement that the renewing of the mind allows one to test and see what is τὸ ἀγαθὸν καὶ εὐάρεστον καὶ τέλειον in 12:2. At this point Paul can expect the church has some idea of what he thinks the good life *looks like*. He has dispatched a cutting judgment on Roman justice that can be creatively embodied in the life of the church at several different levels. He has, moreover, in talking about the nature of the good life, by necessity given some shape to the just life that the church now practices—a life that includes virtues and practices contrary to those of Roman society. Throughout this section Paul's way of life stands in direct contrast to what Moxnes calls the "honor culture" of the Hellenistic polis.[128]

---

128. Moxnes, "Quest for Honor," 203-30. See esp. Dio's orations 44, 66, 31, 77, 78.

Rom 13:1–7 and the Arts of Resistance

Paul has sketched a way of life at odds with the dominant culture. This would not be a problem if the church existed in a vacuum, but of course it does not. It stands in the heart of empires which might pose a threat to this little group whose way of life often stands against accepted norms. If the church adopts the radical stance that Paul lays down in 12:9–21, how should it behave towards the authorities? I suggest that in Rom 13:1–7 Paul is giving councel regarding how the church might navigate such a dynamic. Some account must be given at this point of how this section fits within my reading of Rom 12:9–21 as practice subversive of the dominant culture. This is necessary since this passage has a long history of being seen as Paul's endorsement of the political status quo.[129] How are we to understand it?[130]

Recent studies drawing on post-colonial disciplines have yielded tools for this task, and specifically here I suggest Paul is writing something like a hidden transcript.[131] Below I suggest that Paul has, elsewhere in Romans, already defined the key terms that show up in Rom 13:1–7, so that rather than advocating the status quo he is showing the part that the Roman authorities play in God's providential ordering of the world. Specifically, I think Paul says that God uses those who are in authority in pagan government to *support* the practices of the church. The church, as it were, does not have a part to play in God's providential ordering of the world as much as the world, at times, has a helpful role to play in the performance of the body of Christ. This is Paul's claim in Rom 13:1–7, but he makes it in such a subtle way that it would be virtually undetectable to an outsider.

Instituted By God

The first point, which has not often been pressed, is the subversive nature of claiming that the rulers and authorities of Rome have been established "by God" (13:1). Jewett is right at this point: "That all such officials are divinely appointed needs to be understood rhetorically . . . The issue usually

---

129. Zsifkovits, *Staatsgedanke nach Paulus*, chronicles all the backgrounds that have been proposed for Paul's view of the state.

130. Proposals include a warning not to participate in Jewish zealotism, in revolutionary agitation, not to create unrest for the sake of the Jews in Rome, not to think that Christian enthusiasm of the new age trumps the present one, an attempt by Paul to avoid disloyalty, to placate Rome so he can get to Spain. See Jewett, *Romans*, 788.

131. This is the notion developed by Scott, *Domination*, esp. 45–69 and 202–28.

not raised in the scholarly discussion is precisely who this God is . . . [I]t is the God embodied in the crucified Christ that is in view here, which turns this passage into a massive act of political cooptation."[132] This God of whom Paul speaks and in whom the church makes its only boast (Rom 5:1-2, 8-9) is the God whose Son was executed by the Romans for treason and paradoxically is now worshiped by this strange little gathering as the κύριος of all (Rom 1:4, 7; 5:1 etc.). It is this God's εὐαγγέλιον that Paul proclaims, and not Caesar's.[133]

All this is true. But, against what Jewett implies, this does not mean that the Romans would have found it too offensive. Rome was of course generally fairly tolerant of the gods that her subject nations worshiped, as long as they were also willing to do certain things for Rome.[134] *Of course* not everybody was forced into confessing that Roma ruled the world. *Of course* there were different theologies on this front, and *of course* Rome knew that and tolerated it. Though a necessary first step, this would not have been the treasonous edge to Paul's message.

Authority

Chrysostom makes the observation that what Paul says is not that the current Roman government, nor any of its contemporary embodiments is the subject of Paul's discussion, but authority *itself*.[135] This is an inverse point to that of Jewett and others, who suggest that Paul is saying that the specific rulers in Rome at Paul's time were appointed by God. Both moves achieve the end of avoiding a sanction of all government at all time, but in different ways. The former says that earthly authority itself is appointed by God but leaves the legitimacy of any specific manifestation of it open.[136] The latter consecrates the present manifestation, but leaves the general notion of earthly authority open to question.[137]

I am going to suggest that a nuanced combination of these two views is good description of the passage. Chrysostom's point must be taken seriously, since the discussion is much more general than is usually allowed.

132. Jewett, *Romans*, 789.
133. So, too Horrell, *Solidarity*, 255-56.
134. Cinera, *Religionspolitik*, 1-60.
135. Chrysostom, *Hom. Rom.* 23 (NANF 8: 511).
136. So, with Chrysostom, this is Bockmuehl's argument in *Jewish Law*, 136.
137. This latter is probably the most popular today. For bibliography see the commentaries, and esp. Friedrich et al., "Zur historischen Situation," 131-66.

"Authority" is from God (ἔστιν ἐξουσία ὑπὸ θεοῦ), and anyone who stands against it (ἀντιτασσόμενος τῇ ἐξουσίᾳ) stands against God's command (13:1-2), presumably because God is the ultimate authority (cf. also θέλεις δὲ μὴ φοβεῖσθαι τὴν ἐξουσίαν). No specific authorities are mentioned, and never does Paul say that everyone who would claim to be an authority rightly is so. He simply says that God has established (τεταγμέναι) authority. Again, quite generally, "rulers" (οἱ ἄρχοντες) are not a fear to the good work, but to evil. There is nothing inherently evil about earthly rule.

Jewett, however, is right to point out what Chrysostom glosses over, and that is that Paul says in v. 1 that the authorities that currently exist are instituted by God (αἱ δὲ οὖσαι ὑπὸ θεοῦ τεταγμέναι εἰσίν). In other words, Paul does not seem to have any problem with the church in Rome submitting to the Roman administration as it currently exists. This dovetails nicely with Chrysostom's point, however, for it is not an endorsement of any and all who would claim authority.

Thus I suggest that Paul's claim is that earthly authority itself is established by God (for what purpose we will see below; I do not claim it is simply a "natural" part of the created order) but that any specific instance of authority may be illegitimate.

The Good

It is rarely noticed that in Romans Paul has something like a doctrine of the good. It is not worked out in any sort of philosophical way but nevertheless is pronounced enough that by the time he comes to use the term in our passage the church has been taught a fair amount about it. τὸ ἀγαθόν appears in some grammatical form 22 times in the letter, and three times in significant ways in Rom 13:1-7. The concept's most substantial uses come in chapters that we have looked at, so that there we gain some insight into the nature of the good and specifically the practices that are constitutive of its performance.

We saw that Paul says in Rom 8:28 that "God cooperates in all things toward the good (εἰς ἀγαθόν) with those who love God." The Spirit "works with" (συνεργεῖ) or "cooperates" with the church in her actions and steers them toward the good. But falling as this does in the context of Rom 8, it is clear that this practice of the Spirit toward the good is the practice of suffering with Christ (8:17) and striving to live the practices of the Spirit stated generally in Rom 8:1-17 but outlined specifically as the practices of the church in Rom 12-13. Thus, the actions that aim at the good are, quite appropriately, the practices of the body of Christ. Jewett agrees: "Paul's wording [in Rom 8:28] implies divine and human responsibility in the face of adversity, and in the context of this letter, the 'good' to be accomplished by this cooperation includes the daily work and congregational formation in behalf of the Roman house and tenement churches."[138]

This thesis is corroborated by the fact that most of the references to the good in Romans appear in chapters 12–15, where they are circumscribed by that hortatory context. Most prominent is Rom 12:2 where the good is apposite to "the will of God," along with "the pleasing" and "the perfect." It would appear that Paul uses the latter as synonymous with the good, but the good features far more commonly in his grammar than do the others. Rom 12:2 also gives an indication of what sorts of actions are likely to be instances of actually *doing* the good by exhorting the church members to offer their bodies as a martyrological sacrifice.

Not to be conformed to this world but to be renewed in mind is, as we have said, a comment on the reigning popular epistemology of Rome. To know the world rightly and hence to act for the good was, for the Stoics for instance, to have one's mind stamped with the impressions of the world the way it really is. Out of this, in more or less complex ways, one discerns the good. But, says Paul, it is not *this* world that one should be conformed to both in mind and deed. To offer one's body as a sacrifice is the supreme instance of such non-conformity, and it is therefore a practice whereby one comes to discern the will of God, the good. Once again the good is defined and circumscribed by the martyrological practices of the church.

The instance of the good most proximate to Rom 13:1–7 is 12:9. Here it is closely defined by practices that constitute the unhypocritical Agape. Paul's first recourse after this heading is to implore the Romans to "put off the bad and cling to the good." I suggested there that the language of "clinging" was that of the church's connection with Christ. If this section is about the way that the church practices Christ, then it would appear that there is a close connection for Paul between the practice of the good, the practice of Christ's body, the will of God, and perfection (cf. Eph 4:13: ἄνδρα τέλειον). I think that Paul simply identifies these, in a rather straightforward way, as more or less synonymous terms for the same basic way of life.

That the good is so defined—not as an abstract Platonic notion, but as a certain set of interdependent martyrological and liturgical practices—fits exactly with the parenetic material that follows the more general exhortation to the good in 12:9. Here, however, the good is defined, not just

---

138. Jewett, *Romans*, 527.

as martyrological practices, but specifically as the kind of life that makes for an unhypocritical Agape. In other words, the good for Paul has been rather thoroughly defined as the counter-cultural, non-violent, humble, economically common life of the church.

Because of this rather abundant commentary on the nature of the good already set out in the letter, the nature of the good referred to in 13:1-7 is not an endorsement of Roman rule as broadly instituting some abstract "good" and so therefore a claim that every imperially sanctioned action benefits the advancement of God's will in the world. That this reading has become natural is but another indication of the dearth of ecclesiology in reading Paul, for the good for him is always defined by the church. Thus I suggest that Paul sees rule and authority as granted by God for the purpose of slanting even the non-Christian world toward the Christian good, which is the common good as well, but which is defined by martyrological praxis. This is not to say that authorities thereby make the *world* more just, or more in line with God's will. Rather, in the providence of God they permit the church to practice the good, which is always the world's good. (This is a slightly different position from Yoder's.[139]) They do *not* bear the sword *justly*, but, God's providence makes sure that injustice itself is not in vain.[140] The Roman sword is used by God to make sure that the church can pursue its good. Thus the Roman soldier θεοῦ γὰρ διάκονός ἐστιν ἔκδικος εἰς ὀργὴν τῷ τὸ κακὸν πράσσοντι. In other words, he is directed by God, unwittingly, and, paradoxically, always unjustly (since the whole point is that God uses even injustice for the church's justice), to carry out God's recompense that the just Christian is forbidden, and which the good and the just themselves forbid.[141]

This leaves open the possibility that the Roman soldier might be unwittingly involved in the *Christian's* practice of the good, even if he executes her. For, as we saw in Rom 12:2, the offering of one's body to be sacrificed is one way of practicing the good. And this raises the complex nature of the relationship between the authority which God grants and the Christian good. The *soldier* does not *do* the good, but makes for its possibility. What the soldier does is wicked (hence the church later claimed

---

139. Yoder, *Politics*, 93-111.

140. Thus Horrell's claim in *Solidarity*, 257, that this represents a "universal ethic," cannot stand. Paul nowhere says that everyone should behave like the state nor even that the state is justified in what it does—only that its actions are done for the good.

141. Hence Bruce, *Romans*, 238: "The state thus is charged with a function which has been explicitly forbidden to the Christian." But on my reading this is not the state's "charge" so much as simply what it does.

that one must try to avoid martyrdom so that the enemy would not sin). But God uses this wickedness, which remains evil qua evil and so to be condemned, for the good of the church, which by extension must be the common good.

Moreover, Paul assumes that the good as defined by the practices that he sets out will not directly provoke the Romans to punish; rather, Rome will praise the Christians: θέλεις δὲ μὴ φοβεῖσθαι τὴν ἐξουσίαν· τὸ ἀγαθὸν ποίει, καὶ ἕξεις ἔπαινον ἐξ αὐτῆς (13:4). This is one of the biggest challenges for the anti-imperialist picture of Paul so fashionable these days. This is not to say that Paul does not have a major problem with the Roman Empire, but he does not assume his churches would constantly be living in such a way as to provoke the Romans to action. The actions of the church we have seen in Romans *are* anti-imperial, but in a much deeper way than much current discussion realizes. These are small, tiny actions that no one is going to be particularly upset with even as they undercut the very foundations of Rome. In other words, in 13:4, Paul says: "do the good as I have outlined, do *not* be revolutionaries (in the usual sense). This, in fact, is more dangerous for Rome than outright rebellion, which could be easily put down."

Paying Back Debts

There are further indications here that Paul is being rather crafty. We noted above that in 12:17 he refused to allow the church to pay back evil for evil (μηδενὶ κακὸν ἀντὶ κακοῦ ἀποδιδόντες). This is to reject the common sense that justice is to pay back each what is owed them (see above). When therefore Paul seems to reinstate that maxim in 13:7 by saying ἀπόδοτε πᾶσιν τὰς ὀφειλάς, τῷ τὸν φόρον τὸν φόρον, τῷ τὸ τέλος τὸ τέλος, τῷ τὸν φόβον τὸν φόβον, τῷ τὴν τιμὴν τὴν τιμήν, we have every reason to suspect that we are not to take this straightforwardly. This intuition is confirmed, moreover, when Paul goes on immediately to say "owe (ὀφείλετε) no one anything except to agape one another" (13:8).

These three verses—12:17, 13:7, and 13:8—appear stand together awkwardly. But in them we can discern a coherent picture of Paul's ethic toward the Roman administration, while at the same time allowing Paul to lay claim to the fact that he was not against paying taxes. What Paul advises in 13:7-8 is simply that the church not have debts of any kind, social or economic. The connected nature of these verses is obscured in most translations as it is in the NRSV:

> Pay to all what is due them-- taxes to whom taxes are due, revenue to whom revenue is due, respect to whom respect is due, honor to whom honor is due. Owe no one anything, except to love one another; for the one who loves another has fulfilled the law.

Rather, what Paul says, as the Greek root ὀφειλ- makes very clear in each verse, is to take care of debts so that they owe nothing except agape. Thus we should render the open phrases "Pay back your debts to everyone... be in debt to no one, except to love one another." What is Paul doing?

To a significant extent, it appears he wants the church to be financially independent of the patron-client system that constituted the ancient economy, with the exception of paying taxes.[142] Taxes were only one part thereof. The entire economy of the Roman world was built on the assumption that everyone was going to be in debt to someone else. This was at the base of social relations.[143] And Paul councels the church to get out of it. "Take care of your debts and your social obligations so that you no longer need participate in such *Romanitas*."

Of course, this assumes that the church is largely functioning as a replacement of that economy. This argument can then be corroborated by Jewett's suggestion that the "love" language that Paul uses here is closely connected with the Love Feast. This works very well for my suggestion regarding Paul's call that the church abandon the patron-client system. The only debts that the church should have is the performance of acts of charity toward one another (τὸ ἀλλήλους ἀγαπᾶν) as an alternative economics. Thus Paul highlights here that aspect of the Agape that he commended earlier: making common the needs of the saints (12:13).

Thus, when we take 13:7 along with 13:8, we see that Paul is not reinstituting the definition of justice he has already rejected. Rather, 12:17 still stands as a bulwark against any common Roman ideal of justice.

Submission

At this point it must not be lost that Paul commands the church to submit. The one practical piece of advice that Paul gives in this section is that the Romans, in fact, should pay taxes. Yet that Paul has to commend this practice shows that he expected that it was not a given, especially not in

---

142. In this way I follow, Jewett, *Romans*, 805–6.

143. Crook, *Patronage*, 91–150. Crook does not treat Romans in this work, but his work seems poised to do so.

light of the other things he has said so far in the letter. How can children of God (8:16–17) be subject to any earthly authority? This paragraph seems penned partially to dispatch that sort of thinking. What sort of "submission" he expected beyond the payment of taxes is not clear, and he does not say. But there does not, as I have said, seem to be anything in the practices of the church outlined by Paul in Romans that would have much provoked the Romans. This does not mean that the church practice outlined is not deeply subversive. But it is so in a way that could not matter very much to the authorities. Rome put down harshly any revolutionary activity—open revolts, violence, scheming, and tax evasion. Paul's was not that kind of program. It was much more subtle and intelligent. The practices that fill out the church's life make that clear. But it would always be possible for some hothead to detach the cosmic claims that Paul makes from those humble everyday practices that circumscribe them and call down the Roman police on this insignificant assembly. Paul's exhortations to martyrdom (Rom 8:16–17, 12:1–2) might even make this seem like a good idea. It is this revolutionary zeal that Paul apparently wishes to avoid.

It is important to see the two sides of Paul's carefully crafted paragraph. The rhetoric of the passage is such that, should the letter fall into the wrong hands, it *can* be read as a straightforward endorsement of the status quo. Paul was already persecuted on several fronts, if Acts is to be trusted at all, and so his mission to Spain could easily be jettisoned if he got into more trouble at Rome. So he pens a paragraph on the one hand subversive, on the other hand mundane, even if not always overtly complementary.[144] This is Paul's hidden transcript.

Rom 13:8–14 as Inclusio to Rom 5–8

In this paragraph Paul completes the basic groundwork of an ecclesial praxis and at the same time gives more indications that he intends the material of chapters 12–15 to be the content of the just life of the Spirit described in Rom 5–8, *and* that this life is organically related to the Love Feast. This is best demonstrated by working through the passage backward.

---

144. Elliot, "Strategies of Resistance," 97–122, shows that the common claim of Roman propaganda in the likes of Cicero, Seneca, Plutarch, etc., was that the sword had been put away and that even the worst human being would be spared it. He further notes that "fear" was never considered a good way for rulers to deal, and I might add that, as fear is one of the central popular vices, the claim that a government has intentionally inculcated it in its citizens is far from a compliment.

Romans 12-15 as the Practice of the Body of Christ

After an exhortation to agape (which we have already noted above and to which we shall return) Paul in vv. 13-14 writes two sentences that tie the practical discourse here in Rom 13 back into the more explicitly soteriological discourse of Rom 5-8: ὡς ἐν ἡμέρᾳ εὐσχημόνως περιπατήσωμεν, μὴ κώμοις καὶ μέθαις, μὴ κοίταις καὶ ἀσελγείαις, μὴ ἔριδι καὶ ζήλῳ, ἀλλὰ ἐνδύσασθε τὸν κύριον Ἰησοῦν Χριστὸν καὶ τῆς σαρκὸς πρόνοιαν μὴ ποιεῖσθε εἰς ἐπιθυμίας. Paul has used the language of "walking" (περιπατέω) in 6:4 in describing the "newness of life" the baptized church walks in, and in 8:4 to describe those that live not according to the flesh but according to the Spirit. This is good reason for reading 13:13 as indicating that Rom 12-15 is spelling out the life he set out in those chapters as one dead to sin (Rom 6) and of practicing the Spirit (Rom 8) more generally. περιπατέω signals for Paul the practice of a particular way of life.

Moreover, ἐνδύσασθε resumes the discussion of baptism (and the holy life presumed thereby) from Rom 6. The "clothing" metaphor echoes the ritual of baptism wherein the neophyte is given a clean garment after being dipped as a sign of the new life she has entered.[145]

The command τῆς σαρκὸς πρόνοιαν μὴ ποιεῖσθε (13:14) is a reference back to the long discussion of the flesh in 8:1-14, where the "flesh" is referred to thirteen times in those fourteen verses. The hortatory nature of Rom 13 therefore establishes beyond any doubt the truly hortatory nature of Rom 8:1-11. Paul really does think that life in the Spirit is something that can be *commanded*. The reference to ἐπιθυμία (13:14) draws on Rom 6:12 (cf. also 7:5, 7) as part of Paul's encouragement that the church "not let sin reign in your moral bodies for its obedience of its (the body's) ἐπιθυμίας."

Finally, ἀποθώμεθα οὖν τὰ ἔργα τοῦ σκότους, ἐνδυσώμεθα [δὲ] τὰ ὅπλα τοῦ φωτός, has various resonances of its own with previous parts of Romans. The verb ἀποθώμεθα does not itself occur, but the concept seems to be the same as Romans 6:13: μηδὲ παριστάνετε τὰ μέλη ὑμῶν ὅπλα ἀδικίας τῇ ἁμαρτίᾳ, ἀλλὰ παραστήσατε ἑαυτοὺς τῷ θεῷ ὡσεὶ ἐκ νεκρῶν ζῶντας καὶ τὰ μέλη ὑμῶν ὅπλα δικαιοσύνης τῷ θεῷ. Both verses exhort to a particular sort of action, using the metaphor of "weapons." If I am right concerning the structure of the letter at this point, exactly what that particular action involves is only here in chapters 12-15 becoming apparent. But this exhortation also has certain affinities with Romans 8:13:

---

145. Elsewhere this appears to be exactly the way Paul used the word. See Col 3:10-12; Eph 4:24.

εἰ δὲ πνεύματι τὰς πράξεις τοῦ σώματος θανατοῦτε, ζήσεσθε. The similies πράξεις and ἔργα neatly correspond to each other, and the context of both statements is the eschatological expectation and the demands that are made on the church's current life in light of it.

The constructions in 13:14 with ἐνδυσώμεθα are parallel:

ἐνδυσώμεθα δὲ τὰ ὅπλα τοῦ φωτός
ἐνδύσασθε τὸν κύριον Ἰησοῦν Χριστὸν.

These show that "putting on Christ" is a matter of putting on the weapons of light that *just are* the works (good works or works of light) that are the opposite of τὰ ἔργα τοῦ σκότους. This is important for my thesis that the practices of the church are what constitute it as Christ. For, in both cases, putting on the good works that are Christ is explicitly said to exclude other deeds, named both generally as "the works of darkness" (13:12) and "the thought of the flesh for the passions" (13:14), and specifically as actions such clothing proscribes—ἡ κώμοις καὶ μέθαις, μὴ κοίταις καὶ ἀσελγείαις, μὴ ἔριδι καὶ ζήλῳ (13:13).

There are thus several indications in Rom 13:11–14 that Paul means to resume his earlier and broader discussions and make more concrete and specific the way of life by which the church is constituted. What this also shows, if we had any doubt, is that the three to five (depending on how we count) conceivably independent arguments of Rom 5–8 all basically treat the same topic for Paul. He feels free to use terms from each of those arguments in the same sentences when we get to Rom 12–15. The problem of disobedience, sin, and death in Rom 5 is the same basic condition and corresponding set of actions as the passions in Rom 6 and the flesh in Rom 8. Likewise, the just and obedient life of Rom 5 is the same as the newness of life, obedience, and holiness of Rom 6, and the life of the Spirit in Rom 8. These are all, Rom 13:11–14 helps us see, different aspects and views of the same irreducible sanctification-as-salvation.

Finally, as I have said Jewett is right that the notion of "agape" here is to be taken from the practices that took place at *the* Agape and not from some general notion. If this is so, then by implication both the practices of 13:11–14 and the whole of Rom 5–8 which it calls upon and fills out are tied inextricably to the Eucharistic meal. This is not least because 13:11–14 are conditioned heavily by 13:8–10. So this ends up making a point I have been at pains to press all along—that church practice is that way of life necessary if the Agape is to be unhypocritical. Moreover, here Paul takes up the topic of the life of the church specifically with regard to Torah. The

Torah is fulfilled for the church when it "loves"—when it lives the way that Paul has been articulating. If all of this is required to hold the Agape, then, Paul is saying, of course the commandments of the law will be fulfilled, for Οὐ μοιχεύσεις, Οὐ φονεύσεις, Οὐ κλέψεις, Οὐκ ἐπιθυμήσεις (13:9), etc., will be included in all that has preceded, and also in living μὴ κώμοις καὶ μέθαις, μὴ κοίταις καὶ ἀσελγείαις, μὴ ἔριδι καὶ ζήλῳ (13:13).

Conclusion: Rom 12–15

I have argued that Paul has lead up to his discussion of the way of life necessary for an unhypocritcal Agape in 12:9—15:6 by introducing the liturgical roles that are already practiced in Rome (Rom 12:6-8). The discourse of the body of Christ (Rom 12:3-5) therefore takes its sense from the context of the Eucharistic meal as the place where Christ's body and all of its parts together become visible. So part of my argument in this chapter has had the goal of establishing that the Eucharist is the proper context for understanding what Paul is saying. The body of Christ is not simply a notion of the way that Christ is present in the world through the church in a *general* or metaphysical way, but rather the body and all its parts are formed by the specific contextual dynamics of the Eucharistic Agape. The manifestation of Christ's body in the world is not limited to this liturgical meeting, but extends to relations toward outsiders (12:9-21 and esp. 13:1-7) and to the everyday habits of the church (13:8-14). But the embodiment of Christ beyond the Agape takes its sense from it, in the life that must be lived by anyone who does so liturgically participate. Hence there is every reason to affirm a strong connection for Paul between the Christ's body as church and as Eucharist. In the Agape the church participates in Christ through the Eucharist. That participation is in part constituted by the liturgical roles that make the church Christ's body.

I have made several crucial moves in this chapter for our exegesis of Romans. First, I have argued that Rom 12–15 set out the ecclesial practices that are the content of the broader discussions of Rom 5-8 by anchoring the former to the latter linguistically and thematically. Furthermore, the pneumatic backdrop of the Eucharist that I argue for principally from 1 Cor provides reason to think Paul presumes that the Spirit is intimately involved in these concrete practices, as Rom 8 would also suggest. These are the practices of the Spirit by which the church is urged to put to death the body of sin.

The Practice of the Body of Christ

But we come to this conclusion only by comparative and synthetic work. In Romans 12–15 itself, apart from the exhortation to "boil in the Spirit," Paul does not mention the Spirit. This too is significant for our thesis concerning the centrality of the Spirit in Paul's theological ethics and account of agency. Though we can tell by comparative work that the Spirit is practiced in the church, it is noteworthy that Paul does not comment on the church's inability to so practice without the Spirit, or that the Spirit always has to "go first." The practice of the Spirit cuts through such hyper-Augustinian worries and provides room for genuine human agency, including allowing exhortations full intelligibility. If Paul were going to talk about the "leading" of the Spirit, we might expect it in a discussion of the concrete practice of the community such as we find in Rom 12–15. Yet such qualification is absent. He seems to presume that a good portion of the practice of the church is just a matter of getting on with it.

I have also suggested that the exhortation in 12:9—15:6 grounds the ecclesial life in the dynamics of the Agape so that the latter maybe celebrated unhypocritically. Such an exhortation is only explicable if Paul is concerned that the whole of the church's life be disciplined by its liturgical practice (12:3–8). Rom 12–15 are thus formally much like body-polis tracts. Paul begins his explication of ecclesial polity by a discussion of the body, which serves to inform the ensuing discussion of the activities, virtues, vices, and constitutive practices of the Good Life. Any discussion of human action in Rome in the first century would usually take its sense from such antecedents, and Paul's does so to a considerable extent.

Moreover, the argument of this chapter affirms that at the heart of Paul's theology is the *church*, and specifically one in which both the sacraments and virtues are important. It is plain that any such reading of Paul will cut against much current Protestant hegemony in Pauline studies. But we have also seen in MacIntyre, and in our present chapter in closer looks at figures like Aristotle and Cicero, that in fact action is unintelligible without a community. Neighbors are constituative of human acts. It is no surprise then that as far as Pauline studies can be said to marginalize the church (and it is sometimes quite far!) we have misconstrued questions of agency. The centrality of the church further grounds Paul in a classical account of human agency, and so at this point it is necessary to try to draw together the threads we have collected throughout the various chapters of Romans and ask what comprehensive picture this specifically Pauline model of agency looks like.

5

Some Synthetic and Prospective Conclusions

I HAVE OFFERED A READING OF ROMANS IN TERMS OF A CLASSICAL ACcount of human agency that avoids the pitfalls MacIntyre chronicles in much modern theorizing. That the basic elements of such an account are present has been the burden of the last three chapters. It remains only to say how these elements fit together in a theological account of agency. We only have space in what remains to indicate the contours of this investigation. What follows will raise many more questions than it answers. The complex theological task of attempting to work through these questions—both for reading Paul and for being the church—will have to wait for another study.

First, I return to the two goals named at the beginning of my study. The most basic case that I have been making throughout is that there is plenty of room in Paul for action that can be genuinely called human and that has its place in a journey toward a telos. Paul thinks Christians will be holy, that they will advance in holiness, and I have argued that this involves something like MacIntyre's account of the virtues. I have argued against overriding human agency by the Holy Spirit in some act of instant theosis. Both of these hyper-Augustinian errors are avoided by recovering a classical account of human action and reading central texts of Romans from within that framework.

What, more specifically, have been the further results of this?

The first is the place of the church in Pauline theology. My reading of Romans has made the case for a high ecclesiology both by pointing directly to indicators of such in the text (the Agape, the body of Christ), and by pushing through a reading which presumes church practices even when they are implicit. Especially in readings of Romans, this has not been the norm. Study after study documents the lone individual who comes to faith in Rom 1–4, is sanctified in Rom 5–8, and is then told how to live (sometimes with the view that this has something to do with the church) with other people in Rom 12–15. I have tried to turn these presumptions on their head. Though I decided that the order of this study should follow that of Paul's letter, a good argument could be made for arranging this in reverse order. This would make the point that is often lost on western Protestants that *all along* (i.e., in Rom 1–8) Paul is talking about the concrete practices of the church. I have argued that for Paul there is the closest relation between ecclesiology and Christology, so that the concrete practices of the church *are* the church performing Christ.

More work is called for regarding agency at precisely this point. That the church acts as Christ has sometimes been treated in terms of dual-agency: the Christian somehow acts both as herself and as Christ.[1] But the complex is not this simple, for it is not the individual Christian that acts as Christ but the *church* who does, as Martyn notes.[2] In this regard, the first point to grasp is the discourse of the body as polis as we saw in Chapter 4, for thereby we articulate not just agency as literally corporate but also agency within a classical account. To this, moreover, we have to add that such an agency cannot domesticate divine transcendence. But, what the classical body-polis discussion will not help us with is the fact that the body the church constitutes is the one particular body of a crucified and resurrected Jew. And so we also need to add to our enquiry the third instantiation of Christ's body, the Eucharist. The church receives the very Spirit which constitutes it as Christ in the bread and cup, gifting it with Christ's virtues and demanding a particular way of life. How does the church talk about *this* kind of agency? Several main lines of inquiry suggest themselves, again with no claim to be worked through here.

The first is that Pauline theology should avail itself of the imaginative resources not only of classical body-polis discourse but also of the work done on the notion of the body of Christ (in all its manifestations) in the Tradition, especially the seminal work by Henri de Lubac.[3] De Lubac recovers the notion of Christ's body as a visible community of practice *and*

---

1. See, e.g., Barclay, "Grace."
2. Martyn, "Gospel," 31.
3. Lubac, *Corpus Mysticum*.

Some Synthetic and Prospective Conclusions

as constituted thereby by the Eucharist—both items that I have argued are visible in Romans.[4]

Such work might make us better readers of Paul by teaching us what he means when he says that bodies in the church exist only as body-parts exist—as parts of a whole. This might help us get a sense of the depths of *dependence* and *being-determined-by-others-ness* in Paul's grammar, especially in texts like Rom 12:3-8 (as our analysis of Paul's Greek there indicated). We who think we have something called a "self" that is separate from everything and everybody else, and even from our own body, will always tend to think of such dependence as *that same* separate "self" merely standing in some sort of relation to another separate self. But of course that is to already miss the point. A hand is not a hand in the normal sense if it is not connected to the body, and the body is not a body in the normal way if it does not have a foot. The pneumatic body of Christ is so constituted that its members only have bodies in relation to Christ and to one another. Only in my place as a part of Christ and in relation to my sisters and brothers do "I" have any sense at all. The concept of the body and so the concept of the human being are always already relational "all the way down." MacIntyre in his essay "What is a Human Body?" shows, in a way Paul might agree with, that our concept of *a* human body is always secondary and derivative of the collective of human bodies and ultimately the body politic.[5]

What this means is that the body of Christ for Paul is also *dynamic*. It exists as the church performs the actions that are Christ's actions, derivative of, and conformable to, the Agape. This liturgical performance is the point at which the life of the church comes most clearly into focus, and from this performance derives the way of life that follows in the rest of chapters 12-15. The Agape is the place where the church is habituated to live (not just *a* but) *its* virtuous life, where it receives its cardinal virtues on which all that follows depends.

To say that the church only exists as it practices Christ is to say that the church is contingent and historical. The church does not exist necessarily, or in principle, or ideally. However divinely constituted and sustained, it exists, like everything else, by its actions. This is why the sections on the body of Christ in Paul's letters have a hortatory nature. These actions are formed by and form habits that give them intelligibility. But this is not to put the church in an unduly precarious position, since there is nothing

---

4. This is the direction pressed by Cavanaugh, *Torture and Eucharist*, 207-54.
5. MacIntyre, "Body," 86-103.

deeper and more stable in the world than habits. To say that the church is contingent is simply to say that it is vulnerable, as Christ, to death.

The claim that the church exists by its actions will have to wait to be developed in subsequent work. But for now I think there are several elements of Paul's grammar that must be taken into account. The first is that agency in the church is always a matter of being parts of the other bodies in the church. This means that our action is always tied up with other people and their actions. Second, actions are sometimes said to be given by God. Third, for Paul the gifts also include the agency of the person performing that gift. Hence Paul can encourage the church to vie for certain spiritual gifts and to give instructions about how they should be used (1 Cor 12:31). There thus seems to be a three-part agency involved.

A second major line of inquiry regards the Spirit. I have argued throughout that the Spirit is involved in each and every aspect of the church, even when it is not referenced. My two contentions that for Paul the Spirit is something that can be practiced and that is received (only) in the sacraments (but is at play outside this context) are uncommon, but certainly not without certain parallels in the Tradition, even in interpretation of Paul's letters there. For I have suggested that the Spirit is both determinative of, and determinable by, human behavior. We find St. Chrysostom saying something like this precisely in the context of concrete practices and the Spirit (commenting on Rom 12:6–9):

> See how in every instance Paul aims after higher degrees; for he does not say "give" only, but "with largeness;" nor "rule," but do it "with diligence;" nor "show mercy," but do it "with cheerfulness;" nor "honor," but "prefer one another;" nor "love," but do it "without dissimulation;" nor refrain from "evil" things, but "hate" them; nor "hold to what is good;" but "cleave" to it; nor "love," but to do it "with brotherly affection;" nor be zealous, but be so "without backwardness;" *nor have the "Spirit," but have it "fervent," that is, that you may be warm and awakened. For if you have those things aforesaid, you will draw the Spirit to yourself. And if the Spirit abides with you, it will likewise make you good for those purposes, and all things will be easy from the Spirit and the love, while you are made to glow from both sides.*[6]

For Chrysostom "practicing the Spirit" in such a way "draws" the Spirit and makes it easier for one to so continue. This is especially interesting in that he also has a fully fledged doctrine of the virtues. This is commensurate

---

6. Chrysostom, *Com. Rom.* 21 (*NANF* 8:503).

with the ancient philosophical notion of the πνεῦμα, as we have seen in part, as a substance that determines one's qualities.

Third, Paul's notion of "participation" in Christ belongs right here, at the interplay between the Spirit as, on the one hand, a physical thing and on the other hand something that is in some way determined *by* our corporate practices. This latter element is what Stowers neglects.[7] On his reading, the physical Spirit threatens to betray Paul's grammar by only influencing and not being influenced by church practice. But Chrysostom points out the other side of this that must be in place. One participates in Christ through drawing his Spirit by certain actions (principally worship: the Eucharist); equally, of course, one can cast away the Spirit by others (Rom 8:9–11; cf. 1 Cor 6:9–20; Gal 5:18–21). The Spirit holds the grammar of a sort of holy material whose presence enables some actions and who can be driven away by other actions.

Consequently, I have argued that the Spirit has a very specific place in Paul's theological ethics, namely, the Spirit is the vivifier of Christian bodies as they die to sin. We found at this point both a sort of ascetic theology and realized eschatology. But this dying and rising evinces another MacIntyrian theme—that the Pauline agent is *storied* at a couple different levels. In other words, the Pauline "self" is not comprehensible outside of its place in a larger story. MacIntyre makes this claim about all agents, and so there is nothing particularly interesting about the fact that this is so with Paul. The interesting point is that for Paul the Christian agent is intelligible only as an actor in the story of *Christ*. Any action must be seen from the standpoint of *some* story or stories, but it will be impossible for us to truly describe the Pauline agent apart from the narrative of the dying and rising of the Messiah. *That* will be the story that determines the shape of all others. That the Spirit appears most notably when the conversation turns to such stories is significant. The role of the Spirit appears in the matrix of narrative and action, where it maps one's behavior onto Christ's, both past and present.

The content of this dying and rising should not be mistaken as something overly mysterious. For what brings it about, in the cooperating work of the Spirit, is the ecclesial practice outlined in Rom 12–15. In other words, Pauline ethics are indeed cruciform, but as a kenosis that looks like *this*. Christians don't just die with Christ in a general way, or generally apply a "kenotic principle." By church practices they learn about the cross. This mortification and revivification proceeds through the daily struggle

---

7. Stowers, "Pauline Participation."

against the desires of the flesh—the desire to be considered wiser than others, to get revenge, to possess, and to avoid suffering. The church is the means to making all this possible, not by a magical divine invasion, but by a gathered people that lives with the humble, shares possessions, seeks the honor of the neighbor, is committed to peace, prays, and eats bread and drinks wine together. To so seek the good of the neighbor not only before one's own but *as* one's own is to seek not the private good but the common (Rom 15:2; cf. Phil 2:21). This is, for Paul, what it looks like to suffer with Christ, and this is the activity that "crucifies" the old man (Rom 6:6), not least by Eucharistically receiving the crucified man that the church is.

Such participation is another way of naming the pnumatic and Christic ecclesiology I have been propounding. Such a notion is of course deeply mysterious, and we should not expect to "expound" it fully. Nevertheless, I have indicated some lines where I think it can be, since that the body of Christ is a mystery is not to say that it is wholly ineffable or inscrutable. Indeed, I have contended that around these topics Paul seems to be the earthiest. A large part of understanding the nature of the body of Christ is a matter of *looking* at the church.

In this regard I have already partly remarked upon Paul's theological ethics. But it should now be said that the type of community practice laid out in Rom 12–15 is in part determinative of an account of agency. Rather than first starting with a theory of agency (say, wholly derived from a particular reading of Rom 5–8) and working down to what must be true of church action (as exemplified in Rom 12–15), we must know the character of ecclesial practice and then speak about the nature of those actions. The same is true for MacIntyrian practices. For the details produce the character of the result.

So, what is the relationship between Paul's account of the church in Romans and a MacIntyrian practice? Recall that a practice for MacIntyre is "a coherent and complex form of socially established cooperative human behavior through which goods internal to that practice are realized in the course of trying to achieve excellence in that activity, with the result that the virtues and conceptions of the end and the goods are extended."[8]

In *some* ways Paul's account in Romans can be rightfully adapted into such a schema. This ought to be the case if MacIntyre (even mostly) rightly describes classical action theory and if I am right that the latter is operative in Paul's letters. We can indicate here only the broad lines of such an account, for any practice is potentially infinitely complex.

---

8. MacIntyre, *AV*, 187.

We've seen that for Paul suffering and dying with Christ, as the crucifixion of the evil passions, is the telos toward which the church presses. As it progresses through this journey the church needs certain skills and powers which MacIntyre names virtues, though Paul does not call them this. Such Pauline "virtues" are the character traits (cf. δοκιμή, Rom 5:4) needed to live the Agapaic life that is the best approximation of Christ on the cross. The practices outlined in Rom 12-15 both require such virtues for their stable functioning and train the church in the virtues, for the virtues just are skills at these sorts of tasks. Rom 12-15 sets out the sorts of things that the church exists to be good at, and the sorts of people members will have to be in order to be so.

More specifically, the cooperative behavior Paul names includes a wide variety of different tasks including celebrating the Love Feast, rejoicing, serving the Lord, sharing the needs of the saints, providing hospitality, paying off debts, not judging one's brother, and pursuing peace and edification. Equally, in these chapters Paul names a variety of virtues that sustain and are developed in these activities. The foremost among these appears to be ἀγάπη, since references to it enclose, more or less, the discussion in 12:9—13:14.' Ἀγάπη is both a liturgical meal of shared food wherein Christ is received *and* the character that is formed by (συσχηματίζεσθε, 12:2), and required for, participation in that meal. Beyond the list of the gift-virtues he names, among others, prudence (τὸ φρονεῖν), temperance (τὸ σωφρονεῖν), faithfulness (πίστις), communality (κοινωνοῦντες), endurance (ὑπομονή), peaceableness (εἰρήνη), joy (χαρά), and justice (δικαιοσύνη). A further volume could work out each of these virtues more fully.

If ἀγάπη is most highlighted in Rom 12-15, clearly δικαιοσύνη comes to the fore in Rom 5-8 (and πίστις in 1-4, but I leave that to later work). As such, and given the connections that I have made between the former chapters and the latter, it appears that δικαιοσύνη functions something like a cardinal virtue, summing up the multifold and complex life of virtue under one head. Something like this comes to the surface in 5:1-5 as Paul sets δικαιοσύνη in relation to other virtues, not least πίστις. This is Paul's word, in other words, for Christian otherness, for holiness (cf. Rom 6:19: δικαιοσύνη εἰς ἁγιασμόν). So δικαιοσύνη is set in contrast to "sin" as a

The Practice of the Body of Christ

whole throughout these chapters (cf. 6:7) in the process of describing the new life in Christ.

But a full-fledged and straightforward adoption of MacIntyre's practices for understanding Paul would be a mistake for several reasons. The first is that to presume that a practice is some sort of "neutral" sociological tool through which to "view" what Paul says is to mistake a practice for a merely descriptive "model." No such models exist, and if they did, I'm not sure what we would gain from them.[9] A MacIntyrian practice is a very specific way of inscribing what Craig Heilmann calls a "social ontology."[10] But social ontology in a theological mode names the ecclesial economy of salvation. It tells us about ends, the powers we need to arrive there, what will deter us from arriving, what help we can expect along the way, who "we" are and who "I" am. And, as such, MacIntyre's notion of a practice, without further nuance, is Pelagian. This is not just a theological problem, but *descriptively* it is going to skew interpretation of Paul. To place Paul's ecclesiology into such a schema is thus ultimately to reduce it and domesticate it. MacIntyre's practice has its place in a teleological schema wherein sin as a good-action-deterring-defect plays no part. Thus advancement towards the goal can only be hindered by *error*. As long as the practice continues without detrimental error, internal goods are won, virtues extended, and conceptions of the telos advanced.

But such a historicist account sits uneasily with several elements of Paul's schema. The first sticking point regards ends, and more specifically the fact that beyond the goal of conformity with the crucified Christ sits the final end of conformity with the crucified and *risen* Christ. The ultimate good of glorification is not something that can be achieved within the church qua MacIntyrian practice, however virtuous or perfect one becomes. The closest we come to glorification in this life came out in our discussion of Paul's *partially* realized eschatology, wherein life begins to appear as bodies die to sin, as our discussion of Rom 8 suggested. But one never pursues glorification *as such* as a telos. One never runs directly at it, but rather directly at the cross. Glorification is only something that can be *given* as one pursues crucifixion qua activities of the church (Rom 12–15).[11] Such a dynamic is never present in a MacIntyrian practice.

---

9. Milbank, *Theology and Social Theory*, 101–46.

10. Heilmann, "Nature With/out Grace," 45–55.

11. This raises the question of whether in such a Christian schema glorification is in fact an end external to the practice. See the discussion in Herdt, *Virtue*, 45–72.

Some Synthetic and Prospective Conclusions

For similar reasons a MacIntyrian practice is going to have a hard time making room for the Pauline notions of the Spirit, the body of Christ, the Eucharist, or infused virtues. To adapt Paul to MacIntyre in this straightforward way would consequently be to make him Pelagian. This is not because MacIntyre cannot countenance such theological notions, but because a MacIntyrian practice normally operates on the natural side of a grace/nature contrast. Virtue as ability to attain a telos will always be natural virtue, not infused. My account, however, and this was clear in chapter 1, is headed in exactly the opposite direction. The very nature of Pauline church practice itself, strange as it is, with its joyful martyrology and asceticism, comes as gifted practice. The goal itself is not slowly worked out along the way (though the means may be), but is clearly portrayed as Christ crucified and risen. To push all Paul's theological notions into a MacIntyrian practice, therefore, is to misconstrue a central contention of my reading of Paul, namely, that for him (as with other classical Christian accounts of agency) grace is the condition of the possibility of genuinely human action and not something added to it.

Hence, as an essay arising at least partially out of the apocalyptic school of Pauline interpretation, my hope has been to use MacIntyre to give Paul some much-needed ecclesial development. I hope that by now it is clear that this is necessary not just because it would be helpful to have an account of the church to go along with what Martyn and others have given us. The point is more fundamental. If Hauerwas is right that the church is "the necessary correlative of an apocalyptic narration of existence" and that "the eucharistic community is the epistemological prerequisite to understanding 'how things are,'"[12] it follows that "how things are" is going to include "how Christ is." Because for Paul the church *is* Christ, and because to be the church is to be engaged in a particular community of practice, it follows that Christ is revealed in and through that practice. Of course, there is going to be reciprocal *apocalypsis* involved; it is not all up to practices. The church will learn through hearing about Christ, through consuming Christ, through practicing Christ. But one thing is patent from our reading of Romans: Christ will not be revealed without the church. And this points to a potential problem with a bare statement like Harink's mentioned above that "Jesus Christ *is* the apocalypse for Paul."[13] Gloriously true and necessary as that statement is in the proper context, if spoken in isolation from the church "Jesus Christ" threatens to

---

12. Hauerwas, "Apocalyptic," 112.
13. Harink, *Paul*, 78.

become a vacuous abstraction. What or who is Jesus Christ? What or who is this apocalypse? Paul's answer is: look at the church. Only there do we learn what it means to say that Christ is the apocalypse.[14]

Finally, if we do have a classical account of agency in Paul, with its attendant virtues and room for striving for the good, this will have something to say about Pauline soteriology. I have pressed this claim into the very structure of Romans, for what we have seen, essentially, is that in Rom 5, 6, 8, and 12–15, we are glimpsing four different aspects of one utterly undivisable salvation—more or less from the macro- to the micro-level. This salvation is predicated non-negotiably on both participation in Christ's crucified and resurrected body and—inseparable from it—on the concrete martyrological practices of the daily life of the church. *These four different aspects are impossible to separate soteriologically.* This is salvation viewed from four different angles. Being baptized into Christ (Rom 6) is not separate from being "in Christ" and not "in Adam" (Rom 5). Being in Christ and so being free from sin is only possible by the Spirit that we have been given that conforms us to Christ's martyrological praxis (Rom 8:17, 12:1–2). None of this is ultimately different from living in the kind of society that is described Rom 12:9—15:6: the everyday embodiment of the martyrological praxes of 5:3–4, 8:14 and 12:1.

Thus, for the Apostle, the apocalyptic χάρις, the divine "given," is the *way of life* in the community. Paul is neither an individualist nor a Pelagian. Moreover, I have shown that this way of reading Romans is compatible with what later doctors of the church, especially Augustine and Thomas, were to say about the *gratia Dei*. So it is still possible to say things like "we can do nothing of ourselves" and that "salvation, from beginning to end, is a work of the Holy Spirit." But we can also say things like "salvation requires suffering" and that "holiness is necessary for future blessedness." But this language now finds its place within a properly robust ecclesiology: the only place it is ultimately at home.

To read Paul within this tradition is to call comfortable soteriological assurances into question. We have to learn how to read "labor at (κατεργάζεσθε) your own salvation with fear and trembling" (Phil 2:8) within a tradition and a community that can say that only "by the toil of obedience may you return to Him from whom by the sloth of disobedience

---

14. Eastman, *Mother Tongue*, 17, sees this very clearly: We must address "the question of whether and how the transforming and sustaining power of the gospel, apart from the Law, is mediated over time and made visible in human affairs. Without such visibility, it becomes impossible to describe the history-making intersection of Christ's unique crucifixion and resurrection with the linear narratives of Paul's converts."

you have gone astray" (*Rule of Benedict*, Prologue). The same Benedict still beckons. But if he, St. Paul, and the rest of the prophets have already come, and they were not heeded, it will make no difference if a man is raised from the dead. Yet the grace of God has once again appeared in these latter days and spoken to us in his servants. Dorothy Day used to quote St. Paul that "we are saved by little and by little." We can't find those words anywhere in his letters, but it is true to him nonetheless. There can be no more waiting.

Bibliography

Afanasiev, Nicholas. *The Church of the Holy Spirit*. Notre Dame: University of Notre Dame, 2007.
Andia, Ysabel de. *Homo vivens: incorruptibiliteet divinisation de l'homme selon Irenee de Lyon*. Paris: Etudes augustiniennes, 1986.
Aquinas, Thomas. *Epistolam B. Pauli ad Romanos lectura*. No pages. Online: www.corpusthomisticum.org.
Aristotle. *Works*. Translated by Harold P. Cooke et al. 23 vols. Loeb Classical Library. Cambridge, MA: Harvard University Press, 1926-1955.
Arnim, Hans Friedrich August von, ed. *Stoicorum Veterum Fragmenta*. 4 vols. Leipzig: B. G. Teubneri, 1903.
Aulen, Gustaf. *Christus Victor: An Historical Study of the Three Main Types of the Idea of Atonement*. Translated by A. G. Hebert. New York: Macmillan, 1951.
Barclay, John. "'By the Grace of God I am What I am': Grace and Agency in Philo and Paul." In *Divine and Human Agency in Paul and His Cultural Environment*, edited by John M. Barclay and Simon Gathercole, 140-67. New York: T. & T. Clark, 2006.
―――. *Obeying the Truth: A Study of Paul's Ethics in Galatians*. Edinburgh: T. & T. Clark, 1988.
Barth, Karl. *Adam and Christ: God and Humanity in Romans 5*. Translated by T. A. Smail. New York: Harper, 1957.
―――. *The Epistle to the Romans*. Translated by Edwyn Clement Hoskyns. London: Oxford University Press, 1933.
Beker, J. Christiaan. *Paul the Apostle: The Triumph of God in Life and Thought*. Philadelphia: Fortress, 1980.
―――. *Paul's Apocalyptic Gospel: The Coming Triumph of God*. Philadelphia: Fortress, 1982.
―――. *The Triumph of God: The Essence of Paul's Thought*. Minneapolis: Fortress, 1990.
Best, Ernest. *One Body in Christ: A Study of the Relationship of the Church to Christ in the Epistles of the Apostle Paul*. London: SPCK, 1955.
Betz, Hanz Dieter. *Galatians: A Commentary on Paul's Letter to the Churches in Galatia*. Hermeneia. Minneapolis: Fortress, 1979.
―――. "Transferring a Ritual: Baptism in Romans 6." In *Paul in His Hellenistic Context*, edited by Troels Engberg-Petersen, 84-118. Minneapolis: Fortress, 1995.
Bockmuehl, Marcus. *Jewish Law in Gentile Churches: Halakhah and the Beginning of Christian Public Ethics*. Edinburgh: T. & T. Clark, 2000.
Boer, Martinus de. *The Defeat of Death: Apocalyptic Eschatology in Rom 5 and 1 Cor 15*. Sheffield: JSOT, 1988.
Bosch, J. S. "Le Corps du Christ et les charismes has l'épître aux Romains." In *Dimensions de la vie chretienne: Rom 12-13*, edited by C. K. Barrett et al., 51-72. Rome: Abbaye de S. Paul, 1979.

Bibliography

Brandos, David A. *Paul on the Cross: Restructuring the Apostle's Story of Redemption*. Minneapolis: Fortress, 2006.

Breytenbach, Cilliers. *Versöhnung: Eine Studie zur paulinischen Soteriologie*. Neukirchen-Vluyn: Neukirchener, 1989.

Brockhaus, Ulrick. *Charisma und Amt: die paulinische Charismenlehre auf dem Hintergrund der frühchristlichen Gemeindefunktionen*. Wuppertal: Rolf Brockhaus, 1972.

Brown, Peter. *The Body and Society: Men, Women, and Sexual Renunciation in Early Christianity*. New York: Columbia, 1988.

Bruce, F. F. *The Epistle of Paul to the Romans: An Introduction and Commentary*. London: Tyndale, 1963.

———. "Was Paul a Mystic?" *Reformed Theological Review* 34 (1975) 66–75.

Bultmann, Rudolf. "Adam und Christ nach Römer 5." In *Exegetica: Aufsätze zur Erforschung des Neuen Testaments*, edited by Erich Dinkler, 424–44. Tübingen: Mohr, 1967.

———. *Theology of the New Testament*. 2 vols. New York: Scribner, 1951.

Byrne, Brendan. *Romans*. Sacra Pagina. Collegeville, MN: Liturgical, 1996.

Campbell, Douglas. *The Deliverance of God: An Apocalyptic Rereading of Justification in Paul*. Grand Rapids: Eerdmans, 2009.

———. *The Quest for Paul's Gospel: A Suggested Strategy*. New York: T. & T. Clark, 2005.

Carr, Wesley. *Angels and Principalities: The Background, Meaning, and Development of the Pauline Phrase hai archai kai hai exousiai*. Cambridge: Cambridge University Press, 1981.

Cavanaugh, William. *Torture and Eucharist: Theology, Politics, and the Body of Christ*. Malden, MA: Blackwell, 2006.

Cerfaux, L. *The Church in the Theology of St. Paul*. New York: Herder & Herder, 1959.

Chrysostom, John. *Homilies on the Acts of the Apostles and the Epistle to the Romans*. Vol 1 of *Nicene and Post-Nicene Fathers*. Edited by Philip Schaff. Series 2. Peabody, MA: Hendrickson, 1994.

Cicero. *Cicero*. Translated by E. W. Sutton et al. 29 vols. Loeb Classical Library. Cambridge, MA: Harvard University Press, 1948–2001.

Cinera, Alvarez. *Die Religionspolitik des Kaisers Claudius und die paulinische Mission*. Herders: Freiburg, 1999.

Clark, Elizabeth. *Reading Renunciation: Asceticism and Scripture in Early Christianity*. Princeton: Princeton University Press, 1999.

Cole, R. Lee. *Love Feasts: A History of the Christian Agape*. London: Charles H. Kelly, 1916.

Cranfield, C. E. B. *Romans: A Shorter Commentary*. Grand Rapids: Eerdmans, 1985.

Crook, Zeba A. *Reconceptualizing Conversion: Patronage, Loyalty and Conversion in the Religions of the Ancient Mediterranean*. New York: de Gruyter, 2004.

Cunningham, Lawrence S., ed. *Intractable Disputes about the Natural Law: Alasdair MacIntyre and Critics*. Notre Dame: University of Notre Dame Press, 2009.

De Bruyn, Theodore, ed. *Pelagius's Commentary on St. Paul's Epistle to the Romans: Translated with Introduction and Notes*. Oxford: Clarendon, 1993.

Diogenes Laertius. *Lives of the Eminent Philosophers*. Translated by R. D. Hicks. 2 vols. Loeb Classical Library. Cambridge, MA: Harvard University Press, 1925.

Dodd, C. H. *The Epistle of Paul to the Romans*. New York: Harper, 1932.

Dunn, James D. G. "The Incident at Antioch (Gal 2:11–18)." *JSNT* 18 (1983) 95–122.

———. "The New Perspective on Paul." *Bulletin of the John Rylands University Library of Manchester* 65/2 (1981) 95–122.
———. *Romans*. 2 vols. Word Biblical Commentary. Dallas: Word, 1988.
———. *The Theology of Paul the Apostle*. Grand Rapids: Eerdmans, 1998.
Earl, Donald. *Age of Augustus*. London: ELEK, 1968.
Eastman, Susan. *Recovering Paul's Mother Tongue: Language and Theology in Galatians*. Grand Rapids: Eerdmans, 2007.
Elliot, Neil. "Strategies of Resistance and Hidden Transcripts in the Pauline Corpus." In *Hidden Transcripts and the Arts of Resistance: Applying the Work of James C. Scott to Jesus and Paul*, edited by R. Horsley, 97–122. Atlanta: Society of Biblical Literature, 2004.
Epictetus. *Epictetus*. Translated by W. A. Oldfather. 2 vols. Loeb Classical Library. Cambridge, MA: Harvard University Press, 1928.
Engberg-Petersen, Troels. *Paul and the Stoics*. Louisville: Westminster John Knox, 2000.
Esler, Philip. *Galatians*. London: Routledge, 1998.
———. "Making and Breaking an Agreement Mediterranean Style: A New Reading of Galatians 2: 1–14." *Biblical Interpretation* 3 (1995) 285–314.
Fee, Gordon. *The First Epistle to the Corinthians*. Grand Rapids: Eerdmans, 1987.
———. *God's Empowering Presence: The Holy Spirit in the Letters of Paul*. Peabody: MA: Hendrickson, 1994.
Finlan, Stephen, and Vladimir Kharlamov, eds. *Theosis: Deification in Christian Theology*. Princeton Theological Monograph Series. Eugene, OR: Pickwick, 2006.
Fitzmeyer, Joseph A. "The Consecutive Meaning of *eph' hoi* in Romans 5:12." *New Testament Studies* 39 (1993) 321–28.
———. *Romans: A New Translation with Introduction and Commentary*. Anchor Bible Commentaries. New York: Doubleday, 1993.
Friedrich, J., et al. "Zur historischen Situation und Intenetion von Röm 13:1–7." *Zeitschrift für Theologie und Kirche* 73 (1976) 131–66.
Furnish, Victor Paul. *The Moral Teaching of Paul*. Nashville: Abingdon, 1979.
———. *Theology and Ethics in Paul*. Nashville: Abingdon, 1968.
Gaca, Kathy L. *Early Patristic Readings of Romans*. Edited by L. L. Welborn. Romans through History and Cultures. New York: T. & T. Clark, 2005.
Georgi, Dieter. *Remembering the Poor: The History of Paul's Collection for Jerusalem*. Nashville: Abingdon, 1992.
Gorman, Michael J. *Inhabiting the Cruciform God: Kenosis, Justification, and Theosis in Paul's Narrative Soteriology*. Grand Rapids: Eerdmans, 2009.
Hadot, Pierre. *Philosophy as a Way of Life: Spiritual Exercises from Socrates to Foucault*. New York: Blackwell, 1995.
Hall, Thor. "An Analysis of *Simul Iustus et Peccator*." *Theology Today* 20/2 (1963) 174–82.
Hanby, Michael. *Augustine and Modernity*. New York: Routledge, 2003.
Harink, Douglas. *Paul among the Postliberals: Pauline Theology Beyond Christendom and Modernity*. Grand Rapids: Brazos, 2003.
Harmless, William. *Augustine and the Catechumenate*. Collegeville. MN: Liturgical, 1995.
Hauerwas, Stanley, and David Matzko. "The Sources of Charles Taylor." *Religious Studies Review* 18/4 (1992) 286–89.

Bibliography

Hauerwas, Stanley, and Charles Pinches. *Christians Among the Virtues: Theological Conversations with Ancient and Modern Ethics*. Notre Dame: University of Notre Dame Press, 1997.

Hays, Richard B. *The Faith of Jesus Christ: The Narrative Substructure of Galatians 3:1—4:11*. Grand Rapids: Eerdmans, 1983.

———. *The Moral Vision of the New Testament: Community, Cross and New Creation: A Contemporary Introduction to New Testament Ethics*. San Francisco: HarperOne, 1996.

———. "What is 'Real Participation in Christ'?" In *Redefining First Century Jewish and Christian Identities: Essays in Honor of Ed Parish Sanders*, edited by Fabian E. Udoh et al., 336–51. Notre Dame: University of Notre Dame Press, 2008.

Heilmann, Craig. "Nature With/out Grace: Alasdair MacIntyre and the Ecclesial Formation of Independent Practical Reasoners." ThD diss., Duke Divinity School, 2009.

Hellermann, Joseph. *Reconstructing Honor in Roman Phillipi: Carmen Christi as Cursus Pudorum*. New York: Cambridge University Press, 2005.

Herdt, Jennifer. *Putting on Virtue: The Legacy of the Splendid Vices*. Chicago: University of Chicago Press, 2008.

Horn, Friedrich Wilhelm. *Das Angeld des Geistes: Studien zur paulinischen Pneumatologie*. Göttingen: Vandenhoeck & Ruprecht, 1992.

Horrell, David. "Pauline Churches or Early Christian Churches? Unity, Disagreement, and the Eucharist." In *Einheit der Kirche im Neuen Testament*, edited by A. Alexeev von Anatoly et al., 185–203. Tübingen: Mohr Siebeck, 2008.

———. *Solidarity and Difference: A Contemporary Reading of Paul's Ethics*. New York: T. & T. Clark, 2005.

Hunter, David G. "The Reception and Interpretation of Paul in Late Antiquity: 1 Cor 7 and the Ascetic Debates." In *Reception and Interpretation of the Bible in Late Antiquity*, edited by Lorenzo DiTommaso and Lucian Turcescu, 163–91. Boston: Brill, 2008.

Hütter, Reinhard. "St. Thomas on Grace and Free Will in the *Initium Fidei*: The Surpassing Augustinian Synthesis." *Nova et Vetera* 5/3 (2008) 521–53.

Irenaeus. *The Apostolic Fathers with Justin Martyr and Irenaeus*. In vol 1 of *The Ante-Nicene Fathers*. Edited by A. Cleveland Coxe. 10 vols. Peabody, MA: Hendrickson, 1994.

Isaacs, Marie E. *The Concept of Spirit: A Study of Pneuma in Hellenistic Judaism and Its Bearing on the New Testament*. Heythrop Monographs. London: H. Charlesworth, 1976.

Jewett, Robert. "Are there Allusions to the Love Feast in Rom 13:8–10?" In *Common Life in the Early Church: Essays Honoring Graydon F. Snyder*, edited by Julian Victor Hills et al., 265–78. Harrisburg, PA: Trinity, 1998.

———. *Paul's Anthropological Terms: A Study of Their Use in Conflict Settings*. Leiden: Brill, 1971.

———. *Romans: A Commentary*. Edited by Eldon Jay Epp. Hermeneia. Minneapolis: Fortress, 2007.

———. "Tenement Churches and Pauline Love Feasts." *Quarterly Review* 14/1 (1994) 43–58.

Josephus. *Josephus*. Translated by H. St. J. Thackeray et al. 10 vols. Loeb Classical Library. Cambridge, MA: Harvard University Press, 1926–1965.

Käsemann, Ernst. *Commentary on Romans*. Grand Rapids: Eerdmans, 1980.
Kayne, Bruce N. *The Argument of Romans with Special Reference to Chapter 6*. Austin: Schola, 1979.
Kim, Yung Suk. *Christ's Body in Corinth: The Politics of a Metaphor*. Minneapolis: Fortress, 2008.
Kirby, J. T. "The Syntax of Romans 5.12: A Rhetorical Approach." *New Testament Studies* 33 (1987) 283–86.
Kirk, J. R. Daniel. "Reconsidering Dikaioma in Romans 5:16." *Journal of Biblical Literature* 126 (2007) 787–92.
Kittel, G., and G. Friedrich, eds. *Theological Dictionary of the New Testament* [*TDNT*]. Translated by G. W. Bromiley. 10 vols. Grand Rapids: Eerdmans, 1964–1976.
Koester, Helmut. "ΝΟΜΟΣ ΦΥΣΕΩΣ. The Concept of Natural Law in Greek Thought." In *Religions in Antiquity: Essays in Memory of E. R. Goodenough*, edited by Jacob Neusner, 521–41. Leiden: Brill, 1968.
Konstan, David. *Friendship in the Classical World*. New York: Cambridge University Press, 1997.
Knight, Kelvin. *Aristotelian Philosophy: Ethics and Politics from Aristotle to MacIntyre*. Malden, MA: Polity, 2007.
Knox, John. *Chapters in a Life of Paul*. Macon, GA: Mercer University, 1987.
Lee, Michelle V. *Paul, the Stoics and the Body of Christ*. Society for New Testament Studies. New York: Cambridge University, 2006.
Légasse, Simon. *L'épître de Paul aux Romains*. Lectio divina commentaries 10. Paris: Éditions du Cerf, 2002.
Lendon, J. E. *Empire of Honor: the Art of Government in the Roman World*. New York: Oxford University Press, 2002.
Lenz, John R. "The Deification of the Philosopher in Classical Greece." In *Partakers of the Divine Nature: The History and Development of Deification in the Christian Tradition*, edited by Michael Christensen and Jeffery Wittung, 47–67. Grand Rapids: Brazos, 2008.
Levinson, John. *The Spirit in First-Century Judaism*. New York: Brill, 1997.
Lewis, John G. *Looking For Life: The Role of "Theo-Ethical Reasoning" in Paul's Religion*. New York: T. & T. Clark, 2005.
Liddell, H., R. Scott, and H. Jones, eds. *A Greek-English Lexicon*. Oxford: Clarendon, 1996.
Lietzmann, Hans. *An die Römer*. Tübingen: Mohr, 1928.
Long, A. A., and D. N. Sedley. *The Hellenistic Philosophers*. 2 vols. New York: Cambridge University Press, 1987.
Lubac, Henri de. *Corpus Mysticum: The Eucharist and the Church in the Middle Ages*. London: SCM, 2006.
Luckmann, Harriet Ann. "Pneumatology and Asceticism in Basil of Caesarea: Roots and Influence to 381 CE." PhD diss., Marquette University, 2002.
Lüdemann, Gerd. *Paul Apostle to the Gentiles: Studies in Chronology*. Philadelphia: Fortress, 1984.
Lutz, Christopher S. *Tradition in the Ethics of Alasdair MacIntyre: Relativism, Thomism, and Philosophy*. Lanham, MD: Lexington, 2004.
Lyonnet, S. "Le péché originel et l' exégèse de Rom 5,12–14." *Religious Studies Review* 44 (1956) 63–84.
———. "Le sens de *eph' hoi* en Rom 5,12 et l'exégèse des Pères grecs." *Biblica* 36 (1955) 436–56.

Bibliography

MacIntyre, Alasdair. *After Virtue: A Study in Moral Theory.* Notre Dame: University of Notre Dame, 1981; 2nd edition, 1983; 3rd edition, 2007.

———. "Alasdair MacIntyre on Education: In Dialogue with Joseph Dunn." *Journal of Philosophy of Education* 36/1 (2002) 1–19.

———. *Dependent Rational Animals: Why Human Beings Need the Virtues.* Chicago: Carus, 1999.

———."Hegel on Faces and Skulls." In *The Tasks of Philosophy*, 74–85. Vol. 1 of *Selected Essays.* New York: Cambridge University, 2006.

———."How Moral Agents Became Ghosts, Or, Why the History of Ethics Divided from that of the Philosophy of Mind." *Synthese* 53 (1982) 295–312.

———. *A Short History of Ethics: A History of Moral Philosophy from the Homeric Age to the Twentieth Century.* New York: MacMillan, 1968.

———. *Three Rival Versions of Moral Enquiry: Encyclopedia, Genealogy and Tradition.* Notre Dame: University of Notre Dame, 1991.

———. "What is a Human Body?" In *The Tasks of Philosophy*, 86–103. Vol. 1 of *Selected Essays.* New York: Cambridge University, 2006.

———.*Whose Justice? Which Rationality?* Notre Dame: University of Notre Dame Press, 1989.

Marshall, I. Howard. *Last Supper and Lord's Supper.* Exeter: Paternoster, 1980.

Martin, Dale. *The Corinthian Body.* New Haven, CT: Yale University, 1995.

Martyn, J. Louis. "The Daily Life of the Church in the War Between the Spirit and the Flesh." In *Theological Issues in the Letters of Paul*, 251–66. Nashville: Abingdon, 1997.

———. "De-Apocalypticizing Paul: An Essay Focused on *Paul and the Stoics*." *Journal for the Study of the New Testament* 6 (2002) 61–102.

———. "Epilogue: An Essay in Pauline Meta-Ethics." In *Divine and Human Agency in Paul and His Cultural Environment*, edited by John M. Barclay and Simon Gathercole, 173–83. New York: T. & T. Clark, 2006.

———. *Galatians: A New Translation with Introduction and Commentary.* Anchor Bible 33a. New York: Doubleday, 1997.

———. "The Gospel Invades Philosophy." In *Paul, Philosophy and the Theopolitical Vision Critical Engagements with Agamben, Badiou, Zizek and Others*, edited by Douglas Harink, 13–33. Eugene, OR: Cascade, 2010.

———. *Theological Issues in the Letters of Paul.* Nashville: Abingdon, 1997.

Matera, F. J. *Galatians.* Sacra Pagina 9. Collegeville, MN: Liturgical, 1992.

McCabe, Herbert. *On Aquinas.* New York: Burns & Oates, 2008.

McGowan, Andrew Brian. *Ascetic Eucharists: Food and Drink in Early Christian Ritual Meals.* Oxford: Clarendon, 1999.

McGucken, J. A. "Strategic Adaptation of Deification in the Cappadocians." In *Partakers of the Divine Nature: The History and Development of Deification in the Christian Tradition*, edited by Michael Christensen and Jeffery Wittung, 95–114. Grand Rapids: Brazos, 2008.

Milbank, John. *Theology and Social Theory: Beyond Secular Reason.* Malden, MA: Blackwell, 1990.

Mitchell, Margaret. *The Heavenly Trumpet: John Chrysostom and the Art of Pauline Interpretation.* Louisville: Westminster John Knox, 2002.

———. *Paul and the Rhetoric of Reconciliation: An Exegetical Investigation of the Language and Composition of* 1 *Corinthians*. Louisville: Westminster John Knox, 1992.

Moxnes, Halvor. "Asceticism and Christian Identity in Antiquity: A Dialogue with Foucault and Paul." *Journal for the Study of the New Testament* 26/1 (2003) 3–29.

———. "The Quest for Honor and the Unity of the Community in Romans 12 and the Orations of Dio Chrysostom." In *Paul in His Hellenistic Context*, edited by Troels Engberg-Petersen, 203–30. Minneapolis: Fortress, 1995.

Murphy, Nancy, Brad J. Kallenberg, and Mark Thiessen Nation, eds. *Virtues and Practices in the Christian Tradition: Christian Ethics After Macintyre*. Notre Dame: University of Notre Dame, 2003.

Murray, John. *The Epistle to the Romans: The English Text with Introduction, Exposition and Notes*. New International Commentary on the New Testament 2. Grand Rapids: Eerdmanns, 1968.

Noormann, Rolf. *Irenaeus als Paulusinterpret: zur Rezeption und Wirkung der paulinischen und deuteropaulinischen Briefe im Werk des Ireaeus von Lyon*. WUNT 66. Tubingen: Mohr, 1994.

Nussbaum, Martha C. *The Therapy of Desire: Theory and Practice in Hellenistic Ethics*. Princeton: Princeton University Press, 1994.

Origen. *Commentary on the Epistle to the Romans*. Edited by Thomas P. Halton. Translated by Thomas P. Scheck. The Fathers of the Church 103–104. Washington, DC: Catholic University of America Press, 2001.

Overbeck, Franz. *Über die Auffasung des Streits des Paulus mit Petrus in Antiochen (Gal. 2, 11ff.) bei den Kirchenvätern*. Basel: Darmstadt, 1968.

Parson, Michael. "Being Precedes Act: Indicative and Imperative in Paul's Writing." *Evangelical Quarterly* 60 (1998) 99–127.

Patrologia graeca. Edited by J. -P. Migne. 162 vols. Paris, 1857–1886.

Patrologia latina. Edited by J. -P. Migne. 217 vols. Paris, 1844–1864.

Pervo, Richard. "PANTA KOINA: The Feeding Stories in the Light of Economic Data and Social Practice." In *Religious Propaganda and Missionary Competition in the New Testament World: Essays Honoring Dieter Georgi*, edited by Lukas Bormann et al., 187–94. Leiden: Brill, 1994.

Philo. *Philo*. Translated by F. H. Colson and G. H. Whitaker. 12 vols. Loeb Classical Library. Cambridge, MA: Harvard University Press, 1929–1953.

Pinches, Charles R. *Theology and Action: After Theory in Christian Ethics*. Grand Rapids: Eerdmans, 2002.

Placher, William C. *The Domestication of Transcendence: How Modern Thinking About God Went Wrong*. Louisville: Westminster John Knox, 1996.

Plato. *The Republic*. Translated by Paul Shorey. 2 vols. Loeb Classical Library. Cambridge, MA: Harvard University Press, 2006.

Pohl, Christine. *Making Room: Recovering Hospitality as a Christian Tradition*. Eerdmanns: Grand Rapids, 1999.

Proudfoot, Merrill. "Imitation or Realistic Participation? A Study of Paul's Concept of 'Suffering With Christ.'" *Interpretation* 17 (1963) 140–60.

Reed, Jeffrey. "Indicative and Imperative in Rom 6.21–22: The Rhetoric of Punctuation." *Biblica* 74/2 (1993) 224–57.

Reesor, Margaret E. *The Nature of Man in Early Stoic Philosophy*. New York: St. Martin's, 1989.

Bibliography

Reicke, Bo. *Diakonie, Festfreude und Zelos in Verbindung mit der altchristlicher Agapenfeier*. Uppsala: Lundequistska, 1951.

Ricken, Friedo. "Gab es eine hellenistische Vorlage für Weish 13-15?" *Biblica* 49 (1968) 54-86.

Robinson, J. A. T. *The Body: A Study in Pauline Theology*. Louisville: Westminster John Knox, 1977.

Röhser, Günter. *Metaphorik und Personifikation der Sünde: antike Sündenvorstellungen und paulinische Hamartia*. WUNT 25. Tübingen: Mohr, 1987.

Russell, Norman. *The Doctrine of Deification in the Greek Patristic Fathers*. Oxford: University of Oxford, 2006.

Sanders, E. P. *Judaism: Practice and Belief 63 BCE-63 CE*. Philadelphia: Trinity, 1992.

———. *Paul and Palestinian Judaism: A Comparison of Patters of Religion*. Philadelphia: Fortress, 1977.

Schäfer, Klaus. *Gemeinde als "Bruderschaft": ein Beitrag zum Kirchenverständnis des Paulus*. New York: Frankfurt am Main, 1989.

Scheck, Thomas. *Origen and the History of Justification: The Legacy of Origen's Commentary on the Romans*. Notre Dame: University of Notre Dame Press, 2008.

Schlier, H. *Der Galatierbrief*. Kritisch-exegetischer Kommentar über das Neue Testament (Meyer-Kommentar). Göttingen: Vandenhöck, 1965.

Schweitzer, Albert. *The Mysticism of Paul the Apostle*. Translated by P. Montgomery. New York: Seabury, 1968.

Scott, James. *Domination and the Arts of Resistance: Hidden Transcripts*. New Haven, CT: Yale, 1990.

Scroggs, Robin. *The Last Adam: A Study in Pauline Anthropology*. Philadelphia: Fortress, 1966.

Seneca. *Seneca*. Translated by John W. Basore et al. 10 vols. Loeb Classical Library. Cambridge, MA: Harvard University Press, 1926-1965.

Sharp, Douglas. *Epictetus and the New Testament*. London: C. H. Kelly, 1914.

Sihvola, Juha, and Troels Engberg-Pedersen, eds. *The Emotions in Hellenistic Philosophy*. Dordrecht: Kluwer, 1998.

Smith, R. Scott. *Virtue Ethics and Moral Knowledge: Philosophy of Language After MacIntyre and Hauerwas*. Burlington, UK: Ashgate, 2003.

Sorabiji, Richard K. *Emotions and Peace of Mind: from Stoic Agitation to Christian Temptation*. London: Oxford, 2000.

Stowers, Stanley. *A Rereading of Romans: Justice, Jews, and Gentiles*. New Haven, CT: Yale University Press, 1994.

———. "What is Pauline Participation in Christ." In *Redefining First-Century Jewish and Christian Identities: Essays in Honor of Ed Parish Sanders*, edited by Fabian E. Udoh et al., 352-71. Notre Dame: University of Notre Dame Press, 2008.

Swancutt, Diana. "Sexy Stoics and the Rereading of Romans 1:18—2:16." In *A Feminist Companion to Paul*, edited by Amy-Jill Levine, 42-73. New York: T. & T. Clark, 2004.

Talbert, Charles. "Tradition and Redaction in Rom 12:9-21." *New Testament Studies* 16/1 (1969) 88-91.

Tannehill, Robert C. *Dying and Rising with Christ: A Study in Pauline Theology*. Berlin: Toepelmann, 1967.

Tanner, Kathryn. *God and Creation and Christian Theology: Tyranny or Empowerment?* Minneapolis: Fortress, 1988.

Bibliography

Taylor, Charles. *A Secular Age*. Cambridge, MA: Harvard University Press, 2007.

———. *Sources of the Self: The Making of the Modern Identity*. Cambridge, MA: Harvard University Press, 1989.

Thiselton, Anthony C. *The First Epistle to the Corinthians: A Commentary on the Greek Text*. New International Greek Testament Commentary. Grand Rapids: Eerdmans, 2000.

Vaage, Leif E., et al., eds. *Asceticism in the New Testament*. New York: Routledge, 1999.

Vegge, Tor. *Paulus und das antike Schulwesen: Schule und Bildung des Paulus*. New York: Walter de Gruyter, 2006.

Vlainic, John. "Be What You Are: A Study of the Pauline Indicative and Imperative with Special Reference to Romans 6." In *Kerygma and Praxis: Essays in Honor of Stanley Magill*, edited by Wesley Vanderhoof, 55–76. Winona Lake, IN: Light and Life, 1984.

Vögtle, A. *Röm 8:18-22: eine schöpfungstheologische oder anthropologische-soteriologische Aussage*. Gembloux: Duculot, 1970.

Vos, Johannes Sijko. *Traditionsgeschichtliche Untersuchungen zur paulinischen Pneumatologie*. Assen: Van Gorcum, 1973.

Wasserman, Emma. "The Death of the Soul in Romans 7: Revisiting Paul's Anthropology in Light of Hellenistic Moral Psychology." *Journal of Biblical Literature* 125/4 (2007) 793–816.

———. *The Death of the Soul in Romans 7: Sin, Death, and the Law in Light of Hellenistic Moral Psychology*. WUNT 2 Reihe 256. Tübingen: Mohr Siebeck, 2009.

———. "The Death of the Soul in Romans 7: Sin, Death, and the Law in Light of Hellenistic Moral Psychology." PhD diss., Yale University, 2005.

———. "Paul Among the Philosophers: The Case of Sin in Romans 6-8." *Journal for the Study of the New Testament* 30/4 (2008) 387–415.

Watson, Francis. *Paul, Judaism and Gentiles: Beyond the New Perspective*. Grand Rapids: Eerdmans, 2007.

Weaver, Rebecca Harden. *Divine Grace and Human Agency: A Study of the Semi-Pelagian Controversy*. Macon, GA: Macon University Press, 1996.

Wedderburn, A. J. M. *Baptism and Resurrection: Studies in Pauline Theology Against Its Greco-Roman Background*. Tübingen: Mohr, 1987.

Werner, Johannes. *Der Paulinismus des Irenaeus. Eine kirchen-und dogmengeschichtliche Untersuchung ueber das Verhaeltnis des Irenaeus zu der paulinischen Briefsammlung und Theologie*. Texte und Untersuchungen zur Geschichte der altchristlichen Literatur 6. Leipzig: J. C. Hinrichs, 1889.

Westerholm, Stephen. *Perspectives Old and New on Paul: The "Lutheran" Paul and His Critics*. Grand Rapids: Eerdmans, 2004.

Williams, Sam K. *Jesus' Death as Saving Event: The Background and Origin of a Concept*. Missoula, MT: Scholars, 1975.

Wilson, Jonathan R. *Living Faithfully in a Fragmented World: Lessons for the Church from MacIntyre's After Virtue*. Harrisburg, PA: Trinity, 1998.

Windisch, Hans. "Das Problem des paulinischen Imperativs." *Zeitschrift für die neutestamentliche Wissenschaft und die Kunde der älteren Kirche* 23 (1924) 265–81.

Wingren, Gustaf. *Man and the Incarnation: A Study in the Biblical Theology of Irenaeus*. Philadelphia: Muhlenberg, 1959.

Bibliography

Wright, N. T. "Faith, Virtue, Justification, and the Journey to Freedom." In *The Word Leaps the Gap: Essays on Scripture and Theology in Honor of Richard B. Hays*, edited by Wagner et al., 472–97. Grand Rapids: Eerdmans, 2008.

———. *Justification: God's Plan and Paul's Vision*. Downers Grove, IL: InterVarsity, 2009.

———. "The Letter to the Romans." In *New Interpreters Bible*, edited by Leander Keck, 10:393–770. Nashville: Abingdon, 2002.

———. *Paul: In Fresh Perspective*. Minneapolis: Fortress, 2005.

———. *What Saint Paul Really Said: Was Paul of Tarsus the Real Founder of Christianity?* Grand Rapids: Eerdmans, 1997.

Yoder, John Howard. "Armaments and Eschatology." *Studies in Christian Ethics* 1/1 (1988) 58.

———. *The Politics of Jesus*. Grand Rapids: Eerdmans, 1994.

Zeller, D. "The Life and Death of the Soul in Philo of Alexandria: The Use and Origin of the Metaphor." *Studia Philonica Annual* 7 (1997) 19–55.

Zsifkovits, Valetin. *Der Staatsgedanke nach Paulus in Röm 13, 1–7 mit besonderer Berücksichtigun der Umwelt und der patristischen Auslegung*. Vienna: Herder & Herder, 1964.

www.ingramcontent.com/pod-product-compliance
Lightning Source LLC
Chambersburg PA
CBHW062024220426
43662CB00010B/1470